INDIVIDUALIZING EDUCATIONAL SYSTEMS

SERIES IN ADMINISTRATION

Harry J. Hartley, Consulting Editor

INDIVIDUALIZING EDUCATIONAL SYSTEMS

The Elementary and Secondary School

Implications for Curriculum, Professional Staff, and Students

LLOYD K. BISHOP
New York University

HARPER & ROW, PUBLISHERS
New York, Evanston, and London

INDIVIDUALIZING EDUCATIONAL SYSTEMS
Copyright © 1971 by Lloyd K. Bishop

Library of Congress Catalog Card Number: 79-127338

CONTENTS

PART III The Student and the Educational System 171

PART IV Emergent Professional and Organizational Patterns 223

FOREWORD

Individualized instruction is one of the most talked about and least understood aspects of education. As a result school administrators are faced with a substantial gap in curriculum between expectations and achievements. It has become fashionable, if not a fad, for educators to make claims about how their schools contain individualized programs. Closer observation in many of these schools reveals, however, that there is less there than meets the eye. Who is to blame: the teachers, the principals, or the university preparatory programs? Probably there is enough blame for all of us to share, but the purpose of this book is not to place blame. Its purpose is to provide constructive reforms, to tell why, where, and how schools can reorganize their educational programs and curriculum for student betterment. Professor Lloyd K. Bishop is admirably qualified by training and experience to present this instructional plan.

It appears that conventional approaches to instruction are easier to deplore than to change. Professor Bishop provides the means for change in this volume, a well-organized, comprehensive, cogently written document that is equally appropriate as a guide for educational practitioners and as a text for graduate students. The need for such a book is apparent to anyone who has attempted to determine what individualized instruction really entails, how it can be best accomplished, and what it means for students, teachers, and administrators.

The text represents an excellent balance between conceptual

properties and operational aspects of individualization. Any author who attempts to write a "how to" book on a complex topic in a professional manner assumes a formidable task. Professor Bishop skillfully undertook this task and accomplished it with great success. This book is indeed an important contribution to the profession.

Harry J. Hartley

PREFACE

No concept has had as great an impact upon American elementary and secondary education during the last decade than the concept of *individualizing instruction.* It is the basic contention of this book that educational systems and their related instructional programs, in order to survive in the future, must be more individually and humanistically oriented. Group-oriented instructional programs and materials of a past age are no longer appropriate or effective in meeting the needs of today's youngsters. Professionals equipped with methods and techniques designed only for group consumption in the conventional self-contained classroom must be retrained in order to provide appropriate instructional alternatives for the *individual* as a unique, creative entity. Conventional educational programs are inadequate and obsolete when we consider the diversity of skills, conceptual development, attitudes and values, and capabilities required and rightfully demanded by students for survival in our complex, technological society.

The purpose of this book is to present the major methods and strategies employed by elementary and secondary schools during the past decade for enhancing the individualization of instruction. The concept of individualization is treated in a broad context with program descriptions and techniques encompassing topics in four major areas:

1. Individualization of instructional programs with an emphasis on the major techniques and methods;
2. Individualization of instruction with applications drawn from innovative elementary and secondary school programs;

3. Emphasis on the student as a major force in the educational system; and

4. Emergent professional and organizational patterns with emphasis on the role of the teacher in instructional decision-making.

Essentially, these presentations and descriptions will focus on the development of specific programs and materials, organizational and professional models within elementary and secondary schools, contemporary educational facilities required for individualizing instruction, and the student as a co-participant in the educational enterprise. A balance is maintained between the *pragmatic* in the form of descriptions of existing innovative school programs and the *theoretical* in the form of required future developments in organizational patterns.

This book is written for wide application and for a diverse educational audience. It contains specific and practical material with an eye toward the day-to-day exigencies in school program development as well as broader and more theoretical issues concerned with individualizing educational programs. While a wide range of educational professionals—for example, practicing administrators, college professors, teachers, graduate students—will find the material of immediate and of most value, this does not preclude the usefulness of this volume for the general reader interested in the further sophistication and improvement of American educational systems. This book will also be of value as supplemental material in a wide variety of educational courses, including teacher training programs and administration and supervision courses at both the elementary and secondary school levels.

In addition to the individuals who contributed to major sections of this book as noted in the acknowledgments, thanks is also due to Professor Harry J. Hartley, Head of the Division of Educational Administration, New York University, for his help and encouragement in the final stages of the manuscript preparation. The author acknowledges a close and valued friend, W. Deane Wiley, Dean of the School of Education, Southern Illinois University, for his critical review of several chapters of this book.

Lloyd K. Bishop

ACKNOWLEDGMENTS

The author wishes to express gratitude to several contributors to various chapters of this book. The program descriptions of two nongraded elementary schools contained in Chapter 4 were extracted in part from previously printed material by permission of the Claremont Unified School District, Claremont, California.

Special recognition is also made to several colleagues who contributed to various chapters of this book.

Chapter 5   —Rudolph Wilson, School of Education, Southern Illinois University
Chapter 6   —Dr. Joseph Forcinelli, Claremont High School, Claremont, California
Chapters 7, 8, 9—Geraldine Turner, Fine Arts Area Chairman, Claremont High School, Claremont, California, and Alice Ritchie, Claremont High School, Claremont, California

INTRODUCTION

The development and organization of educational programs in American school systems have been geared traditionally toward groups of students, as illustrated by the typical self-contained classroom. Children may leave home as individuals—yet, from the moment they enter a school bus or a school door, they are organized as a group and thus subjected to all aspects of group life, group norms, and general group conditions. In turn, teaching methodology has been the response of schools required to deal with these faceless groups of children. In many school programs individuality and individual recognition, if not neglected completely, become secondary considerations.

In recent years, instructional methods and organizational patterns within elementary and secondary schools have reflected a strong desire to develop more effective techniques for coping with the individual differences and individual needs of both professional staff and student. It has been recognized in some quarters that there is an urgent and justifiable demand for schools to become more humanizing social institutions that are capable of developing creative and imaginative techniques for recognizing the individual within conventional organizational situations. This seems particularly germane when we consider a culture such as ours which is experiencing extreme technological advances, tendencies for dehumanization of the individual, and prophetic overtones of the "big brother" society.

It is not surprising that one of the most pervasive themes dominating American education during the last decade has been the concept of individualization of instruction. No other concept has had greater influence or greater impact upon the development of modern educational systems and the implementation of concomitant instructional changes. Consider the following propositions:

1. That learning takes place individually; therefore, curriculum and methodology should be organized around the individual child. The quest for ways to individualize learning and instruction is the most important innovating force influencing the development of present day educational systems.
2. That students must come in contact with different levels of learning and have the opportunity to work together to discover the relationships of various disciplines as aspects of one world. Fragmentation and compartmentalization of subject matter must be replaced with interdisciplinary and multidisciplinary approaches with the concomitant interaction of the instructional staff.
3. That there are no time limits or space limits on when or where a student can learn—with or without the teacher and the formal classroom. In fact, there are no age limits; for education to be internalized, students must learn that true education is a continuing process. This is the ubiquitous nature of true education and learning.
4. That the educational program must be dynamic and in a constant state of evaluation and change in order to survive. It must be adaptable, flexible, and capable of meeting the demands of a complex, technological, and changing culture. Thus, the educational program contributes to the individual, to the community, and to society.[1]

The preceding premises evoke dynamic educational procedures and contain powerful implications for any community and its school system desiring to provide the best possible education for its children.

In an operational sense, each individual student is on his own track and has a personalized course of instruction designed for him. He progresses at his own rate—a rate governed by his background, interest, and ability. He competes primarily with himself and only generally with the group. "His own track" takes him not

---

[1] These propositions and the following generalizations concerning the characteristics of an individualized instructional program were extracted in part from a brochure entitled: *Anniston Educational Park, Master Plan* produced by Caudill, Rowlett, Scott, Houston, Texas, 1968.

only into group situations but also provides him with opportunities to work alone doing research, reading, or studying, frequently with the aid of electronic and mechanical teaching equipment and often without the presence of the teacher. Most importantly, the teaching of facts and the drudgery of rote memorization is replaced by procedural discovery and conceptualization. The student may, in some instances, depend on the computer to keep up with the intricacies of his schedule, to review or retrieve past information, and to follow his development, both academic and behavioral. The *individual* is the focal point around which the school is organized.

Along with the individualized approach to education comes the need for guidance. The teachers become specialists geared to the individual's interests and needs, and the problem-solving process of the students is enhanced by the relationship between counselor and student as they plan, follow through, and evaluate the student's total educational program.

Grade levels as goals and ends are removed. A program geared to learning on a continuous nongraded basis is developed. Why? Because students are different. The usual tenth grade class contains students achieving at eighth, ninth, tenth, eleventh, and even twelfth grade levels in one aspect or another of their school work. An eleventh grader may be in the ninth grade for spelling, the tenth for arithmetic, the eleventh for language, and the twelfth for paragraph and word meaning. This pattern can be completely reversed by another student. Thus, contemporary educational programs must be designed to break the conventional graded lock-step and to permit each student to make progress in the various subjects as rapidly as his ability, initiative, and performance will permit.

The nongraded system also offers the possibility of an inter-disciplinary approach to the curriculum. Students having different backgrounds can be scheduled to attend any large group presentation, lecture, or film, although each might have a different point of reference. A "class" viewing a film on Michelangelo may be composed of art students, science students, and history students. At the end of the film, the class can break down into small groups to discuss what they have just seen. Consider the possibilities for depth and breadth of discussion and the growing awareness by the students that all subjects can be related to one another as fragments of a whole. Ideas and concepts are related across disciplines rather than being compartmentalized within disciplines. Thus, the educational program and its curriculum become more closely related to the "real" world rather than fragmented into isolated packages and disassociated from the totality of life, as is often the case in many conventional school programs.

Individualized instructional programs must be developed in a flexible school environment. The flexible school provides an atmosphere which encourages greater interaction between students and their peers, between students and teachers, and among professional staff. There are no walls to fragment learning by dividing subject matter, teachers, and students into rows of similar cell-like rooms. There are no halls to funnel youngsters from room to room at the callous call of a bell. Each student finds his own place, creates his own path, and has more opportunity to cross paths with others. Indeed, a young person is better prepared for "real" life if he has been exposed to as many ideas, people, and situations as possible and if he has been able to accept or reject them at his own discretion.

Individualized instructional programs must also have facilities which relate in name only to typical educational facilities. The Instructional Resource Center (IRC) is the heart of each major subject area. In essence, the instructional resource center is a common base which serves as an individual place of study for each student. This facility houses the materials, supplementary readings, references, teacher-initiated instructional materials, and texts for each instructional area. Related to the IRC are faculty offices which can be used for academic counseling and where individual relationships between student and teacher can develop. Large group and small group instructional facilities and laboratories also relate to the IRC and provide the student, within the school program, a well-rounded, total instructional system.

Multiple interactions and multiple instructional exposure is a major part of the individual's education in a program based on techniques for individualizing instruction. The more open the school's climate, the greater the opportunity for students and professional staff of similar interests to work together. This in turn will enhance understanding and provide opportunities for students to develop self-motivation and individual responsibility.

Thus, individualization requires an organization which allows the student to engage in activities uniquely appropriate to his own style and rate of learning. In this type of organization, instruction promotes independence, provides opportunities for study beyond the regular curriculum, and permits maximum use of instructional resources. The curriculum must be designed to meet the individual requirements of each child at his particular level of ability, achievement, and progression. In applying such a premise to the day-to-day operations of a typical school program, it is not difficult to understand the resultant frustration expressed by administrators and teachers when it is considered that most conventional programs have only accommodated group, not individual, interactions and processes.

This book concentrates on the impact of the concept of individualization on educational innovations in elementary and secondary schools in general and on the need to explore practical as well as theoretical methods for meeting the individual differences of students and teachers within these schools. This book also will focus on various techniques and methods for individualizing instruction which have been recognized as being successful in a wide variety of elementary and secondary school situations in recent years.

The book is separated into four major sections. Part I deals with the general topic of individualization of instruction and emphasizes several contemporary trends, methods, and techniques which have been developed recently to meet the individual differences of student and professional staff. Part II emphasizes several operational techniques which have been employed in some elementary and secondary schools in attempts to provide greater individualization in specific instructional areas. Chapters in this section are devoted to the development of a nongraded elementary program, as well as secondary programs in the humanities, English, and the fine arts. The central thematic material for these chapters is based on such techniques as team teaching, flexible schedules, or instructional (behavioral) objectives as vehicles for providing greater student participation and individualization in the instructional system of the school.

Part III emphasizes the role of the secondary school student as a co-participant in the educational enterprise and the opportunities afforded through various methods of individualizing instruction for allowing students greater latitude for individuality and freedom of expression. Consideration is given to the student's role in instructional policy and decision-making, curriculum development, the development of an individual's responsibility for his education, and the creation of more humanizing, student-oriented educational environments. The questions raised here are: What is the typical secondary school really like from the perspective of the student? Does the conventional school structure impede or enhance the development of creative skills and individuality? Can teachers provide instructional environments for the development of the creative potential of the individual student? Are there realistic and operational alternatives in developing more creative and humanizing school programs?

Part IV is devoted to the concept of teacher professionalism, differentiated staffing models, and other unique organizational schemes which provide greater creative and functional arrangements for coordinating school activities while placing emphasis upon the individualization of instructional systems. Concepts of educational change and critical leadership priorities necessary for creating climates for instructional change and innovation are also treated.

Although this book may raise more questions and issues than it objectively answers, the author submits that it is time that educators attempt to explore alternative solutions to many problems faced by American elementary and secondary schools. The social scene today furnishes ample evidence of the discontent on the American campus and the obvious inability of education to cope with these rising problems. Anyone interested in the continued survival of American educational institutions as vital instructional forces in our society must be willing and eager to explore and develop alternative solutions. This book is written in recognition of this need in order to provide educators, students, and laymen with a framework for developing more creative school programs that will be capable of meeting the demands of today's youngsters in preparing for leadership positions in the twenty-first century.

INDIVIDUALIZING EDUCATIONAL PROGRAMS

Techniques and Methods

INDIVIDUALIZING INSTRUCTION: CONTEMPORARY TRENDS IN ORGANIZATIONAL PATTERNS

2

INTRODUCTION

The purpose of this chapter, as well as Chapter 3, is to serve as an introduction to several contemporary trends and methods for individualizing instruction which have been employed by elementary or secondary schools during the past few years. This presentation is not intended to be an exhaustive list of various techniques nor will it contain an in-depth or intensive treatment of these programs. Rather, it is an introduction to concepts and basic definitions. Broadly based examples are given which are representative of activities in the various areas. The main purpose is to stimulate and incite interest in a wide variety of methods and techniques for individualizing instruction, thereby providing the reader with a general framework for pursuing individual topics of interest in greater depth as he is motivated to do so.

Essentially, this is a survey and synthesis of various techniques that have been employed in individualizing instructional programs in recent years. It may also serve as a ready reference for brief descriptions of methods that are gaining wider application and are finding more acceptable positions in American education.

The methods and techniques to be covered in these two chapters will be organized under four broad categories:

1. *Organizational Patterns.* These are techniques for individualizing instruction which have their greatest effect, or place

primary emphasis, upon the organizational or structural features of a school's program. These are:

Team teaching
Nongraded instruction
Flexible scheduling
Large group–small group instruction

While it is recognized that these programs have their roots in the curriculum and may greatly influence curriculum development within any school, it is proposed that they are primarily organizational schemes which provide techniques for rearranging the basic components and structural features of a school. A school employing a flexible schedule or a team teaching program as a vehicle for reorganizing the resources of the school may not necessarily develop new approaches to instruction and curriculum development. Instructional change may, in fact, depend more on the ingenuity of the leadership within the professional staff in utilizing the new organizational scheme. Essentially, the position is that the development and implementation of change programs categorized as fundamentally "organizational programs" do not necessarily guarantee the development of changes in instructional methodology. Programs which basically effect the organizational elements of a school do not guarantee fundamental changes in teacher behavior or attitude in relation to the instructional process or individuality of teaching and learning.

2. *Curriculum Development.* These are techniques for individualizing instruction which place their primary emphasis upon curriculum development and the teaching-learning process. These are:

Continuous progress curriculum (performance curriculum)
Individualized learning materials
   Teacher prepared: UNIPAC
                   Learning Activity Package
                   Esbensen Pac
   Commercially prepared: Individually prescribed instruction
                      AIR-Project PLAN
                      Computer based resource guides
Instructional (behavioral) objectives
Independent study programs

3. *Educational Technology.* These are techniques for indi-

vidualizing instruction which place primary emphasis upon educational technology. These are:

Computer assisted instruction (CAI)
Audiovisual media
Programmed instruction
Teaching machines

4. *Educational Facilities.* These are techniques for individualizing instruction which raise serious questions concerning the present design of educational facilities. These are:

Large group-small group instructional space
Independent study space
Instructional resource center
Instructional materials center
Team planning and teacher office facilities

ORGANIZATIONAL TECHNIQUES FOR
INDIVIDUALIZING INSTRUCTION

TEAM TEACHING (COOPERATIVE TEACHING)

The oldest and perhaps best known of all the techniques employed in the past decade for creating individual approaches to instruction is team teaching (sometimes referred to as cooperative teaching).[1] This teaching method, as well as specific team programs, has dominated the education literature for the past several years.

---

[1] The more recent use of the concept of team teaching in education is generally attributed to J. Lloyd Trump and Dorsey Baynham, *Guide to Better Schools: Focus on Change* (Chicago: Rand McNally & Company, 1961). This volume reported the results of a study dealing with staff utilization conducted by the National Association of Secondary School Principals. Also, in 1957 the Fund for Advancement of Education financed the efforts of the Education Faculty of the Claremont Graduate School, Claremont, California, to design a teaching team program for improving the quality of teaching and counseling and the use of time and talents of teachers. In 1958, under the auspices of the Fund, the Teaching Team Program conducted a one-year pilot study at this institution. In 1959 the Ford Foundation granted support to several universities in the United States (e.g., Claremont Graduate School, Harvard University) to conduct further studies of team teaching programs. The design of these pilot studies has established several hypothetical advantages of teaching teams as well as various types of models. These team models have been stated in several progress reports distributed by these funded programs.

Simply, team teaching can be defined as the use of multiple teaching personnel for any given group of students in a given instructional area. This suggests one teacher will be "teamed" either with other teachers of equal responsibility and status or with differentiated responsibilities and status.[2] Inherent within the definition is also the requirement for paraprofessional personnel, teaching assistants, clerical assistants, technicians, or other supplemental instructional aides. Conceptually, team teaching also implies wide variations in patterns of classroom organization utilizing multiple instructional personnel.

> Any intelligent discussion of team teaching must begin by making clear what it actually is, for in visiting so-called team teaching programs around the country, I have seen too many examples of what it is not—part-time practices, with teachers tacitly or openly agreeing, "Your turn today; mine tomorrow."[3]

Rationale. The usual arguments in favor of team teaching might be briefly summarized as follows: (1) By combining their specialties and talents, teachers can offer a far richer educational experience than their students might otherwise receive. (2) Through a variety of grouping possibilities, teachers can provide their students with differentiated instruction more closely associated with the individual student's abilities. (3) Students with particular requirements can be given specialized attention. (4) More capable students can pursue their particular interests more effectively during individual study periods than in a self-contained classroom. (5) The formation of teams can also avoid duplication in the use of audiovisual media, guest speakers, or other supplemental instructional materials. (6) It furnishes teachers with more unscheduled time to plan and prepare curriculum, to read and develop professionally, and to relax and be creative.[4]

Conventional Program Design. At present, the concept

---

[2] Chapter 12 of this volume contains a more complete description of a differentiated staffing model.

[3] William Georgiades, "Team Teaching: A New Star, Not a Meteor," *NEA Journal* (April, 1967).

[4] Jack R. Fraenkel and Richard E. Gross, "Team Teaching: A Note of Caution Is In Order," *NEA Journal* (April, 1967).

"team teaching" does not communicate any universally recognized model for designing teams. Theoretically, there are as many different team programs as there are schools that have implemented the technique. The following description, extracted from the Ford Foundation's experimentation in team teaching, might serve as a representative sample of general directions in creating more conventional team programs.

In its essence, team teaching is an instructional unit within a school. . . . This unit is a combination of: (1) a distinct student group, (2) a small faculty group with complementary talents responsible for teaching the student group, and (3) certain persons who assist the teachers and students. For purpose of description of this unit, the student group may be regarded as the student team, the faculty group as the faculty team, and the assistants as auxiliary personnel.

First, a secondary school student team comprises a clearly identifiable group of from ninety to one hundred and eighty students who have chosen a similar program of courses, such as college preparatory or vocational; an elementary school team consists of from 150 to 200 students of particular ages or grades. Each student team is assigned to a faculty team.

Second, a faculty team consists of teachers whose talents and specializations complement one another. In the secondary school, it comprises three to six teachers who have the same daily conference period. Each of the members represents a certain academic discipline, or subject area; some of the members possess, or agree to acquire, skills in auxiliary areas such as remedial reading or counseling.

Each faculty team has an elected or appointed leader who accepts responsibility for coordinating his team's efforts. He is paid a stipend above his normal pay for this responsibility. In the secondary school he is given an extra period, in addition to his conference period, to plan and to coordinate team activities; in the elementary school for the same purposes he is relieved of teaching from time to time by an auxiliary teacher.

Third, auxiliary personnel for the team include teacher aides, auxiliary teachers, and laymen with special talents needed in school programs. . . . An aide is a noncertificated person from the community who works with the team on a paid part-time basis. He may do clerical duties for team teachers, such as typing, filing, mimeographing, phoning, taking attendance, answering correspondence. . . . On occasions, he may perform certain routine aspects of teaching, such as correcting tests, arranging field trips, proctoring examinations . . . and administering examinations. . . . A strong effort is made to move the eligible teacher aide on to the teaching team as a teacher intern during his second year.[5]

Secondary Team Models. Because most conventional secondary schools are organized into classes according to academic subjects, that is, English, history, or math, and by grades, departures from these basic patterns might be used in suggesting various team models. Essentially, teaching teams can be developed by exploring various possibilities along the extremes of a continuum employing conventional secondary organizational characteristics. At one extreme of the continuum, an interdisciplinary team can be formed with several teachers from various academic subjects. Several teams could be formed at each grade level. The example below shows a hypothetical tenth grade interdisciplinary team composed of English, history, math, and science teachers.

TEAM I

Interdisciplinary Team

Grades	9	10	11	12
		English		
		history		
		math		
		science		

At the other extreme of the continuum, a team can be created that consists of two or more teachers with auxiliary personnel from one academic discipline and with students from several grade levels. This might appropriately be referred to as a nongraded team. By moving along the continuum from one extreme to the other, several combinations of teams can be formed by rearranging these basic components.

It is not necessary to confine teams to academic curricular areas. Many excellent teams have been developed where nonacademic or elective curriculum has been included in the basic team design. An interdisciplinary, nongraded humanities team composed of six teachers representing English literature, fine arts,

[5] Claremont Team Teaching Program, Fourth Annual Report to the Ford Foundation, 1962–63, Claremont Graduate School, Claremont, California.

TEAM II

Nongraded Team

Grades	
9	English
10	English
11	English
12	English

political science, philosophy, mathematics, and physics was created in one high school.

Human Considerations in Teams. Inherent in any teaching endeavor are the factors of interpersonal relations and human interactions. The importance of this factor is accentuated particularly in team teaching situations, where teachers must work together closely and regularly. Administrators and teachers who develop team programs must be sensitive to the human elements which exist in team interactions. In establishing criteria for selection of team members, perhaps no factor is more important than that of *compatible* relationships among team members.

Team composition may differ widely in specific instances concerning student age and subject area, but in each team design the complementary talents, abilities, and interests of teachers are essential considerations. The curriculum philosophy of the school, the administration, and the teacher will influence the grade, the level, and the subjects involved in the team approach, but these considerations are no more important than the compatibility factor of the team members. "Each team member must be pliable enough and professional enough to work as a vital part of a team. The rugged individualist may be an excellent teacher in certain settings, but if he becomes a member of a teaching team, he must learn how to remain excellent as he works cooperatively with fellow teachers. In a real sense, the teaching team is a functioning social unit."[6]

Considerations for Team Effectiveness. The literature is replete with suggestions concerning team effectiveness. However,

---

[6] M. P. Heller, "Overcoming Pitfalls in Team Teaching," *Civic Leader* (January, 1967).

schools should be cautioned that merely following the acceptable criteria or copying any particular team model will not guarantee success. Generally, basic considerations for team teaching success include arrangements for cooperative staff planning and preparation time, use of paraprofessionals and instructional assistants, provision of adequate materials, proper and ample audiovisual media, adequate preparation of the teachers involved, and a proper climate of administrative support and encouragement. Research indicates that support from the administrative staff is vital to a school's success in team teaching.[7]

The following questions may be useful in providing guidelines for success in developing and implementing teaching teams:

1. Are the teachers suited for team teaching? Are some teachers most effective when they work alone? How important is the factor of teacher insecurity in developing team relationships?
2. Is the administration committed to experimentation and change? Will there be superintendent and board support? Will sufficient funding be provided to support the program?
3. Are the educational facilities suitable for, or adaptable to, team operations? Can space be converted for appropriate large group and small group rooms? Can a variety of learning activities take place at different times without disrupting the routine essential to the school's operation?
4. Is the team program being planned in order to integrate other appropriate innovations currently in use? Is teaming most effective within or across subject lines?
5. Will student learning benefit from team teaching? Will the team composition enhance individualized study and independent study programs? Can all students benefit from large and small group instructional arrangements?
6. In the present climate of innovation, is there a danger that team teaching, as well as other secondary instructional changes, could become "form without substance?" Will the program, once implemented, become an end in itself rather than the means to an end? What precautions can be taken within the administrative staff to prevent this from happening?

The most persistent problems encountered in team teaching programs are generally attitudinal rather than mechanical, physi-

---

[7] Wilfred E. Belleau, Jr., "A Study of Team Teaching in the Senior High Schools of California" (unpublished doctoral thesis, The University of Southern California, Los Angeles, 1965).

cal, or financial. Personality problems, communications problems, and coordination problems can be solved if teacher attitudes are positive and if the teachers truly are functioning as a team.

Evaluation of Team Teaching. Research evidence is scanty concerning the question of whether team teaching is demonstrably more effective in producing learning than the conventional classroom situation with only one teacher who operates independently. Of the experiments conducted, most studies indicate no significant difference in achievement between the experimental (team teaching) groups and the more conventional groups.[8] Only a few studies show that more effective learning occurred under the team approach.[9]

Serious doubts can be raised about most of these studies, however. Greatly improved student performance as measured by standardized achievement test is not the most important objective of team teaching. Teaching basic methods of inquiry and cultivating a desire to learn are much more significant. The purpose of education is not to pile up a storehouse of information in each student's brain, but to give him the tools with which to think. Unfortunately, most current techniques of evaluation are designed to measure the piling-up process.[10]

Because of methodological arguments surrounding statements such as the foregoing, it may be that team teaching has not yet been properly evaluated against the correct objectives. There is

---

[8] Studies which show no significant difference are: D. E. Christensen, "Experimenting with Geography Teaching by Television," *Journal of Geography* (February, 1965); Darrell Holmes and Lois Harvey, "An Evaluation of Two Methods of Grouping," *Educational Research Bulletin* (November 14, 1965); Philip Lambert and others, "A Comparison of Pupil Achievement in Team and Self-Contained Organizations," *Journal of Experimental Education* (Spring, 1965); I. Zweibelson, M. Bahnmuller, and L. Lyman, "Team Teaching and Flexible Grouping in the Junior High School Social Studies," *Journal of Experimental Education* (Fall, 1965).

[9] The following studies show some appreciable difference in the team teaching group: Thomas A. MacCalla, "Coordinated Instruction of Senior High School United States History and American Literature Classes" (unpublished doctoral thesis, The University of California, Los Angeles, 1964); Wanda Riggle, Lawrall Jensen, and Matthew F. Noall, "Teacher-Team Project, Roosevelt Junior High School, Duchense County School District, Utah" *NASSP Bulletin* (January, 1961); Scott Thomson, "An Analysis of Achievement Outcomes: Team Teaching and Traditional Classes" (unpublished doctoral thesis, Stanford University, Stanford, 1963).

[10] Fraenkel and Gross, *op. cit.*

little evidence to suggest that team teaching has created any adverse effects upon students or the learning process and there is some indirect evidence to suggest that benefits are derived from successful team programs. Teams provide greater opportunities for teacher and student interaction, as well as opportunities for more instructional flexibility than is typically manifest in the conventional self-contained classroom.

NONGRADED INSTRUCTION

In its simplest form, nongraded instruction can be divided into two general dimensions: (1) A nongraded program eliminates the conventional grouping of students by chronological age into arbitrary grade levels. Instead, students of different chronological ages are grouped together according to their development, achievement, or ability in a particular subject. (2) Nongrading is particularly useful as a method of scheduling basic skill subjects such as reading or math so that a student may proceed up a carefully constructed series of steps in that particular subject at his own rate (continuous progress).[11]

Student Variability—Rationale for Nongraded Schools. The nongraded school is based on the premise that there is a great deal of difference among students of the same chronological age and that these differences cannot be properly treated within the arbitrary grouping patterns found in the graded self-contained classroom. Without this prerequisite of wide student variability, the need for the nongraded organization would be less essential. Attempts to break the lock-step pattern of the conventional classroom are most often attempts to adjust better to the individual differences that exist among students. One study, using a typical cross-section of students who had been in the New York City schools for seven semesters, reported that the range in educational age was from six to fifteen years, although these students had entered school at the same time and had received the same number of months of schooling.[12]

---

[11] See the section in Chapter 3 on continuous progress instruction for a detailed description of this program.

[12] Gertrude Hildreth, "Individual Differences," (Encyclopedia of Educational Research).

Nongrading is not a method of instruction. Rather, it is a method of organization, an administrative device that rejects the conventional age-grouping of students in favor of grouping patterns based on individual needs. However, merely eliminating conventional grade designations and grouping students by developmental age or achievement rather than by chronological age does not fulfill the purpose of a nongraded instructional program. In order for this organizational device to have significance, it must provide for each student a path of individual progress suited to his educational needs. The essence of nongrading is continuous progress and *continuity of progress*. Each student has the opportunity to progress as rapidly as he is able; he is neither held back nor pushed ahead by an organizational system based upon the implicit assumption that students of similar chronological age are similar in all other respects.

A further purpose of the nongraded program has been to achieve more effective utilization of teaching strengths. In this program the teacher no longer operates in isolation. He is part of a team, each member of which can contribute to the professional growth of the other. Ideas are exchanged, new teaching methods evolve, problems are attacked with concerted action, the teacher has an audience of peers to stimulate him to greater efforts on behalf of the student and to reward him with approval for what he does well. In short, the teacher also is provided with an opportunity for continuous progress.

FLEXIBLE SCHEDULING[13]

In American secondary schools, at least until recently, three related conventions concerning the arrangement of the school day endured through many changes in educational philosophy and method: (1) All classes in secondary schools ordinarily have met on identical weekly time patterns, that is, for the same number of meetings per week and for the same length of time per meeting (six or seven periods per day). (2) Each high school class has generally met at the same time and for the same length of time

---

[13] For an in-depth treatment of the applications of flexible scheduling in secondary schools, the reader is referred to W. Deane Wiley and Lloyd K. Bishop, *The Flexibly Scheduled High School* (West Nyack, New York: Parker Publishing Co., 1968).

each day of the week (45- or 50-minute periods). (3) Secondary school students have generally been expected to be in class, under the supervision of a teacher, every school day. These classes have usually contained from 15 to 40 students with 22 to 25 students identified as the ideal maximum enrollment for each class.

In the conventional educational environment, strong philosophical assumptions have prevailed concerning the need for control of the students (the traditional school schedule is an excellent control mechanism), the student's innate interest in school, the learning process, and the teacher's role in the instructional program. Essentially, the conventional school program stresses the idea that students are irresponsible, that they dislike school, that learning can take place only in a formal, self-contained classroom where a teacher is present, that the teacher is the sole guardian of the instructional enterprise, and that all students must be in school and under supervision all day, every day. Furthermore, in this homogenized environment we also specify that students of similar chronological ages have the same needs and skills, that they have the same preparation and capacity for learning, and that they have similar interests and motivations for being in school. All of these conventions and traditional assumptions concerning secondary schools are being examined by the development of a novel approach to the arrangement of the school day. The *flexible (modular) schedule* opens up new opportunities for curriculum development, for instructional improvement, and particularly for greater recognition of individual student strengths.

Rationale. The conventional six-period day has long been the graveyard of educational change and, rightfully or wrongfully, secondary principals have used its restrictive features as an excuse for not doing much about the instructional program. In 1962-1963 the Stanford School Scheduling System (SSSS) was opened on an experimental basis in a few selected schools. The desire of some of these schools to break from conventional scheduling methods and to implement more experimental instructional practices may be summarized as follows:

1. To provide a better opportunity to develop a comprehensive curriculum in terms of more elective offerings in areas of the curriculum such as art, music, drama, humanities, speech, debate, business education, industrial education, and homemaking.

2. To be able to accommodate additional student course requests—at least seven per student—without scheduling a conventional seven-period day.
3. To be able to use time as a variable in the learning process in contrast to a conventional schedule where time is a constant and the learning process is adjusted to fit a fixed time pattern.
4. To enhance the professionalization of the classroom teacher by providing more time during the school day for teachers to prepare for classes and to bring teachers into a tutorial relationship with their students.
5. To provide an opportunity for change in teacher methodology by implementing a schedule that would better facilitate such practices as team teaching, large group–small group instruction, and independent study.
6. To attempt to inculcate in each student a sense of responsibility for his own education. This is based on the proposition that only as the individual student understands his personal need for education will true education take place.[14]

The School Day. Flexible scheduling creates greater opportunities for variety in the daily schedule than the conventional schedule permits. The schedule is not limited to the basic time unit (period) traditionally used in designing secondary programs. Instead, it employs a new, more flexible unit. Borrowing a term from architecture, the designers of flexible scheduling divide the school day into *modules* rather than into the conventional six or seven periods. The module, generally 18 to 22 minutes in length, is flexible in that it may be used singly or in any number of combinations. Thus, classes may meet for any number of modules per day, depending on the instructional activity to be performed.

Because of its length, few classes will meet for only one module. However, it is common for classes to meet for two, three, or four modules, with some laboratory-oriented courses even meeting for five or six. Typically, 15 to 25 modules will be found in a school day, again depending on the length of the module employed and the number of courses in which each student is allowed to enroll. It is not uncommon in some schools to have students enrolled in as many as eight or more different courses. Class sessions do not always begin and end simultaneously; some classes are dis-

---

[14] Lloyd K. Bishop, "Computerized Modular Scheduling: A Technical Breakthrough for More Flexible School Programs," *Kappa Delta Pi Record* (October, 1968).

missed while others remain in session. The traditional school bell is often eliminated. Students are generally allowed a few minutes of passing time between classes; however, for most students and teachers there are blocks of unscheduled time between classes.

The School Week—Course Structures. This restructuring of the school day brings with it significant changes in the school week and in the structuring of any particular course throughout the week. Courses may now meet for different lengths of time on different days of the week and classes seldom meet every day of the week. For example, an English class might meet for two modules of large group instruction on Monday, for three modules of small group discussion on Wednesday, and for four modules of laboratory (individualized project) activities on Thursday. Some classes will meet three days a week, twice a week, or possibly only once a week. A course may also meet twice in the same day. Although this type of schedule is rare, teachers on occasion can employ this technique to advantage.

In addition to the variability of course structuring, the opportunity also exists to schedule courses with varying weights, that is, to schedule them for different numbers of modules per week. Some courses can meet for as few as two or three and others for as many as 16 (or more) modules per week. Generally, there is a direct relationship between the length of the module used in a school's program and the number of modules assigned a particular course. However, courses assigned large numbers of modules (12 or more) can become extremely difficult to schedule when generating the master schedule.

Flexible scheduling also offers new possibilities for the development of variable class size, that is, the organization of courses into meetings of related large group instruction, conventional-size groups, and very small groups and/or individual tutorials. Class size can then be matched with the appropriateness of the instructional method to be employed (lecture or discussion), knowledge concerning the student group, and the amount of time required to conduct a particular instructional task. This variability of class size related to instructional methodology usually is distributed throughout the week in time ratios of 15–20 percent large group instruction, 30–35 percent small group discussion sessions, and 15–20 percent laboratory activities. Also inherent within the concept of flexible scheduling is the assumption that each student should have some part of the school week unscheduled so that he can participate in an independent study program.[15] Under ideal conditions, approximately 65–75 percent of the student's school week would be spent in formal in-class instruction, with approximately 25–35 percent unscheduled time for participation in independent or individualized study.

It is the author's contention that the most successful and sophisticated flexible schedules to date are computer-generated, although some school systems have employed hand-made flexible schedules. Due to the complexity of flexible schedule-building, the hand-made schedule may seriously limit the number of choices and instructional alternatives available to the school's program. Frequently, the hand-made schedule also limits the number of students who can participate in the flexible program. Computer scheduling is not, by any means, a completely mechanical process, although this assumption is often made by the scheduling novice. In any school employing computerized techniques, the professional staff is able to make significant adaptations within the computer-oriented master schedule and with individual student schedules as particular instructional problems arise. Of perhaps even greater significance is the amount of professional involvement required within a school which elects to develop a computerized flexible schedule. Department chairmen, along with their teachers, must be involved continually and extensively throughout the developmental stages of the program. Thus, by utilizing flexible scheduling as a vehicle for change, many school staffs have been able to create more significant curricula and provide unusual opportunities for developing creative and individualized instructional programs. Two examples of a weekly program in a flexible schedule system are shown in Tables 2.1 and 2.2 below.

LARGE GROUP–SMALL GROUP INSTRUCTION

One of the basic assumptions in the design of many flexible schedules is that most subjects, when properly taught, will provide each student with exposure to four fundamental types of instruc-

---

[15] For a more detailed description of independent study, see the section in Chapter 3 on this topic.

tion each week. These are: (1) large group instruction, (2) small group discussions, (3) independent study, and (4) laboratory activities. Therefore, the concept of large group–small group instruction has become endemic to the design of a more individualized school program.

It is frequently assumed that one of the most flagrant viola-

TABLE 2.1

Student Weekly Program of Classes in a Computer-Generated Flexible Schedule

Modules[a]	Monday	Tuesday	Wednesday	Thursday	Friday
1	Fr. PE[b]		Fr. PE		Fr. PE
2	Fr. PE		Fr. PE		Fr. PE
3	Fr. PE	Type 1	Fr. PE	Type 1	Fr. PE
4		Type 1		Type 1	
5	Math 9		Math 9	Math 9	Math 9
6	Math 9		Math 9	Math 9	Math 9
7	Eng. LG[c]	Int SS[d]	Eng. SG	Int SS	Eng. SG
8	Eng. LG	Int SS	Eng. SG	Int SS	Eng. SG
9		Int SS	Eng. SG	Int SS	Eng. SG
10	Lunch	Lunch	Lunch		
11				Lunch	Lunch
12	Frnch 1A	IRD LG[e]	Frnch 1A		Frnch 1A
13	Frnch 1A	IRD LG	Frnch 1A		Frnch 1A
14				Frnch 1A	
15	Type 1		Type 1	Frnch 1A	
16	Type 1		Type 1	Frnch 1A	Lang Lab
17		Fr. PE	IRD Lab		
18	Lang PE	Fr. PE	IRD Lab	Int SS LG	IRD Lab
19		Type Lab	IRD Lab	Int SS LG	IRD Lab
20		Type Lab	IRD Lab		IRD Lab

[a] Periods of time—20 minutes in length
[b] Freshman Physical Education
[c] English Large Group-Small Group Instruction
[d] Introduction to the Social Sciences
[e] Industrial Research and Development (Industrial Education Program)

tions of the principle of individualization is the large group. However, when placed in proper perspective with other instructional activities, large group instruction can become a functional and important aspect of any instructional/learning system. When large group instruction is structured as one aspect of a *total instructional system*, and if the basic components of the system are appropriately integrated and interrelated into the methodology and instructional planning of the professional staff, then large group instruction, as

TABLE 2.2

Teacher's Weekly Program and Assignments in a Computer-Generated Flexible Schedule

Modules[a]	Monday	Tuesday	Wednesday	Thursday	Friday
1		Int SS SG1[b]		Int SS SG1	
2		Int SS SG1		Int SS SG1	
3		Int SS SG1	Att. Check	Int SS SG1	
4		Int SS SG2		Int SS SG2	
5		Int SS SG2		Int SS SG2	
6		Int SS SG2		Int SS SG2	
7					
8		Int SS SG3		Int SS SG3	
9		Int SS SG3	Int SS SG4	Int SS SG3	Int SS SG4
10	Int SS LG	Int SS SG3	Int SS SG4	Int SS SG3	Int SS SG4
11	Int SS LG		Int SS SG4		Int SS SG4
12					
13		Int SS SG5		Int SS SG5	
14		Int SS SG5		Int SS SG5	
15		Int SS SG5		Int SS SG5	
16	Int SS LG	Int SS SG6		Int SS SG6	Int SS LG4
17	Int SS LG	Int SS SG6	Int SS LG3	Int SS SG6	Int SS LG4
18		Int SS SG6	Int SS LG3	Int SS SG6	
19					
20					

[a] Periods of time—20 minutes in length
[b] Introduction to the Social Sciences

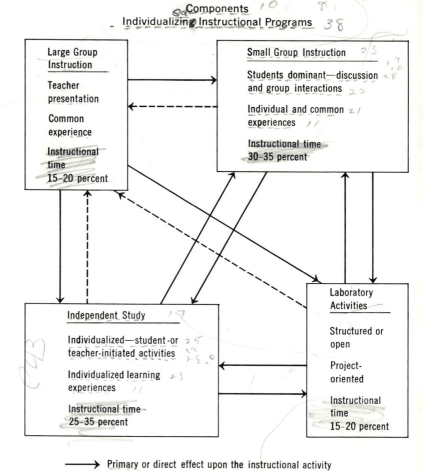

Components
Individualizing Instructional Programs

FIGURE 2.1
Basic Model—Instructional Learning System

well as other instructional modes, can perform a significant role in the individualization of instruction.

As indicated in the model (Figure 2.1) the relationship among the components of the system must be maintained in proper perspective and sufficient planning and continuity should be provided between each instructional activity. If proper continuity between the four instructional phases is maintained, the student will be prepared for each large group session. If this preparation is appropriately developed, the large group activity can be conceived as an "individualized" segment of the total instructional process for any particular student.

Characteristics of Large Groups. The size of the large group will be predicated more on the facilities within the school than any other factor. After the initial experience of conducting large groups, some teachers have indicated that a group of 300-350 students is feasible and educationally defensible. The seating accommodations of the facility used, physical arrangements, supplemental equipment, audiovisual requirements, and an adequate PA system are more critical considerations than the number of students who attend.

Essentially, the large group is a teacher-dominated, teacher-lecture type of activity. Therefore, if the teacher has a well-prepared presentation, the size of the group is not important. (Due to psychological factors created by large groups, many teachers may wish to have much smaller audiences—perhaps only 75 to 150— during their initial experience with large group instruction.) Generally, a large group can be defined as any group of students brought together for formal instructional purposes where the group is larger than that found in the conventional classroom situation.

> Obviously the effectiveness of large group instruction, as with any instructional technique, is dependent upon the talent and ability of the teacher engaged in it. . . . Some teachers, . . . are completely unable to work effectively in large groups. There is something foreboding to some teachers about facing a large group of 150-300 students at one time. In some instances this same person may be quite effective in small discussion groups. This obviously points to the need for team work among several teachers with varying skills and abilities. Also, team teaching and large group arrangements are pratically compatible because all teachers on a team are not required to meet all large group meetings. While one teacher is presenting material in his area of expertise, the other teachers may be preparing for their presentations in their respective areas of ability and interest.[16]

Purposes of Large Groups. Basically, large group activities can be separated into two categories: (1) those representing *instructional* purposes and (2) those which are primarily *institutional*

---

[16] Wiley and Bishop, *op. cit.*

in nature. For instructional purposes, large groups can be effectively employed for such activities as lectures, presentation of instructional material or other supplemental presentations, critiques of student work where it applies to the total group, general testing, diagnosis, and evaluation; review, repetition, and remediation; and films, entertainment, and stimulation.

Institutional purposes of large groups might include such factors as the conservation of teacher time and talent, particularly useful in conjunction with team teaching; the control of sequencing and pacing of course content; the provision of a common experience for students which may be especially useful in terms of heterogenous groupings; the allowance of some diversity in instruction; and the provision of maximum preparation time and enhancing of instructional efficiency.

Small Groups. While small group activities are generally placed in the same context as large group instruction, the two instructional modes actually have very little in common. Many of the generalizations made concerning large group activities do not apply or are, in fact, contrary to effective small group discussion techniques. When the group is operating as a genuine small group, teacher and student behavior is fundamentally different from that found in the typical classroom.

Characteristics of Small Groups. The basic premise of small group instruction is that in the conventional classroom teachers talk too much and too little opportunity exists for significant dialogue and interaction among students. Contrary to large group instruction, the size of the small group is extremely critical. For the most effective interaction and the involvement of all students, group size should not be larger than 12 to 15 students, with the ideal number only eight or ten. When this small number of participants meet consistently as a group, it is difficult for any single member to remain isolated from interaction or involvement, either psychologically or physically, for any length of time. This generalization cannot be made concerning the conventional classroom, where timid or reticent students are often unwilling or unable to participate in group discussions and are able, due to the size of the class, to remain isolated.

The fundamental and characteristic event in the small group

is *discussion* (discussion is interpreted broadly to include as well debate, dialogue, extensive group interaction, and exchange of ideas, beliefs, and values). The small group meeting should not be used for reading, writing exercises, memorizing, lecturing, examinations, or other typical classroom events. The most productive small group is one where the teacher is passive and the students, through interaction and dialogue, assume a dominant role. Generally, the students are allowed to set the task for each group session with guidance, when necessary, provided by the teacher. The leadership role passing from teacher to students creates a threatening environment for those teachers who require passivity and acquiescence from students.

The physical location and facilities for small groups are less essential than for large group instruction. Small group interactions can be developed in any reasonably quiet and isolated environment. Preferably, the conventional classroom is not used but rather a smaller room without the usual classroom paraphenalia. More rapid and genuine group interactions can be created if the usual desks, tables, or other physical barriers are omitted.

After the group has been meeting consistently for a period of time, it is not uncommon for a group dynamic to develop among the participants. If this emotional and psychological phenomenon can be appropriately harnessed, many productive activities and greater sensitivity toward each participant can occur. One of the benefits of the small group process is the opportunity to allow individuals to develop closer, more sensitive, and more genuine relationships with each other. An attempt is made to break down the façade, or psychological screen, that many individuals develop in group situations and that inhibits them from authentic interactions and relationships with their peers. Furthermore, an opportunity develops for genuine exchange of ideas, allowing the individual student to see that others share similar concerns, feelings, frustrations, and anxieties. A rapport and closeness can exist between the student and his peers and between the student and his teacher which is seldom found in the conventional classroom. Thus, the small group adds one additional and necessary dimension to the individualization of instructional programs in the elementary and secondary school.

SELECTED BIBLIOGRAPHY

Bair, Medill, and Richard G. Woodward. *Team Teaching in Action.* Boston: Houghton Mifflin Co., 1964.

Bales, R. F. "The Equilibrium Problem in Small Groups," in Talcott Parsons *et al.* (eds.), *Working Papers In The Theory of Action.* Glencoe, Ill.: Free Press, 1953.

Beggs, David W., III (ed.). *Team Teaching—Bold New Venture.* Bloomington, Ind.: Indiana University Press, 1964.

Beggs, David W., III, and Edward G. Buffie (eds.). *Nongraded Schools in Action.* Bloomington, Ind.: Indiana University Press, 1967.

Brown, Frank. *The Nongraded High School.* Englewood Cliffs, N.J.: Prentice-Hall, Inc., 1963.

Bush, Robert N., and Dwight W. Allen. *A New Design for High School Education: Assuming a Flexible Schedule.* New York: McGraw-Hill Book Co., 1964.

Davis, Harold S. *Team Teaching Bibliography.* Cleveland, III.: Educational Research Council of Greater Cleveland, 1964.

Glatthorn, Allan A. *Learning in the Small Group.* Dayton, Ohio: Institute for Development of Educational Activities, 1966.

Goodlad, John I., and Obert H. Anderson. *The Nongraded Elementary School.* New York: Harcourt, Brace & World, Inc., 1959.

Hare, A. Paul. *Handbook of Small Group Research.* New York: Macmillan Co., 1962.

Hare, A. Paul *et al.* (eds.). *Small Groups: Studies in Social Interaction,* rev. ed. New York: Alfred A. Knopf, 1967.

Manlove, Donald C., and David W. Beggs, III. *Flexible Scheduling.* Bloomington, Ind.: Indiana University Press, 1965.

Peterson, Carl H. *Effective Team Teaching.* West Nyack, N.Y.: Parker Publishing Co., 1966.

Petrequin, Gaynor. *Individualizing Learning Through Modular-Flexible Programming.* New York: McGraw-Hill Book Co., 1968.

Polos, Nicholas C. *The Dynamics of Team Teaching.* Dubuque, Iowa: Wm. C. Brown Company, 1965.

Polos, Nicholos C. (ed.). *Team Teaching and Flexible Scheduling for Tomorrow.* New York: MSS Educational Publishing Co., 1969.

Schein, Edgar H., and Warren G. Bennis. *Personal and Organizational Change Through Group Methods.* New York: John Wiley & Sons, Inc., 1965.

Shaplin, Judson T., and Henry F. Olds (eds.). *Team Teaching.* New York: Harper and Row, Publishers, Inc., 1964.

INDIVIDUALIZING INSTRUCTION: CONTEMPORARY TRENDS IN CURRICULUM, TECHNOLOGY, AND FACILITIES

3

CURRICULUM TECHNIQUES FOR INDIVIDUALIZING INSTRUCTION

While significant strides have been made in rearranging the organizational and physical components of elementary and secondary schools with programs such as team teaching, flexible scheduling, and nongraded grouping patterns, to date only minimal progress has been made in curriculum development activities which offer specific content or subject matter methodologies for practical applications in individualizing instruction. Educators have devoted considerable energy to attacking the problems associated with the physical and mechanical features of schools, but they continue to fail to provide viable alternatives for the more abstract but substantive elements of subject matter and instructional methodology. This is particularly evident in any search for specific, well-developed, and operationally tested programs for individualizing curriculum and instructional content in both elementary and secondary schools.

For example, the concepts and theoretical assumptions associated with the continuous progress curriculum seem to be philosophically sound and educationally defensible. The reader, however, will have difficulty locating many schools in the United States with programs actually designed to allow all students the opportunity to progress through the school's curriculum at their own rate and according to their individual abilities and interests.

The educational problems associated with a continuous progress curriculum may appear to be insurmountable for some educators. What happens to the student who completes all the school has to offer and is only fifteen years of age? Does he continue on to college? Will the university accept him? Does his family and the community support this type of individual progression and advancement? What about his emotional and psychological development? These questions and many more are only indicative of a great number of concerns which may be generated by discerning administrators and teachers when faced with the desire to develop operational approaches from the theoretically oriented programs that are forcing their way into "modern" educational jargon.

Furthermore, the present use of either teacher or commercially prepared individualized learning materials such as UNIPACs or Individually Prescribed Instruction (IPI) does not guarantee a school staff success in developing individualized programs. Although these techniques appear to offer promise for the future refinement of individualized instructional methodology, they still remain very much in the realm of instructional experimentation. At this writing little is known concerning their potential, their final contribution to the needs of the individual child, or their impact upon the further sophistication of the learning process.

These comments are not designed to discourage a school staff from exploring various techniques for individualizing subject matter content. They are meant to suggest the need for discovering more appropriate techniques, through more broadly based research and more general program development on a nation-wide basis.

CONTINUOUS PROGRESS CURRICULUM

In design, the continuous progress plan permits students to progress through a school's curriculum at rates and in directions more nearly commensurate with their individual abilities and interests than do conventional, group-oriented programs. The continuous progress school must deal with such instructional problems as curriculum planning and materials development. The plan makes extensive use of large group–small group instruction, cooperation and teaming among the teaching staff, and considerable use of independent study. New concepts and learning materials must be clarified, including programmed materials which permit each student to progress at his own rate.

The curriculum is generally designed around specific, individualized units of instruction (generally programmed materials) which allow the individual student the opportunity to progress in each subject as rapidly as he is capable of doing.[1] Each student is on his own "track" and has a personalized course of instruction designed for him. He progresses at his own rate—a rate governed by his background, interest, and ability. He competes primarily with himself and only generally with the group or other students. This individualized approach takes him not only into group situations for interaction and verbal exchange but also allows him opportunities to work on his own, doing research, reading, or studying with the use of electronic or mechanical teaching equipment and without the presence of the teacher.

The continuous progress program has also been identified with other names which seem to communicate the philosophical intent of this plan. Synonyms such as self-paced larning, individual learning rates, sequential learning program, performance curriculum, or discovery approach are often applied to this instructional plan. Regardless of the name, this curriculum plan is based upon the *individual differences* that are recognized in students and it attempts to adjust the curriculum and course content to the individuality of the student rather than adjusting the student to the program.

Generally, two major dimensions are required in developing a continuous progress program.

1. The curriculum must be organized so that students can progress through the curriculum content moving from concept to concept without artificial barriers interrupting the logical sequence of work. If the knowledge of one concept is needed to perform the task or to learn a succeeding concept, the concept must be organized in a vertical sequence. Such a sequence requires the presentation and learning of concept "A" before concept "B" and concept "B" before concept "C". It should be understood that not all curriculum areas require complete vertical sequencing of concepts.
2. The curriculum must be organized so that the student can progress through the curriculum at his own rate of speed commensurate with his abilities, motivation, interest and other factors relating

---

[1] See the section of this chapter dealing with individualized learning materials.

to individual differences. In other words the curriculum unit must have provisions for individual differences and progress.[2]

One of the most difficult problems in applying these generalizations to practical situations is to provide the teacher with sufficient alternatives in dealing effectively with large numbers of students. Even the diagnosis of individual differences may be difficult, much less the organization and administration of individualized units of instruction.

One method of facilitating more individualized methods is the preparation of prepackaged individualized learning units which require a minimum of teacher participation for their use. These materials are usually "program"-oriented and are primarily conceived for self-instruction. Although these units can be employed independently of direct teacher contact, the teacher still performs an integral role in the learning process in terms of overall supervision, diagnosis, remediation, and prescription.

Prepackaged individualized instructional units designed for a continuous progress curriculum are usually characterized by the following components:

1. *Broad Educational Objectives*—These objectives relate the purpose of the unit to the objectives of the total course.
2. *Specific Unit Behavioral Objectives*—These objectives are specifically oriented to the purpose of the unit and to the expected behavior of the student upon completion of the unit.
3. *Specific Concepts, Sub-concepts, and Skills To Be Learned*—A concept is a complete and meaningful idea that is found in the mind of a person. The major concepts and sub-concepts to be learned by the students should be in writing . . . the concepts should be stated (written) in simple, concise sentences. In this way, the concept can be given a specific meaning which then becomes common for all students. In some curriculum units, skills are also emphasized. A skill is the performance of a task such as playing an instrument or doing a setting-up exercise. There are degrees or levels of performance associated with the skill development.
4. *Teaching-Learning Activities*—These activities consist of all those which are to be performed or engaged in by the teacher and the student and are necessary to reach the understanding of the concepts or competency required in the program objectives.

---

[2] Glen F. Ovard, "Developing an Individualized, Continuous Progress Curriculum Unit Emphasizing Concepts and Behavioral Objectives "(unpublished paper distributed by the IDEA Materials Center, Anaheim, California), n.d.

5. *Teaching-Learning Resources*—This consists of all materials, supplies, books, equipment, objects, artifacts, personnel—in short, all
   resources—which are used by the teacher and/or the student while
   engaged in any of the teaching-learning activities.
6. *Performance Measure*—This includes all instruments or means by
   which the specific behavioral objective is measured. The measurement
   instrument can involve oral or written tests, completion of a project,
   ability to play a score without error, or other observable performances.
7. *Provisions for Individual Differences and Continuous Progress*—Each
   individual student is different in his ability, interests, motivational
   patterns, and needs. It should be recognized that as a member of
   society the student needs a minimum competency or understanding
   in a given curriculum area. The degree of competency of each
   individual student must be defined. Two basic standards must be
   considered: A *quantity standard* must be built into the unit or become supplemental to the unit. As related to the curriculum unit, the
   following questions might be asked: What must every student know?
   What must some students know? What must student "A" know?
   What is necessary for all students? What is necessary for student
   "A"? The understanding of a concept or the competency skill is also
   defined in measurements of quality. The *quality standard* is concerned
   with the degree of competency. As related to the behavioral objective,
   the following questions might be asked: Must all students demonstrate the same proficiency? If so, what level is satisfactory—100
   percent, 90 percent, 80 percent, 70 percent, etc? Are some concepts
   or skills so fundamental that 100 percent competency must be
   established prior to progressing to the next concept or skill? If the
   same degree of quality competency is not required of all students,
   what is expected of each individual student?[3]

INDIVIDUALIZED LEARNING MATERIALS (UNITS)

   The instructional techniques to be presented in this section
are representative of several attempts to operationalize and apply
in practice the theoretical and philosophical assumptions inherent
within the concept of a continuous progress curriculum. The development of individualized learning materials, referred to as
"learning packages," have become an integral and functional aspect
of any school program where serious attempts toward continuous
progress are made. The development of learning packages usually
can be categorized into two broad areas: (1) teacher-initiated and
teacher-prepared materials, developed within any specific school
program, and (2) commercially prepared materials, developed out-

---

[3] *Ibid.*

side of a specific school program and more generalized in format and design.

Teacher-Prepared Materials. Several formats are available to teachers who wish to create their own individualized learning units. Three independently developed sets of material are representative of these formats: (1) The Esbensen Pac, a student assignment sheet used in the Duluth Public Schools; (2) the Learning Activity Package (LAP), developed by the Nova School in Fort Lauderdale, Florida; and (3) the *UNIPAC*, a format designed by the staff of the IDEA Materials Center, Anaheim, California. The UNIPAC will serve here as an example of one type of teacher-initiated prepackaged instructional unit.

A UNIPAC is a self-contained set of teaching–learning materials designed to teach a *single concept*. It is structured for individual and independent learners who are performing at the same general level of instruction. The essential component of the UNIPAC is a single major learnable idea, skill, or attitude. Specific learning objectives are listed for the student and stated in behavioral terms (words or phrases which describe observable enroute or terminal performance). Diversified media, materials, and methods are provided for the learner; evaluation through pre-test, self-test, and post-test is included so that the learner may measure his progress toward the achievement of the objectives. Suggestions are also provided for quest activities or supplemental study.

> UNIPACs are designed to help students achieve at their own best learning rates. Given UNIPACs, students will be able to achieve measurable performances under given conditions, at or above specified minimum levels, and at rates which are individually unique to each student.
>
> When the student with the assistance of a teacher selects a particular UNIPAC in his sequential learning program, he takes a pretest based on the behavioral objectives in that UNIPAC. If the pre-test results indicate that he is ready for the concepts or skills of the UNIPAC, he selects from suggested learning materials and activities in the UNIPAC those which fit his own unique learning style. Behavioral objectives, which are contained in his UNIPAC, guide him as he learns. When he feels that he has achieved one behavioral objective, he proceeds to the next one and again selects from suggested learning materials and activities.
>
> When the student feels that he has achieved all of the behavioral objectives in his UNIPAC, he takes a self-test. If the self-test results indicate that he is ready for teacher evaluation, the student can re-

quest the post-test for his UNIPAC. Upon successful completion of the post-test, the student may proceed to this next UNIPAC or he may participate in quest activities. If the student elects to participate in quest, he defines a problem for in-depth or in-breadth study, and he conducts his research in order to achieve some level of resolution of his problem.

During the entire learning sequence the teacher provides as many opportunities as possible for a student-teacher and student-student interaction during conferences and seminars. Small learning teams, made up of from two to six students are formed whenever feasible. The teacher *monitors* each student's progress, *diagnoses* learning problems, *prescribes* possible alternative learning materials and activities, and evaluates each student's progress in achieving the stated behavioral objectives.[4]

As a result of individualizing instruction through the use of UNIPACs and other related materials, the teaching–learning act can become much more personalized both for the teacher and for the student.

Before UNIPACs or other individualized learning units can be used effectively, performance criteria must be established for each course in which the instructional units will be prepared.[5] These performance criteria in turn will permit specific performance levels (competency levels) to be established in order to guide the student in the prerequisite learner attributes, abilities, and achievement necessary for successful completion of the particular "learning unit."

Conventional teaching is too frequently a guessing game between student and teacher ("guess what the teacher is thinking"), with the teacher seldom defining in explicit terms (behavioral terms) the outcome or level of performance required for success. Stating objectives and expected performance in behavioral terms does not mean that these units of instruction are either mechanistic or limited as to their humanistic orientation. It simply means that precise instructional goals must be specified in certain instances.

---

[4] The concept of the UNIPAC and the description and generalizations concerning its use were developed by the staff at the IDEA Materials Center, Anaheim, California. Materials and information concerning the development of individualized learning packages (UNIPACS) may be obtained by writing the IDEA Materials Center, 730 North Euclid Street, Suite 304, Anaheim, California 92801.

[5] See the section in this chapter concerning behavioral objectives.

Too often teachers rely on vague generalities and defend their use on humanistic or creative grounds.

Commercially Prepared Materials. Since 1966, the Learning Development Center of the University of Pittsburgh and Research for Better Schools, Inc., have been cooperating in the development, field testing, and dissemination of Individually Prescribed Instruction, generally referred to as IPI, Although to date the IPI materials have been developed only for elementary schools, there is important carryover into secondary programs.

IPI is an instructional system based on specific objectives and correlated with diagnostic tools, teaching materials, and methods. It represents one specific way of providing for the wide range of differences that exist in classrooms. Certainly it typifies what can be done to help resolve the age-old problem of providing for each student, each day, his own program of studies.

Materials designed for the individual student have been created in elementary mathematics, reading, science, handwriting, and spelling. Operationally, these materials are designed to allow the student to proceed at a rate of speed dependent on his own capacities; they also are tailored to his learning needs and to his unique characteristics. The student places himself on a "learning continuum" by taking both placement tests and pre-tests. The curriculum material is arranged in sequential order and the assignments are given by prescription to fit his individual needs. The student's mastery of the curriculum is judged by curriculum-oriented tests and post-tests and he is required to perform at a level of 85 percent.[6]

There are six characteristics that distinguish IPI from conventional elementary school procedures:

1. The curriculum materials provide detailed specifications of educational objectives.
2. There is ample organization of methods and materials to attain these objectives.
3. The program carefully determines each student's present competence in a given subject before initiation into the IPI materials.

---

[6] The information contained here dealing with Individually Prescribed Instruction (IPI) was extracted from a bulletin entitled, "Individually Prescribed Instruction," distributed by the Research for Better Schools, Inc., Philadelphia, Pennsylvania, and from the Learning Research and Development Center, University of Pittsburgh, n.d.

4. The program provides individual daily evaluation and guidance of each student.
5. Provisions are made for frequent monitoring of student performance in order to inform both the student and the teacher of progress toward an objective.
6. Materials are provided for continual evaluation and strengthening of the curriculum and instructional procedures.[7]

A program sponsored and developed by the Center for Curriculum Planning, State University of New York at Buffalo, offers what may prove to be a very useful and productive source of individualized materials for elementary and secondary schools. This project has developed a series of computer-based resource units, generally referred to as resource guides, covering a wide variety of topics and subject areas typically found in most schools. The emphasis is on the use of electronic computers in developing information storage and retrieval systems for providing more individualized resource units oriented toward the individual student.

The teacher, or student, may "call-up" a resource guide by choosing from a list of specific objectives which he feels is pertinent to a particular unit of instruction. The list of instructional objectives available are organized according to the classification scheme described by Bloom, *The Taxonomy of Educational Objectives, Parts I and II.*[8] Space will not permit a detailed description of this approach to individualizing instruction.[9]

Air—Project Plan.[10] Project PLAN is a cooperative demonstration program in computer-managed individualized instruction involving the American Institutes for Research (AIR) and fourteen independent school districts. The word "PLAN" itself is indicative of the operational aspects of the program and stands for a "Program for Learning in Accordance with Needs."

This is not a program of computer-assisted instruction (CAI).

---

[7] *Ibid.*

[8] Benjamin S. Bloom, ed., *Taxonomy of Educational Objectives* (New York: David McKay Co., 1956).

[9] For more information concerning individualized computer-based resource guides, the reader should write to Professor Robert S. Harnack, School of Education, State University of New York at Buffalo, New York.

[10] The description of Project PLAN was extracted in part from an unpublished paper by William M. Shanner, "PLAN, A System of Individualized Instruction," printed and distributed by Westinghouse Learning Corporation, 100 Park Avenue, New York, N.Y., 10017, n.d.

The student does not interact directly with the computer, nor does the computer actually administer or teach the student any of his instructional program. On the contrary, student-teacher interaction is maintained in the classroom. The student utilizes currently available instructional materials. The computer is brought into the program as an aid for the teacher. It becomes an information system which records the student's learning and academic history and his program of studies, scores his tests and examinations, and furnishes this information to the teacher on a retrieval basis. On a day-to-day basis, the computer monitors the progress of the student through the program. In other words, the computer is concerned with the non-instructional or managerial aspects of the program. The students learn from currently available instructional materials in organized learning situations. The teacher facilitates learning by assisting the students on an individual or group basis as problems arise.

With reference to the individualized instruction aspect of the program, this does not mean that the students learn in *isolation*. Rather, from Project PLAN's point-of-view individualized instruction is defined as the assignment of appropriate learning tasks to students according to their needs and to what they are able to accomplish and the assignment of appropriate ways of accomplishing these learning tasks. So the individualization in this system applies to the assignments and the methods of achieving these assignments rather than to learning in isolation. Students may learn through independent study, small group discussions, large group activities, or teacher-led activities, whichever is most appropriate. By systems approach, it is intended to indicate that all the relevant factors in the situation are considered, not just selected aspects. In other words, the whole educational program of a student is treated, rather than just specific parts of the program. Thus, Project PLAN deals systematically with educational programs from grades one through twelve and across the board in all academic areas. Project PLAN deals with guidance aspects as well as with academic aspects. It is a computer-managed system of individualized instruction which accounts for the total educational activities of the student.

It should be noted that Project PLAN is not involved in the development of instructional materials. Project PLAN is dedicated to the utilization of commercially available materials. The curriculum aspects of this program involve the writing in and coding of commercially available materials to the requirements of the computer-managed system of individualized instruction so that a student's progress can be monitored by the computer. In essence, Project PLAN attempts to determine whether or not greater learning can be effectuated on the part of the individual student by the use of a computer-managed system of individualized instruction and by use of the same instructional materials as are utilized in typical group-instruction classrooms.

The system starts with the administration of a series of placement tests to a student. On the basis of their results, the place in the scope and sequence in each particular subject matter area where each student is best able to learn is identified. At this point, an assignment is given to each student based upon behavioral objectives which are classified at this level. These objectives are organized into a module which represents about a two-week assignment of materials in a particular subject. Parallel with each module are several Teaching–Learning Units (TLU), because there may be several ways for mastering the objectives in the module. It is the desire here to identify the learning style of the student and then to select the most appropriate instructional materials to help him master objectives by the way in which he can learn best. After learning, the student is tested to see how well he can perform each objective. These test results are reported in decision-making terms so that the student is either advanced to the next group of objectives or he is re-cycled through those objectives which he has failed to master and is given remedial or reinforcing work in order to bring him up to mastery level. Then the next module is assigned and the cycle is repeated.

The role of the teacher also changes in a program of individualized instruction. One of the major purposes of the computer-managed program of individualized instruction is to free the teacher from non-instructional activities in the classroom to relate to students in an instructional way. Here, the teacher's task in the classroom is to facilitate learning. It might be pointed out that students actually do not learn from teachers; they learn from materials. In much the same way, sick people do not get well from doctors but from medication. The doctor, however, is important in prescribing and facilitating the proper kind of medication, just as the teacher is very important in facilitating learning through the proper utilization of instructional materials in the classroom. Thus, this program is designed to maximize the amount of time that a teacher has for working with students who have learning problems in order that the teacher may facilitate that learning.

INSTRUCTIONAL (BEHAVIORAL) OBJECTIVES

One essential component contained in all of the various methods for individualized learning units is the necessity for communicating precise, explicit instructions. It has long been recognized that teachers are often enigmatic, somewhat esoterical, and content with vague generalizations which do not always impart explicit, clearly understood goals concerning a particular learning assignment. The purpose of employing instructional or behavioral objectives is to make clear to teachers, students, and other interested persons what it is that needs to be taught.

After a specific concept or idea has been identified around which an individualized learning unit will be developed, it is necessary to provide the student with clear, concise directions if we expect him to operate in a self-instructional mode. Behavioral or instructional objectives are, essentially, precise, easily understood directives for the learner.

A behavioral objective contains three essential elements: (1) the *performance expected* of the learner (based upon the performance criteria established for the unit of instruction), (2) the *conditions* under which the performance will occur, and (3) the *level of proficiency* the learner is expected to attain.

Most educators would agree that one of their primary responsibilities is the teaching of concepts to students. To perform this task, teachers must communicate many instructions. Behavioral objectives are merely a written form of these instructions, stated in clear, concise terms so that the student understands explicitly what is expected of him. If students are to progress independently through a school curriculum, they must have immediate access to the objectives or instructions necessary for this progress. The student must know what he is expected to perform and what is the acceptable level of performance (behavior) at the conclusion of the specific unit of instruction. Inherent in the concept of behavioral objective is the functionality and importance of self-evaluation based upon clearly defined performance criteria.

A well written instructional objective should specify under what conditions and to what extent a certain kind of student performance can be expected to take place.

Performing means doing. A student who performs something does something. Here are two statements. Which one is expressed in terms of student performance?

A. *The student will have a good understanding of the letters of the alphabet, A through Z.*

B. *The student will be able to pronounce the names of the letters of the alphabet, A through Z.*

Statement "B" tells what it is that the student will be able to do. He will be able to pronounce the names of the letters of the alphabet, A through Z. Statement "A" tells us that the student will have a good understanding of the letters of the alphabet. But this is not very clear. We cannot tell what it is that the student is supposed to be able to do as a result of this understanding.

Let's try another pair of statements. Which one is expressed in terms of student performance?

A. *The student will have an adequate comprehension of the mechanics of punctuation.*

B. *Given a sentence containing an error in punctuation, the student will correct the mistake.*

Statement "B" tells what it is that the student will do. He will correct the error in punctuation. Statement "A" is rather cloudy. We cannot tell what it is that the student is supposed to do as a result of his comprehension.

At this point, an objection may be raised, Isn't the person who is comprehending something doing something? Isn't intellectual performance an acceptable kind of student performance? Certainly. The difficulty is that mental activity, as such, is not directly observable. We cannot literally open up a person's head and see the thinking that is going on inside. If it is to be of use to us, a statement of performance must specify some sort of behavior that can be observed.[11]

INDEPENDENT STUDY[12]

Generally, for those schools which have implemented independent study programs, this term has become associated with a

---

[11] Thorwald Esbensen, "Writing Instructional Objectives," unpublished paper distributed by IDEA Materials Center, Anaheim, California, n.d.

[12] The material presented in this chapter on independent study was extracted in part from W. Deane Wiley and Lloyd K. Bishop, *The Flexibly*

learning situation during the school day which allows the student some unscheduled, out-of-class time (Table 3.1). The student may develop personal skills or interests either individually or in informal interaction with others (students or teachers) as he chooses. The key to this program is characterized by the attainment of

TABLE 3.1

Student Program Indicating Unscheduled Time Designed for Independent Study (IS) (Flexible Scheduling)

Modules[a]	Monday	Tuesday	Wednesday	Thursday	Friday
1	IS	Biol LG	Eng LG	Biol	IS
2	IS	Biol LG	Eng LG	Biol	IS
3	IS				IS
4	US Hist LG	Psych	US Hist SG	Psych	US Hist SG
5	US Hist LG	Psych	US Hist SG	Psych	US Hist SG
6		Psych	US Hist SG	Psych	US Hist SG
7	Jr. PE	IS	Jr. PE	IS	Jr. PE
8	Jr. PE	IS	Jr. PE	IS	Jr. PE
9	Jr. PE	Journ	Jr. PE	Journ	Jr. PE
10	LUNCH	Journ	LUNCH	Journ	LUNCH
11	IS	Journ	IS	Journ	
12	IS	LUNCH	IS	LUNCH	Lang Lab
13	Biol Lab		Biol Lab		IS
14	Biol Lab	Eng SG	Biol Lab	Eng SG	IS
15	Biol Lab	Eng SG	Biol Lab	Eng SG	IS
16	Jwlry	Eng SG	Lang Lab	Eng SG	Jwlry Lab
17	Jwlry	IS			Jwlry Lab
18	Germ 3	IS	Germ 3	Germ 3	Germ 3
19	Germ 3	Jr. PE	Germ 3	Germ 3	Germ 3
20		Jr. PE			

[a] Periods of time—20 minutes in length

Scheduled High School (West Nyack, N.Y.: Parker Publishing Co., 1968). For a more in-depth discussion concerning the development and implementation of independent study programs, the reader is encouraged to obtain this book.

some degree of freedom from constant supervision. The student is allowed time to make some choices about his school activities during the school day without constant restrictions and constraints from adults or his peer group. During independent study time, students may carry on various activities either individually, in small peer groups, or with teachers. A student may read, write, discuss, contemplate, listen to records and tapes, memorize, practice, experiment, analyze, investigate, or converse and interact with other students both formally and informally. He may also, on occasion, just relax—an opportunity seldom afforded the student in the conventionally controlled school day. Thus, independent study emphasizes the individual's role in learning. It implies that students who react favorably to this environment possess potential for self-initiative, self-discipline, and self-evaluation.

Independent study generally becomes a fundamental aspect of the instructional program in those schools that implement some type of flexible or nongraded schedule. One basic dimension of a computer-based flexible scheduling system is that of allowing students about 25-30 percent unscheduled time during each school day. This concept maintains that students can develop mature, self-disciplined judgment and be responsible for some educational decisions. Independent study not only allows students to develop responsibility but also allows them to work in a school atmosphere and with materials and falicities which are more appropriate for a highly complex, specialized, and individualized curriculum. Independent study fills an extremely useful and necessary role in any school program designed to provide greater degrees of individualization to students and professional staff.

It should be emphasized that a school does not have to institute a flexible schedule, a team teaching program, or any other organizational innovation in order to implement an independent study program. Some schools with otherwise conventional programs have developed very effective independent study activities for their students. A primary requisite prior to the implementation of such a program, however, is the rearranging and development of appropriate educational facilities for students. The conventional school library with its austere atmosphere is no longer adequate to meet the demands of this program. Instructional resource centers are required in at least the major academic areas—English, history, mathematics, and science. The "open laboratory" concept may also be employed, where various laboratory facilities within the school are opened and available for student use during the school day. Facilities appropriate for this type of activity are typing and business laboratories, shorthand laboratories, foreign language laboratories, industrial education facilities, art rooms, and music facilities.

TECHNOLOGICAL DEVELOPMENTS FOR INDIVIDUALIZING INSTRUCTION

It is undoubtedly presumptuous to attempt a survey of the extensive developments in the past few years in the area of educational technology and, more particularly, in its impact upon instruction. It is apparent that such technological developments as audiovisual media—particularly educational television (ETV)—various types of programmed instruction, and teaching machines have made significant in-roads into elementary and secondary instructional programs. The concept of programmed instruction alone has revolutionized instructional techniques in some schools and has had a profound influence on the role of the teacher. It is evident that the possibility of inculcating the concept of individualized instruction in the classroom will be further enhanced through further refinements in "programmed" or self-instructional materials.

In an attempt to limit the field of educational technology, a central theme has been adopted—that of computers. This selection is made because the computer represents a segment of the technology explosion in education which will have perhaps the greatest single impact on instruction in coming years. The computer also will have a more universal application in many phases of the educational process, including planning, budgeting, decision-making, educational management and administration, as well as in the important area of instruction.

COMPUTER-ASSISTED INSTRUCTION (CAI)

In both educational research and actual instruction, the computer is likely to have a profound effect on education in the coming years. What makes the computer a potentially important —perhaps revolutionary—instructional tool is precisely the fact that it offers a technology by which, for the first time, instruction can be geared to the specific abilities, achievements, and progress of individual students. The wide range of material that can be presented by the computer, combined with the high degree of control of experimental conditions and the ease of varying the course presentation, provide unusual opportunities for creating individualized instructional programs.

Essentially, the concept of computer-assisted instruction (or computer-based instruction) employs a rapidly developing computer technology to supplement or, in some cases, actually to replace the teacher for some specialized learning skills. CAI learning systems have been successful as individualized teaching tools in areas such as developing problem-solving skills, drill and practice (learning factual information), and general retrieval of information. Because of the inordinant amount of factual information that can be stored and then later recalled by the student, the computer must be seriously considered as a significant teaching tool. Obviously, with its application some of our "time-honored" techniques of instruction, as well as the role of the teacher in the instructional process, will change drastically as computer-based instructional systems become more prominent. In many respects, in terms of its potential impact upon education CAI as an instructional tool is analogous to Gutenberg's invention of the printing press.

The Computer as an Instructional Tool.   To understand the usefulness of computers in instruction, it might be helpful to review briefly the concept of programmed instruction and teaching machines. Computer-assisted instruction is, to a great extent, an extension of programmed instruction and the application of the relatively simple teaching machine. This technique presents to the student a series of multiple-choice questions or statements which the student must answer by pushing one of a choice of keys. If the student is right, the machine presents the next question. If he is wrong, the machine records the error and requires the student to try again. The machine keeps each question on which the student makes an error before him until he finds the right answer. The student must get the correct answer to each question before he can go on to the next. When he does give the right answer, the apparatus informs him of this and the next question or statement is selected.

The concept of "intrinsic programming" has also been created; this allows the student to move in alternative directions with the material. If the student assimilates the new material, he moves ahead; if not, he is "branched" to a remedial presentation. Early proponents of programming hoped that the process would teach more effectively than human teachers, but this has not been demonstrated. However, it does appear that programmed teaching can free the teacher from much of the drudgery involved in presenting straightforward factual material and in drilling students. This seems particularly promising now with the advent of computers for instructional purposes.

A description of a computer-based schoolroom may provide useful insights into the function of the computer as an instructional tool.

At the System Development Corporation, we have built an experimental computer-based schoolroom called "CLASS" which stands for "Computer-Based Laboratory for Automated School System." CLASS is a rather unusual schoolroom in that each student works in a separate small cubicle which has equipment allowing him to receive visual and auditory instruction through film projectors, tape recorders, or television. The student is able to respond to the material being presented through a special switchboard, or set of buttons, which is connected to our Philco 2000, a medium-sized modern computer. The student's response is instantly transmitted to the computer which has in it a program for recording the response, for analyzing it, and for determining what instructional material should be presented next to the student. On the basis of this program, the computer transmits a signal back to the student which instructs him about the film frame or auditory grouping to which he should next attend. As the student progresses through the instructional material, the computer is able to specify the sequence of materials to meet his particular needs. That is to say, as the student responds to the instructional items, his progress is constantly monitored and wherever items are being missed or trouble appears, the computer analyzes the difficulty and presents to the student items of sequences of material which attempt to remedy it. [13]

---

[13] Launor F. Carter, "Computers: Their Impact on Instruction, on Educational Planning, and on the Curriculum," distributed by the System Development Corporation, Santa Monica, California, 1964. See also, John G. Caffrey, "The Impact of the Computer on School Systems" and John G. Caffrey, "Computers and Decision Making in Education," System Development Corporation Santa Monica, Calif. 1965.

CAI—Applications, Advantages, Limitations. For instructional purposes the computer can be employed as a "monitor of the learning process, and in some cases, the actual presenter of instructional situations and materials."[14] When appropriate soft-ware has been developed and the computer is properly programmed, it can provide powerful applications for teaching and learning.[15] Consider the degree of monitoring capability that is possible; the computer will:

1. Engage in two-way communication with a student by means of natural language messages.
2. Guide the student through a program of tasks, helping him where he has difficulty, and accelerating his progress where he finds little challenge.
3. Observe and record significant details of the student's behavior, including steps undertaken in performing tasks, time taken for particular steps, and values of varying psychological and environmental qualities.
4. Simulate the operation of a physical, mathematical, or social process responding to variations in parameters.
5. Analyze and summarize performance records and other behavioral records of individual students and also groups of students.[16]

Within basic classroom instruction, the concept of individualization is generally considered to have two main functions: (1) the proper selection of student activities to provide appropriate levels of challenge and to respond to specific deficiencies in student performance, and (2) the capability for individualized remediation (or providing individual remedies for individual deficiencies). Both of these functions are considerably enhanced and basically inherent within the structure of a CAI learning system.

Even in a routine recitation each student works directly with his own communication station and recites individually in direct relation to the system. The repertoire of exercises in a single computer

[14] G. Ernest Anderson, "Computer-Assisted Instruction: State of the Art," *Nation's Schools* (October, 1968). This edition of Nation's Schools provides an excellent series of articles on computer applications in education and instruction.

[15] "Soft-ware" is the concept employed in computer language to designate a computer program or specific computer instructions and directions. Unfortunately, the computer, as a machine or tool, is no more useful than the program or instructions that are written for it.

[16] E. N. Adams, "Computer-Assisted Instruction," *Computers and Automation* (March, 1966).

can span a great range of difficulty. Thus every student can work on material appropriate to his ability. The logical power of the computer permits complex processing of the student's response to reveal individual deficiencies, and to determine what assignment should be given next. Thus each student as he works receives immediate individualized feedback whenever he runs into difficulty.[17]

Furthermore, the computer offers unusual advantages in the teaching of skill subjects such as mathematics or foreign languages. Conventional classroom instruction is characteristically inefficient and unproductive in dealing with these subjects. Where a high level of skill is desired, where student abilities vary considerably, and where students need individual recitation and drill, the computer is far more efficient and effective than the classroom environment. The simulation of complex processes is another avenue for computer exploitation in instruction. One could construct a computer program which allows the student to manipulate the process parameters and thus to experiment with a model of the particular system. Another computer application to instruction and the learning process is the computer's capacity for high-speed monitoring, recording, and analyzing of data. This could be either instructional data or the monitoring of student behavior.

There are certain significant limitations in CAI learning systems that should be mentioned. One is that the computer system can respond only to a very specific predetermined program. It cannot devise on-the-spot solutions or alternatives. It has a very limited ability to "think" or to understand partial meanings or responses. The most serious limitation to many school systems is the general cost of computers. Presently the cost is prohibitive to most schools; however, in the near future this factor should change considerably.[18] The continued development of time-sharing facilities is making it economically feasible for a school to have access to a large, highspeed computer, via terminals, without the expense of an "in-house" installation. Another of the limitations to this system lies in the knowledge base and training of teachers. Will they know how to apply the computer and its program to the individualization of instruction once CAI systems become commonplace? And finally,

---

[17] *Ibid.*

[18] See *Nation's Schools* (October, 1968). One article in this series dealing with computer applications in education offers definitive cost information concerning computer-assisted instruction.

little research has been done concerning the importance of class-room interactions on the socialization process; these may be seri-ously altered in a CAI instructional system.

EDUCATIONAL FACILITIES AND INDIVIDUALIZING INSTRUCTION

With significant changes in instructional methodology and organ-izational innovations, educators have been forced to re-define basic concepts concerning the appropriateness of instructional facilities. For example, in some schools the conventional classroom which seats 30 to 35 students is practically obsolete. It is no longer appropriate to assign a particular teacher to a specific classroom. Rather, any given teacher may occupy several different facilities throughout the school week, depending on the specific instructional activity or task to be performed. Large group instruction will take place in the school's large group room, a facility shared with sev-eral other teachers who also are employing large group techniques. Small group instruction will take place in small, informal seminar rooms. Laboratory instruction will be held in rooms suitable to this instructional mode, and individual study will be most effective in the resource centers, the instructional materials center, or in the teachers' office area.

With the advent of specific techniques for individualizing instruction, school architecture must adjust considerably. If we ex-pect teachers to act as professionals, to engage in the individualiza-tion of instruction, and to confer with individual students, then suitable office space must be provided. The concept of the teacher occupying an otherwise empty classroom during his "preparation period" is unrealistic and obsolete.

INSTRUCTIONAL RESOURCE CENTER (IRC)

The heart of the instructional program, particularly when de-veloping independent study programs, is the Instructional Resource Center. Each IRC serves a precisely defined group of courses typi-cally within one discipline. The operation of the IRC, including its equipment and materials, is under the control and direction of the teachers who offer the courses which the resource center serves. While the library remains materials-oriented, the IRC is program- or instruction-oriented and is different from the library in terms of the materials it contains. The IRC is usually available to students at their discretion during independent or individual study although formal assignment is possible.

The IRC may also serve as an administrative center where the distribution of materials can be made, where students may return papers, where testing materials are stored and student records are maintained. It can also serve as an instructional information center where teachers file all assignments and requirements as much in advance as possible. This facilitates make-up work for those students who want course information after absences.

It is important that the professional staff is not assigned to the resource center for supervisory purposes, even though many administrators are prone to make these assignments. It has been found that paraprofessionals or other semi-professional aides can provide adequate supervision and control in these facilities. Teachers should be left free to perform more important instructional responsibilities. However, in an ideal situation, the teachers' office area will be adjacent to the IRC. Then, if a student has a question, he can locate quickly a teacher who can help him with a solution.

INSTRUCTIONAL MATERIALS CENTER (IMC)

The concept of the conventional school library with its typical school librarian is an anachronism in the modern school designed for individualized instruction. Not only have study facilities become more decentralized, but they are also more specialized than the typical services which the library can provide. In this respect another facility of unique importance to the school program is the Instructional Materials Center.

> In any good school, many IMC functions are performed. The school library provides books, reference books, and periodicals; guidance in selection and use of these resources; and supervised study facilities. The audiovisual department provides equipment and materials for classroom use. The bookstore issues, receives, and repairs texts. . . . All of these functions and many additional activities, on a greatly increased scale, are performed in the IMC. Thus, the IMC becomes the center for much of the learning activity of the [modern elementary or secondary school].[19]

---

[19] Robert L. Egbert and John F. Cogswell, "System Design for A Continuous Progress School: Part III, The Instructional Materials Center," distributed by System Development Corporation, Santa Monica, California, 1964.

Also located with the IMC is the materials production center, a facility designed for the development of graphic materials, programmed learning units, specific individualized learning materials, and other teacher aids. This center should be managed by professional or semi-professional personnel who are knowledgeable in subject matter but who are technically oriented to graphic production, videotape production, the creation of audiofilm series, and other special production needs. Planning rooms are also necessary if more joint planning is to be done by the professional staff. The audiovisual center will grow rapidly and provisions within the IMC must be made for film and video viewing both by groups and individuals.

INDEPENDENT STUDY CARRELS

Independent study carrels can be located in the IMC, the resource centers, laboratories, classrooms, and any other semi-quiet areas about the school plant. These carrels should be conceived as general purpose, multi-sensory study environments where students can call on electronic and mechanical teaching aids as needed. However, it is logical that not all carrels will be specialized with video and audio feedback capabilities (referred to as a "wet" carrel). Carrels need many devices for the individualization of instruction but not all devices are needed simultaneously. Each carrel can be highly specialized as to function and location within the school plant. Decisions concerning the number of "wet" or "dry" carrels will inevitably be a function of the total instructional program designed by the school.

SUMMARY: AN INSTRUCTIONAL SYSTEM FOR
INDIVIDUALIZING INSTRUCTION

The individualization of instruction goes beyond the physical and organizational arrangements of a school; the concept has a functional impact upon the designing of curricula and the instructional program. It also has serious implications for teachers, administrators, and other personnel who are primarily engaged in developing and implementing specific instructional programs. Individualized instruction calls for a *particularistic* curriculum rather than a *universalistic* curriculum. This suggests that the opportunity for individual mastery of common subject material will exist, as well as the provision of personalized instruction for the student that is unique to his ability, motivation, and interest.

Because each student becomes a unique entity and the instructional program can be tailored to fit him and his special requirements, individualization is a type of instruction in which the student engages in activities appropriate to his own learning style. Once this instructional program is properly conceived, several ancillary support techniques will be developed to provide for more flexible schedules, nongraded concepts, large and small groups, independent study, and team teaching. Thus, individualized instructional programs will promote independence and the development of responsibility, provide for unique opportunities for study beyond the regular curriculum, and permit maximum use of instructional facilities.

Individualized programs have serious implications for conventional classroom organization. Consider the monolithic structure created by the traditional classroom environment and its impact upon professional staff development. This organizational system is detrimental to the professional development and needed interaction of teachers. Perhaps the greatest disadvantage is found in the utilization and development of professional strengths and individuality. Inasmuch as the conventional classroom forces the teacher into isolation, the teacher is deprived of discourse with his colleagues, out of which can arise common purposes, instructional improvement, and curricular innovation.

The self-contained classroom and its concomitant instructional procedures also impede significant developments in the teaching–learning process. Issues concerning time and its relationship to instruction, individual student learning rates, and interaction processes cannot be adequately considered. Furthermore, the traditional classroom cannot differentiate between the size of the group and the specific instructional task or activity to be conducted. The system is inflexible and does not accommodate student individuality or professional decision-making.

The concept of individualized instruction calls for the evolvement of an integrated instructional-learning system in elementary and secondary schools which can accommodate, both in theoretical design and practical application, the complex requirements demanded by the recent development of several contemporary instructional techniques. This system requires flexibility and a capacity to adjust to the complexities of specific requirements of individualization. The following generalizations and philosophical assumptions are offered as a summary and synthesis of the major functional components of this instructional system for individualizing secondary or elementary school instructional programs.

The Instructional-Learning System (See Figure 3.1). Within this teaching-learning system, when individualizing instructional programs it is the assumption that each subject, when properly taught, will include four basic modes of instruction for all students: large group instruction, small group discussion, individual or independent study, and laboratory instruction. Further, it is assumed that through the act of teaching:

1. Some experiences and learnings will be common to all students.
   Technique: Large group instruction
2. Some experiences and learnings will be unique or individualized for specific students.
   Technique: Independent study
   Open laboratories and clinics
   Small group discussion
3. Some experiences and learnings for some students will be more in depth in some curricular areas.
   Technique: Individualized independent study
   Directed readings program
   Teacher-assigned or student-initiated
   Independent study projects
4. Learning experiences and instruction will require variability throughout the school day, week, or year to include:
   Class size
   Instructional time
   Professional staff
   School facilities and resources
   Variable course structures
   Team teaching
   Large group instruction
   Small group discussion
   Open laboratories
   Contractual course arrangements
   Independent study programs
   Instructional materials center
   Curricular resource centers

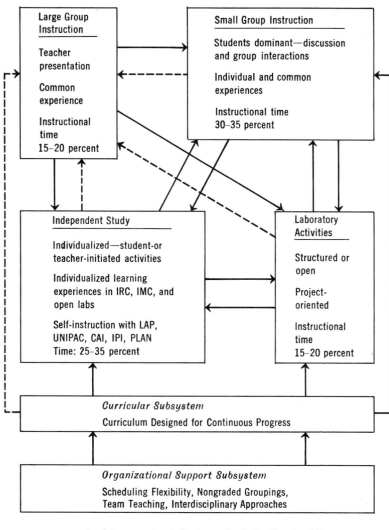

Components
Individualizing Instructional Programs

Large Group Instruction

Teacher presentation

Common experience

Instructional time 15–20 percent

Small Group Instruction

Students dominant—discussion and group interactions

Individual and common experiences

Instructional time 30–35 percent

Independent Study

Individualized—student-or teacher-initiated activities

Individualized learning experiences in IRC, IMC, and open labs

Self-instruction with LAP, UNIPAC, CAI, IPI, PLAN
Time: 25–35 percent

Laboratory Activities

Structured or open

Project-oriented

Instructional time 15–20 percent

Curricular Subsystem
Curriculum Designed for Continuous Progress

Organizational Support Subsystem
Scheduling Flexibility, Nongraded Groupings, Team Teaching, Interdisciplinary Approaches

⟶ Primary or direct effect upon the instructional activity

----⟶ Secondary or indirect effect upon the instructional activity

FIGURE 3.1
Expanded Model—Instructional Learning System

5. The learning experience is founded upon a curriculum which is concept-oriented or concept-centered. Fundamental concepts are identified within each subject matter area and become the basis for structuring the curriculum and expected learning activities for all students within a curricular area.
6. A curriculum is developed which offers achievement opportunity for all students, regardless of ability or academic potential.
7. The learning experience should be a plan of continuous progress for all students; all students should have the opportunity for continuous study in all subject matter fields throughout their school years.

SELECTED BIBLIOGRAPHY

Association for Supervision and Curriculum Development. *New Dimensions in Learning: A Multi-Disciplinary Approach.* Washington, D.C.: NEA, 1962.

Association for Supervision and Curriculum Development. *New Insights and the Curriculum.* Washington, D.C.: NEA, 1963.

Association for Supervision and Curriculum Development. *Perceiving, Behaving, Becoming: A New Focus for Education.* Washington, D.C.: NEA, 1962.

Banghart, Frank W. *Educational Systems Analysis.* London: The Macmillan Co., 1969.

Beggs, David W., III and Edward G. Buffie (ed.). *Independent Study.* Bloomington, Ind.: Indiana University Press, 1965.

Bennis, Warren G., *et al.* (ed.). *The Planning of Change.* (2nd ed.) New York: Holt, Rinehart and Winston, 1967.

Bloom, Benjamin S., *et al.* (eds.). *Taxonomy of Educational Objectives, I and II.* New York: David McKay Co., 1963.

Bruner, Jerome S. *On Knowing.* Cambridge, Mass.: Harvard University Press, 1962.

Bruner, Jerome S. *Toward a Theory of Instruction.* Cambridge, Mass.: Harvard University Press, 1966.

Burck, Gilbert. *The Computer Age.* New York: Harper & Row, Publishers, 1965.

A Climate for Individuality, Washington, D.C.: AASA, ASCD, NASSP, and NEA, 1965.

Ellsworth, Ralph E. and Hobart D. Wagner. *The School Library: Facilities for Independent Study in Secondary Schools.* New York: Educational Facilities Laboratories, 1963.

de Grazia, Alfred and David A. Sohn. *Revolution in Teaching: New Theory, Technology, and Curricula.* New York: Bantam Books, 1964.

Johnson, B. Lamar. *Islands of Innovation Expanding.* London: Glencoe Press, 1969.

Kahn, Herman and Anthony J. Wiener. *The Year 2000.* New York: The Macmillan Co., 1967.

Mager, Robert F. *Preparing Objectives for Programmed Instruction.* San Francisco: Fearon Publishers, 1962.

McLuhan, Marshall. *Understanding Media: The Extensions of Man.* New York: McGraw-Hill Book Co., 1965.

Miles, Matthew B. (ed.). *Innovations in Education.* New York: Bureau of Publications, Teachers College, Columbia University, 1964.

National Society for the Study of Education. *Individualizing Instruction, Sixty-first Yearbook, Part I.* Chicago: University of Chicago Press, 1962.

National Society for the Study of Education. *Theories of Learning and Instruction. Sixty-third Yearbook, Part I.* Chicago: University of Chicago Press, 1964.

Trump, J. Lloyd and Delmas F. Miller. *Secondary School Curriculum Improvement.* Boston: Allyn and Bacon, Inc., 1968.

INDIVIDUALIZING INSTRUCTION

Applications in Elementary and Secondary School Programs

Part II of this book will present several specific methods for individualizing instruction which have been successfully employed in innovative school programs. Various methods for individualizing educational programs were treated essentially in a theoretical context in Chapters 2 and 3; this section will describe these techniques in an operational context as developed and implemented in actual situations. Nongrading and flexible scheduling are the underlying organizational patterns employed by the elementary schools and the high school in which several of these instructional programs were developed. Although these concepts permeate much of the program description in the following chapters, this does not preclude the treatment and utilization of other unique procedures for individualizing instruction. Thus, the programs to be described also include references to the use of team teaching, behavioral objectives, instructional resource centers, open labs, contract teaching, interdisciplinary approaches to curriculum development and staff utilization, and independent study.

It must be emphasized that the presentation of these programs is not intended to serve as an "instructional model" for interested schools to adopt or imitate. The purpose is to present the reader with a few representative examples of unique and creative activities in elementary and secondary schools for individualizing instructional programs.

Chapter 4 describes the development of two different nongraded team teaching programs implemented at the elementary school level. Chapter 5 reports the development of a high school English program and Chapter 6 relates the rationale and creation of a high school humanities program. This program, in addition to employing an interdisciplinary team, includes courses in Philosophy and the History of World

Religions. Chapter 7 contains a general overview of an art program where the development of a flexible schedule enhanced the further exploration of instructional change and individualization of instruction in the school's art curriculum. As extensive curriculum development was undertaken by the art staff, it became necessary for these teachers to consider more critically other theoretical and philosophical issues concerned with the learning process and the nature and purpose of schooling in our contemporary society. In Chapter 8 the application of a simplified systems model is employed in making an analysis of the learning process in the art program. Chapter 9 completes this part of the book with an in-depth analysis of the design of a high school ceramics course in which several of the concepts and methods for individualizing instruction presented throughout this volume are applied in a practical and operational context in curriculum development.

The author is again indebted to the individuals who contributed to the various chapters of this section of the book. Their presentations, based on first-hand knowledge and involvement in the development and implementation of these programs, will provide the reader with greater insight into the possible applications of several approaches to individualizing instruction. Mr. Rudolph Wilson, author of Chapter 5, is presently involved in the teacher training program, School of Education, Southern Illinois University at Edwardsville, Illinois. Dr. Joseph Forcinelli, author of Chapter 6, is a teacher and humanities team leader at Claremont High School, Claremont, California. Mrs. Geraldine Turner and Mrs. Alice Ritchie, co-authors of Chapters 7, 8, and 9, art artists and members of the faculty at Claremont High School, Claremont, California.

A NONGRADED TEAM APPROACH
TO ELEMENTARY INSTRUCTION

4

INTRODUCTION

Since the advent of the graded, self-contained classroom, educators have been seeking ways of improving the defects of this organizational system. Particularly in the past few years many school staffs have recognized the need for changes in the elementary school. The visible evidence of this response has been the proposal of several organizational schemes for elementary schools. One which has gained widespread support and popularity among schools is the nongraded, team approach to organizing instructional programs at the elementary level. A brief consideration of the typical elementary education program confirms the reality of the above concern.

Typically, the elementary school is organized into a number of graded classrooms to which children are assigned on the basis of chronological age. As a child grows older, he progresses through succeeding grade levels at a pace little different from that of other children his age. While grouping often occurs within the classroom unit, it seldom transcends the lock-step nature of the conventional elementary school grade-level organization. Little consideration can be given to the needs of the individual child in spite of a recognition that children of similar chronological ages differ considerably with respect to intellectual capacities, mental skills, and motor abilities.

In the typical school, a teacher is assigned to each self-contained classroom to instruct the children of that class in all subject matter and skills considered appropriate for that age. Implicit in the assignment is the assumption that the teacher is equally capable and interested in all areas of instruction. More often than not, this assumption is fallacious and, indeed, unrealistic in view of the rapid growth in the amount of knowledge in mathematics, science, and the social sciences. The teacher's effectiveness in meeting the expectations held for him is further diminished by a disproportionate burden of clerical duties which intrude upon his teaching time.

Schools typically do not utilize resources from outside the school. However, because of the increasing complexity and breadth of knowledge, in order to function at maximum effectiveness a school must go beyond its own staff in order to augment its instructional program in specialized areas. In science, for example, only by using appropriate persons from the community can the school make available to interested students knowledge about missiles, astronomy, oceanography, and other important fields of current interest. Some communities count more specialists among their population than others, but certainly every community has some persons whose special knowledge can enhance the school program.

In 1848 in Quincy, Massachusetts, the first generally recognized graded organization was adopted. Otto indicates that by 1860 the graded system was so widespread that most towns and cities had elementary schools organized on the graded basis.[1] This was the forerunner of the basic elementary school organization of today. In a short time (some 20 years later), schools were devising plans that would hopefully avoid some of the disadvantages inherent within the graded school plan.[2] The graded school did not seem to provide a scheme whereby the individual differences and needs of each student could be given full consideration. In response to this deficiency many attempts have been made to improve the typical graded elementary school. Nongraded approaches to instruction, as well as team teaching programs, are further attempts to

---

[1] Henry J. Otto, "Elementary Education III: Organization and Administration," found in Walter S. Monroe, *Encyclopedia of Educational Research* (New York: The MacMillan Co., 1950).

[2] The Department of Elementary School Principals, *Elementary School Organization: Purposes and Patterns* (Washington, D.C.: National Educational Association, 1961).

find more individualized methods of organizing students, teachers, and curricula within the often rigid confines of the elementary school.

Generally, the nongraded school is designed to implement a theory of continuous pupil progress. Since the differences among children are great and since these differences cannot be substantially modified, the school's structure must facilitate the continuous educational progress of each child. Therefore, a longer period of time will be required for some students than for others to achieve certain learnings and to attain certain developmental levels.[3] In turn, the concept of continuous pupil progress assumes some form of a nongraded organizational pattern in which individual progression is based on physical, social, and emotional factors as well as chronological, mental, and achievement factors.

INITIAL ORGANIZATION AND DESIGN

The nongraded plan calls for the removal of age-grade labels and the mixing together of children of different ages but similar abilities. It is a way of scheduling basic skill subjects—particularly reading—so that a student may proceed along a carefully constructed series of steps or levels in that particular subject at his own rate. Naturally, when we propose that students cross traditional grade-level lines, the resultant thought of mass confusion and disorganization can be frightening. Coupled with the fact that the child may also be at different levels in each subject area, we can easily see why some administrators and teachers become reticent toward such a plan before it has a chance to start.

However, it is possible to organize a successful nongraded plan, and many teachers and administrators have found that this organization stimulates them as well as the children. In one school a very simple program was designed.[4] The staff, consisting of 33 members, was organized into seven teams:

1. The leadership team—this included the principal, pupil personnel consultant, and instructional consultant.

---

[3] John Goodlad and Robert Anderson, *The Nongraded Elementary School* (New York: Harcourt, Brace, and World, 1959).

[4] A. Haas, "First Year Organization of Elmcrest Elementary School: A Nongraded Team Teaching School," *American School Board Journal* (October, 1965).

2. The resource team—this included teachers in art, music, library, physical education, and reading, and the dental hygienist and school nurse.
3. The kindergarten team.
4. Teams I and II for six- and seven-year-olds.
5. Team III for eight- and nine-year-olds.
6. Team IV for ten- and eleven-year-olds.

Another attempt at nongrading, which is somewhat more flexible than the above plan, allows a school to be organized into a series of overlapping teams. Each team has students with staggered chronological ages, for example:

Team I   5-, 6-, 7-year-olds
Team II   7-, 8-, 9-year-olds
Team III 9-, 10-, 11-year-olds

This can even be expanded to provide two-year overlapping sequences, for example:

Team I   5, 6, 7
Team II   6, 7, 8
Team III 7, 8, 9, and so on.

This overlapping obviously allows for greater flexibility in assigning students to the individual team members. Depending upon the size of the elementary school, several teams may be necessary at each succeeding level. The number of individual teams would also be a consideration in determining the number of teachers assigned to each team. There is no optimal number for determining the size of the teacher team or the number of students assigned, although the two generally are directly related. Team composition should be determined more by the interest and compatibility of the teachers involved and by the ability and achievement range of the students. However, the more teachers with wider ranges of abilities and skills that are assigned to a particular team (composed of at least 3 or 4 teachers), the more flexibility the team will be capable of generating in terms of meeting individual student needs. The placement of teacher aides and student teachers is also fundamental to this concept of team teaching.

Although many different organizational schemes may be used in a nongraded plan, there are a few basic points common to all. They discard the age-grade designation of classes and labels. They allow for more teacher-to-teacher interaction and also more teacher-to-administrator interaction. They require teachers who are flexible and who are conscientiously looking for new and better instructional methods and techniques. They require frequent re-evaluation of individual students and new placement of these students within the various instructional teams. They require parents who are well-informed and sympathetic to the program. Given the presence of the majority of these factors, the nongraded program can be organized in an effective manner.

EVOLUTION AND DEVELOPMENT OF A NONGRADED PROGRAM (K-6)[5]

THE INITIAL STAGE

The nongraded program at Sycamore Elementary School evolved in response to several concerns: (1) greater individualization of instruction, (2) further enrichment of a program promoting self-direction for the children, and (3) more effective use of staff professional strengths and other educational resources in the community. Accordingly, in 1960 the educational faculty of a nearby university proposed an experimental design for a nongraded, team teaching plan which the Ford Foundation approved and partially financed for three years at this school.

The instructional organization of the school in this initial stage consisted of three teams:

Team I included all 5-, 6-, and 7-year-olds and 5 teachers.
Team II included all 8- and 9-year-olds and 4 teachers.
Team III contained all 10-, 11-, and 12-year-olds and 4 teachers (see Figure 4.1).

With the exception of the kindergarten, the children in each team were grouped into multigraded classes by their previous teachers. The staff tried to balance these heterogenous groups with equal distribution of boys and grils, achievement levels, and behavior characteristics. Each year approximately one-half remained with their teachers for a second year. Once assigned to a team, pupils were regularly re-grouped within the team to maximize the effectiveness of the program. These groups varied in size from one student to the entire team.

---

[5] This material was extracted in part and edited from previously published material by permission of the Claremont Unified School District, Claremont, California.

Ages

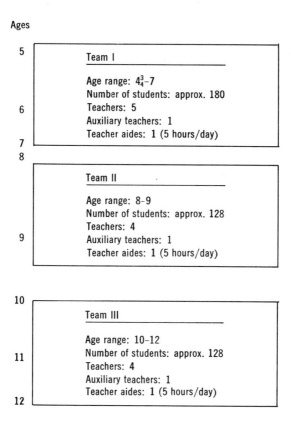

5

6

7

8

Team I

Age range: $4\frac{3}{4}$–7
Number of students: approx. 180
Teachers: 5
Auxiliary teachers: 1
Teacher aides: 1 (5 hours/day)

Team II

Age range: 8–9
Number of students: approx. 128
Teachers: 4
Auxiliary teachers: 1
Teacher aides: 1 (5 hours/day)

9

10

11

12

Team III

Age range: 10–12
Number of students: approx. 128
Teachers: 4
Auxiliary teachers: 1
Teacher aides: 1 (5 hours/day)

FIGURE 4.1
Initial Nongraded Organizational Design

In composing teacher teams, the members of the staff were grouped according to the age level of their prospective students. When recruiting new members for a team, an effort was made to find persons with complementary teaching strengths. During this initial stage the principal appointed one team leader for each team and assigned him the responsibility for improving instruction and for shaping the efforts of the team on behalf of the students. Ideally, the three leaders were to receive some time for planning and meetings in addition to a small stipend.

Each team was provided an auxiliary teacher and a teacher aide. The auxiliary teacher substituted for members of the team who were absent on sick or personal leave. Each team was also allowed twenty extra days of auxiliary teacher time to be used by the team, as necessary, to permit members to plan curriculum and to attend meetings and conferences. The teacher aide performed clerical duties and other routine tasks and tutored special groups in the classroom under the supervision of the regular teachers.

EVALUATION OF THE INITIAL STAGE

The experiment, spanning five years, confirmed the belief that team organization offered greater opportunities for individualized instruction and more effective use of teaching resources. A self-evaluation by the entire staff during the fourth and fifth years of the initial stage also raised several questions about the structure of the nongraded program.

1. Are the two major factors currently employed, that is, the age level of the pupils and the teaching strengths, the most important criteria for grouping teachers into teams?
2. If nongrading of the instructional program is justified, as it is thought to be, should the age range of students in a team be limited to two or even three years?
3. Some children may profit more from not having movement built into their programs. Can the instructional organization of the school provide adequately for these students at the same time that it is providing for the others who benefit from an organization requiring movement?
4. Is it possible to give elementary teachers time during the school day to plan and to solve special instructional and curricular problems?

PROGRAM MODIFICATIONS

The staff members suggested that the personal compatibility and philosophy of a group of teachers may be more vital to the effectiveness of the team than the fact that they teach children of similar age or that they complement the academic strengths of one another. Thus, the existing faculty was re-grouped according to mutual choice and outlook and based on compatible work relations. No one attempted to proselytize or alter another's way of working with the children.

The teachers agreed that the opportunity to have children for at least two years was an excellent idea. They knew the students better and they also enjoyed the stability of a class nucleus from the previous year. In spite of a certain amount of nongradedness which was accomplished by nongrading within the three teams, the staff felt there definitely remained three grades in the school:

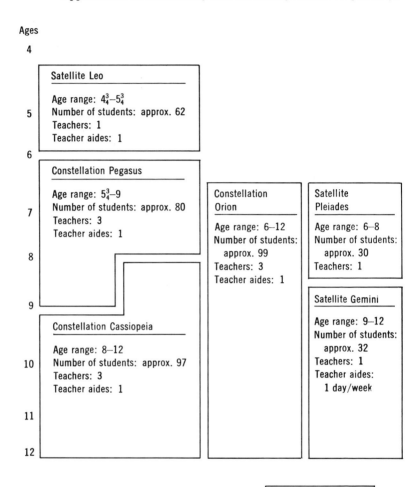

Modified Nongraded Organizational Design

Grade Team I, Grade Team II, and Grade Team III. The staff decided to assign children to newly formed teacher groups according to the preferences of each teacher as to the age of his pupils.

The results of this decision were threefold: (1) three teams in which the chronological age span of the pupils was at least four years, (2) two self-contained groups of children with a difference of more than two chronological years, and (3)two classes of five-year-old pupils (kindergarten). In order to accommodate the new organization and to disassociate from the old concept of "team," the names of constellations and satellites were adopted as names for the new groups (see Figure 4.2).

Within the framework described above the staff made provisions for the student who needed a program with minimum movement. Teachers with the same need created self-contained rooms to serve these children for whom movement would be less desirable. These groups were Satellite Leo (5-year-olds), Satellite Pleiades (6-, 7-, and 8-year-olds), and Satellite Gemini (9-, 10-, and 11-year-olds). In the latter case, the adults rather than the children moved; two teachers shared the class, one teaching her specialties in the morning, the other in the afternoon. Not all of the children who were assigned to these classes needed a program requiring a minimum of physical movement; Other important considerations were also involved in their placement.

To provide teachers with time during the school day to plan and to solve curricular problems, the faculty created the position of supporting teacher. The supporting teacher had no regular assignment of pupils and could be on call to all other teachers to assume their assignments and to provide released time for special curricular and instruction work. One of the regular staff members volunteered for the role of supporting teaching in the afternoon. The school district hired another experienced teacher for the complementary half-time position in the morning. The two supporting teachers played a far greater role than simply relieving teachers who wanted to plan programs, prepare written evaluations, or attend professional conferences. Throughout the school the supporting teachers added classes on a regular basis in mathematics, reading, spelling, science, art, and music. They worked with smaller groups in remedial reading and spelling. They administered standardized tests such as the California Test of Mental Maturity and the California Achievement Test, as well as developmental tests for new pupils.

Thus, two half-time teachers combined to fill one full-time

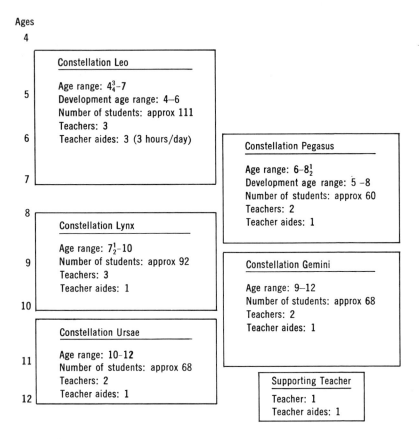

Ages

Constellation Leo

Age range: $4\frac{3}{4}$–7
Development age range: 4–6
Number of students: approx 111
Teachers: 3
Teacher aides: 3 (3 hours/day)

Constellation Pegasus

Age range: 6–$8\frac{1}{2}$
Development age range: 5 –8
Number of students: approx 60
Teachers: 2
Teacher aides: 1

Constellation Lynx

Age range: $7\frac{1}{2}$–10
Number of students: approx 92
Teachers: 3
Teacher aides: 1

Constellation Gemini

Age range: 9–12
Number of students: approx 68
Teachers: 2
Teacher aides: 1

Constellation Ursae

Age range: 10–12
Number of students: approx 68
Teachers: 2
Teacher aides: 1

Supporting Teacher

Teacher: 1
Teacher aides: 1

FIGURE 4.3
Final Nongraded Organizational Design

teaching position on the staff, an innovation which encouraged greater use of qualified teacher resources within the community.

The next year the organization changed somewhat to accommodate a few realignments and newcomers to the staff, but it adhered to the same basic principles of the previous year (see Figure 4.3). The most important refinement of the program was the creation of a means of reporting to the parents that was consistent with the school's goal of individualization. The institution of a written evaluation in February and June, like the parent conference earlier in the year, increased the communication between teacher and parent. It not only deepened the teacher's knowledge of the student, but also fostered self-evaluation by the student. Four pages of description of the pupil's performance in his school program provide information not transmitted by conventional letter grades. The report creates a new climate of commitment. The goal is satisfaction from work, rather than quantitative analysis of "satisfactory work" as reflected in grades.

AN APPROACH TO THE NONGRADED PRIMARY PROGRAM[6]

Oakmont Elementary School has a student population of 430 and a certificated staff of 13.5 classroom teachers, augmented by special teachers in vocal and instrumental music, speech, and learning assistance. The local district provides one five-hour-per-day teacher aide who serves as librarian and coordinator of instructional materials. Federal funds are being used to provide the services of a one-third-time learning assistance specialist and three additional teacher aides who work primarily with under-achieving students. In addition, the school is fortunate to have a corps of volunteer helpers from local colleges, PTA mother's groups, and three students from the local high school.

The school plant was constructed in 1950 and is traditional in every respect, with the exception of a war surplus building which is used exclusively as the learning assistance center. Movable walls, flexible spaces, and other innovations usually associated with team teaching programs are as yet not available to the Oakmont teachers. Teacher determination and smallness of plant, plus a local district philosophy encouraging individual schools to improve existing programs, are the factors responsible for progress to date. The Oakmont School Nongraded Primary Plan is an excellent example of what can be done to provide a flexible program under the limitations of a tight budget and an inflexible building.

PROGRAM DEVELOPMENT

A few teachers at Oakmont became interested in a nongraded system. Whatever could be found in the literature was read and materials were collected from schools where existing programs were already in operation. The idea was discussed at staff meetings and an effort was made to apply the knowledge gained from

---

[6] *Ibid.*

reading and from the experiences of other schools to this situation.

Teachers were concerned by the wide range of achievement among the children in their rooms. Coincidentally, an overcrowded second grade combined with this concern to illustrate the restrictions placed upon the educational program by the conventional method of grade placement. There were children in the second grade who would have benefited from being placed in the first grade, where there were more children at a stage of maturation similar to theirs. However, such a move could not occur because it was felt that a change downward in placement would be perceived by the child as a sign of failure.

The teachers recognized that the normal spread of almost a year in chronological age within a given grade often worked to the detriment of the younger child, although he might be progressing well in relation to his own development. Consequently, by the chance of his birthdate, a child might proceed obscured or even inhibited by an arbitrary age-grade placement.

In view of the wide range of developmental levels within any age group, some criteria for grouping other than age was seen by the teachers as necessary in the interests of the child's mental health and his need for continuous progress without repetitions or leaps. Thus, it was the decision of the staff to work toward a nongraded program of instruction at the primary level.

The first steps were taken in the direction of cooperative teaching and movement of children between grade levels. A boy who had been retained in kindergarten visited a first grade room and participated enough to show that he could now work well with some of the first grade children. His stay was increased gradually until he was remaining there for the full day. A similar arrangement was made for a girl. Their progress encouraged the movement of other children between grade levels.

Five teachers agreed to regroup the children for math instruction. They created five alternatives for placement where only three—Book I, Book II, and Book III—had existed before. The success of these first probing efforts to break through the rigidity of conventional grade placement encouraged these teachers to propose a plan of nongraded organization for instruction at the K-2 level to be implemented in the next school year.

The Primary Department consisted of approximately 180 children, aged five, six, and seven, and five teachers. The teachers comprised a team with mutual responsibility for all the children. One of the teachers was designated team leader. The total group of primary students was divided among the five teachers. The teacher to whom the child was assigned was called the "Planning Teacher." The planning teacher was the person with primary responsibility for the child and assumed a major role in guiding the child's progress, conferring with parents, and reporting progress. The child spent the major portion of his school day with his planning teacher. Assignment of children to a planning teacher was determined alphabetically, with attention given to balancing of age levels within the Primary Department.

The nongraded teaching team planned instruction, shared decisions concerning grouping, assigned children to the planning teachers, and developed curriculum appropriate to the nongraded program. The major effort was directed toward insuring individualized instruction and continuous progress for each child and maintaining flexibility of grouping.

The facilities available for use by the team included four standard-size classrooms, one large room, and an adjoining outdoor play area. Because of the limitation of these facilities it should be pointed out that the term "team" as used in this description refers to the group of teachers who share guidance and instructional responsibilities for a group of children. As used here, the term does not imply "team teaching" as commonly practiced.

During the following year, the nongraded primary organization extended to include the third grade. This expansion brought two more teachers into the primary team. With this number of persons participating, it was necessary to create two teams named by the age range of the pupils within them: the 5-8 team and the 7-9 team. Close cooperation was maintained between the two teams, and regrouping of students occurs between teams as well as within teams.

In a move to establish articulation between the nongraded primary and the graded intermediate department of the school, as well as to increase flexibility of instruction, a fourth grade teacher was included in the 7-9 team. Now it is possible to place primary students with this teacher for some subjects and to bring fourth grade students into the nongraded team for certain types of instruction. The teachers of the graded portion of the school constitute the 9-12 team. The leader of this team meets weekly with the primary team leaders and the principal, providing for an extension of the type of communication so important at the primary level.

A TYPICAL TEACHING DAY

Perhaps the effect of the Oakmont nongraded organization upon the teacher's daily life can be most effectively described by presenting the schedule for a typical teaching day. As one looks at this schedule, he will see that in many ways it resembles the routine of the teacher in a conventional organization, but there are important distinctions—particularly the methods of grouping children in planning groups across age levels and the flexible regrouping of children for special instruction made possible by the cooperative planning of the several teachers in the team.

The following represents a typical daily schedule of the 5-8 or the 7-9 teams:

8:45— 9:00 The children meet as a group with their planning teacher for roll-taking, purchasing of lunch tickets, reading of announcements, etc.

9:00— 9:40 The children are regrouped among the seven teachers of the primary department for arithmetic instruction. During regrouping there is an intermingling of pupils between the two teams described in the preceding section.

9:40— 9:55 Recess

9:55—11:30 Pupils are regrouped among the seven teachers for language instruction.

11:30—12:15 Lunch

12:15— 2:00 Pupils meet with the planning teacher for instruction in social studies, science, music, and art. During this large block of time groups can be combined for large group instruction. Combining groups can free a teacher for planning.

2:00— 2:30 During this period some seven- and most eight-year-olds remain for either enrichment programs in some subjects or for remedial instruction.

STUDENT PLACEMENT

"With which teacher or group of teachers will this child experience the greatest degree of success?" is the main criterion of pupil placement. A secondary consideration is the nature of the group itself: "In what type of peer group will this child profit most?" These criteria admittedly are highly subjective but staff decisions take into consideration all of the available objective instruments such as development, achievement, or scholastic appitude tests.

One technique for student placement in a nongraded team program may be accomplished in the following manner. In the spring the principal prepares a large pocket chart (approximately four feet by five feet) which corresponds in design to the school's organization for the coming year. The teachers prepare a card for each child with his name, photograph, and birthdate. Then the principal meets with each teacher to decide where their students should be placed for the next year. These initial decisions are registered by inserting the child's card in an appropriate pocket on the chart. Following the tentative placement of everyone in the school, the principal meets with each team group to evaluate and to modify the decisions. Also, other teachers who taught the children in previous years are consulted by the principal and the current teachers.

Finally, the principal posts the pocket chart in the teachers' workroom or lounge, and the entire faulty is encouraged to evaluate the decisions. The chart remains there for two or three weeks, and if a staff member disagrees with a placement, he registers his dissent by placing the child's card on its side in the pocket. Further consideration is then necessary before a final decision can be made. Placement is not irrevocable. Changes can and do occur as needed throughout the school year. Student placement by this process is obviously much more time-consuming than by previous elementary scheduling methods; however, other less time-consuming alternatives do not appear as satisfactory in terms of achieving proper student assignments to the appropriate nongraded team.

INDIVIDUALIZED INSTRUCTION

The sole purpose for the nongraded organization, its major emphasis and impact upon instruction, and all of the plans necessary to implement this program derive from one single, dominant theme; the individual needs of each child in his quest for self-discovery. One of the major concerns of the teachers should be the way the child feels about himself, his successes, and his failures, rather than how others feel about him. The teachers are interested in his uniqueness rather than in how he fits into a standardized, arbitrary grade level.

Since graded textbooks are often incompatible with these goals, new materials are necessary for instruction. Rich and varied content is important in the nongraded school. Perhaps teachers might follow the admonition of Jerome Bruner: "Discovery, like surprise, favors the well prepared mind."[7] Packaged programs may be used freely to help supplement specific disabilities or to coordinate studies throughout the school. However, the best materials for individualized instruction may be the *teacher-prepared* materials, and this may become necessary in order to achieve the degree of individualization desired. New and unusual units of instruction designed by the teacher especially for a specific group of children provokes high interest and can allow for a larger spread of capabilities. New techniques for learning by tactile and kinesthetic means such as sandtrays and sandpaper, by aural devices such as the tape recorder, or by visual aids such as the tachistoscope or controlled reader may be usefully adapted for the classroom. The children should be offered more opportunities and more time to grow. This approach allows for creative growth of the teacher as well as of the child.

One obstacle to the individualization of instruction felt not only by the teacher in the nongraded school but also by the conventional grade-level teacher is progress reporting. If a child's educational path is to be charted individually, some method must be developed to report his progress in terms of his movement along that path rather than in terms of achievement compared to other children in his group. Many nongraded programs have departed from the use of the traditional report card in favor of an instrument which attempts to allow the teacher to evaluate the child's progress individually. One such instrument designed by a school staff was called the *Primary Continuous Progress Profile*. It contained a combination of checklist items and continual dia-

---

[7] Jerome S. Bruner, *Toward a Theory of Instruction* (Cambridge, Mass.: Harvard University Press, 1966).

grams. The instrument reported the child's mastery of specific tasks within each subject area and indicated his point of beginning and his degree of progress.

EVALUATION AND EDUCATIONAL LEADERSHIP

We might consider briefly the problems in evaluating innovative programs such as nongraded schools. Feedback as to the success or failure in any program very often is one of its most important aspects. The principal must become aware of difficult areas in which potential problems may exist or where teachers may need support. At the end of the first year one nongraded school identified the following critical elements in the program:

1. There is a need for more careful selection of staff members.
2. There is a need for continuous in-service programs to assist staff members in implementing nongraded team teaching concepts that will promote continuous progress for each pupil.
3. There is a need to keep members of the community informed concerning changes in the educational program.
4. Outside agencies or individuals should be brought into the school to help measure and assess the program in a more scientific and objective way.

The role and function of the principal as an educational leader in establishing and maintaining the nongraded school is most important. The old adage, "So goes the principal, so goes the school," has serious elements of truth. It is through his leadership ability that the program will succeed or fail. He is the facilitator who must satisfy teachers, parents, and his superiors all at the same time for the benefit of the students. It is not an overstatement to say that the principal who involves himself with the nongraded program must be committed, have deep faith in this approach to learning, and be willing to suffer set-backs from time to time.

The organization of the nongraded school must bend with the inevitable changes in the staff, student composition, and community. It strives toward individualization for the student and for the teacher. It is flexible, with a different meaning for each teacher and each child at various times.

THE ENGLISH PROGRAM AND THE
INDIVIDUALIZATION OF INSTRUCTION

5

The individualization of instruction has put certain demands on both the secondary school and the family. In traditional schools, parents as well as administrators can be concerned about individualizing instruction as long as it stays within the confines of a conventional six-period day.

The irony of this situation rests upon the student's ability or inability to find time to work with teachers or peers. Most likely, the teacher dedicatedly remains after school—heroic a task as it might be—to promote individual instruction, only to find himself in competition with a school bus, an extracurricular activity, or a dentist's appointment.

Yet, state guideliness on the teaching of English, administrators and English conferences will demand that teachers begin to look at curricula and to develop positive steps toward individual instruction with an emphasis on student behavior, goals, and personality. At the same time, these areas do not ask for gimmicks but rather that teachers take a positive step towards looking at the total education of a secondary student and answering the questions of what, why, and why not.

One area in which new steps have been taken in the individualizing of instruction is English education. Traditionalists have advocated that spelling, reading, and grammar be the parameters within which all education in English takes place. The educator has asked that integrated learning be exposed to the student and that a better approach through the implementation of a humanistic approach to learning be utilized rather than merely reading, writing, and spelling.

Thus, the administrators introduce flexible scheduling, an approach to the individualizing of instruction. Flexable scheduling offers the English curriculum a much greater innovative opportunity for learning.

THE ENGLISH CURRICULUM AND FLEXIBLE SCHEDULING

The English teacher finds that he has time to work individually with students, to implement and evaluate new and ongoing programs, and to design daily intricacies of English education that used to be heard only at English conferences.

Flexible scheduling does not limit a teacher's understanding of himself and his students; it does help to explain and understand changing human behavior and behavioral trends. It helps make a student in an English classroom aware of his learning limitations and discover methods by which to improve himself. It also helps to nurture positive reinforcements in the student who excels, as this student finds that his only competition is himself.

Certainly, one could continue and draw from experience with both students and teachers laudatory comments about the excellence of flexible scheduling as it is concerned with the English curriculum. However, the attempt here will be to show the flexibility of the program, the possibility for innovative curricula, and the attitudinal effects of flexible scheduling as it affects students and teachers in an English program.

With the magical words "flexible scheduling" comes its progeny: team teaching, large group instruction, small group learning, independent study, teacher conferences, curriculum meetings, workshops, departmental decentralization, greater teacher autonomy, and even continued traditional teaching in a flexible school. If an English staff is unprepared for the implementation of this new technique, flexible scheduling may die in its conception because of rigidity, conformity, or just plain stubbornness. Teachers and administrators, given the responsibility to nurse the progeny to maturity, may cheat in the performance of their duties. What appears to be a well-balanced, well-nourished program may have the side effects of apathy, rebellion, and disgust. An English staff, when given more direct articulation of a new program, must be reminded of a point made by Louis J. Halle in *Society of Man,* in which he observes that we all live simultaneously in two worlds of teaching and practice—"The orderly conceptual world and the chaotic existential world."[1] Flexible scheduling is somewhat between the two worlds—a dangerous position in which to grow to maturity! The teacher, given the power to amend the teaching world, must demonstrate an affection for developing new trends in English education.

To an English teacher, a program of flexible scheduling seems easy. Keeping the traditional concept of a school day in mind, he sees that he might teach, at the most, 15 hours a week as compared to a traditional 25 hours a week. The teacher will also think about the excellent opportunity he might have to perform such teaching duties as posting grades and grading papers at school, realizing that his additional unscheduled time at school will give him a chance to bowl every night. After the administrators emphasize that the reason for the fewer modules, or hours, is not for "free time," the reorienting of the teacher to the program begins.

If looked at closely, we find that traditionally what has been taught in the English curriculum does not help to make a student aware of his social responsibility. *Silas Marner,* if taught as outlined in an unemotional teaching guide for the novel, does not give students the feeling of awareness that they so desperately need in a rapidly changing world. The question of deciding the fate of *Silas Marner* depends on today's world.

Doctor Johnson of Illinois University gives an insight to curriculum from which flexible scheduling might receive its impetus:

> However puzzled we may be about education relevance for students who will dominate the first decade of the next century, we can do better than to comprehend the line on which we (the teachers) find ourselves now. The implication is of a social environment of grinding interfaces, increasingly urban and increasingly global; a reduction of the discrete blocks of education, work and leisure into a new kind of fluidity from which more complex life time mixes can be made, the rapid rate of intellectual and institutional obsolescence; the sensitization to inequality, with a compensatory leveling-up rather than leveling-down philosophy; the mounting use of organiza-

---

[1] Louis J. Halle, *Society of Man* (New York: Harper & Row, Publishers, 1965).

tion for the social sharing of individual risks and the increasing dominance of men by tool, word and by number.[2]

The English teacher in a flexibly scheduled school is not primarily concerned with the traditional goals set by rigid traditional curricula. He has a responsibility to develop a relevant curriculum that will help lead a student towards self-articulation; and the curriculum meeting the educational and social needs at the high school level is diverse. Teachers, being an entity with teaching weaknesses as well as strengths, also begin to discover their diversity. No more do they have five classes covering the same material during the school day. No more do students lock-step themselves and, because of this built-in rigidity, become bored and feel useless. The English curriculum puts demands on the teacher and on the students. Teachers, rather than accept the curriculum of past years, now devise new courses to fit the individual student's needs and the strength of the teacher. Courses such as Art of the Film, Correct Writing and Speaking, Humanities, Developmental Reading, Seminars for Individualized Instruction, Reading Improvement and Composition, The Art of Great Speeches, Creative Writing, Negro Literature, and Folk-Rock Poetry now can be elected by students. Since the courses were designed by individual teachers, the effect of interested teachers is laudatory. Not only has the teacher written the course, he has also designed the structure of the course.

Electives such as those mentioned above are constantly changing. Depending on the school budget and student interest, the courses may die at conception or continue to be nourished with sensitivity to the program in terms of student needs, teacher needs, and societal concerns. Within the confines of the regular courses, teachers as well as students find greater flexibility for curriculum development and relevancy of content in a flexibly scheduled program. In the ninth grade curriculum, for example, teachers are not in lock-step. The levels of study vary because of the individualization of instruction. A teacher whose teaching strength is drama and teaching weakness poetry, finds that he has time to schedule his teaching units so that his fellow teacher whose

---

[2] Eldon L. Johnson, "Education: Cutting Edges for Social Change," *Educational Record* (Fall, 1968).

strength is poetry may be utilized during the time that he can exchange his drama strength. The drama teacher who is directing a play which will be taught in the ninth grade can send out a notice to all ninth grade teachers and they can schedule their classes for viewing of the play without total school disruption. If students from back-to-back English classes are acting out scenes from a play, all other students might be given an opportunity to see these scenes during the school day.

The curriculum in a flexibly scheduled high school, therefore, offers greater opportunity for the utilization and development of a

TABLE 5.1

English Teacher's Weekly Program in a Flexible Schedule

Modules[a]	Monday	Tuesday	Wednesday	Thursday	Friday
1			Eng SG 1		Eng Lab 1
2			Eng SG 1		Eng Lab 1
3			Eng SG 1		Eng Lab 1
4		Eng LG 1			Eng Lab 1
5		Eng LG 1			
6				Eng Sem 9	
7			Eng SG 2	Eng Sem 9	Eng Lab 2
8			Eng SG 2	Eng Sem 9	Eng Lab 2
9			Eng SG 2		Eng Lab 2
10		Eng SG 3		Eng Lab 3	Eng Lab 2
11		Eng SG 3		Eng Lab 3	
12		Eng SG 3		Eng Lab 3	
13				Eng Lab 3	
14					
15					
16		Dir Stud		Dir Stud	
17		Dir Stud	Eng Sem 9	Dir Stud	Eng Sem 9
18		Eng SG 4	Eng Sem 9	Eng Lab 4	Eng Sem 9
19		Eng SG 4	Eng Sem 9	Eng Lab 4	Eng Sem 9
20		Eng SG 4		Eng Lab 4	

[a] Periods of time—20 minutes in length

teacher's strength. It also helps the new teacher become exposed to different teaching styles. If there is no class conflict, the teacher is able to observe another teacher's class during the school day and there is greater opportunity for developing team approaches to instruction.

VARIABILITY OF TEACHER SCHEDULES (see Table 5.1)

Individual teacher's schedules will vary considerably. Some teachers who elect a three-module, three-times-per-week pattern find that they may teach only on Monday, Wednesday, and Friday. Tuesday and Thursday can be devoted to pupil conferences, cirriculum meetings, and observation. The teacher who elects this traditional teaching schedule (this 3×3 time pattern is considered "traditional" in the flexible schedule because class size normally will not vary and the time period is uniform throughout the week) is usually one who is timid about large group instruction, has not convinced himself of the flexibility of the program, or wants a free schedule for greater lengths of time.

However, within the confines of a 3×3 time pattern, the teacher can have greater flexibility than in the conventional six-period-per-day schedule. Whenever he wants to have smaller class sizes, he can excuse half of his students for independent study, send half of his students to the English Resource Center, or find an empty classroom or a pleasant place in which the students can work on a pre-assigned project.

The following diagrams reveal some of the flexibility that can be built into a traditional 3×3 schedule. Diagram 1 shows all the students meeting three times a week. The teacher may lead the

DIAGRAM 1

3 Modules:	Monday	Wednesday	Friday
	30 students in class	30 students in class	30 students in class

DIAGRAM 2

3 Modules:	Monday	Wednesday	Friday
	15 Group A in class	15 Group B in class	30 Total group in class
	15 Group B Resource Center Independent Study	15 Group A Resource Center Independent Study	

discussion during the class time or he may have students lead the discussion. He may also have various groups working on a project within the confines of three modules.

Diagram 2 shows the flexibility of the teacher's program. The teacher meets with half of the class, Group A, and sends the other half, Group B, to the Resource Center for independent study where prescribed work is placed on a bulletin board. The student may also have the choice of independent study in which he decides what he should be doing. On Wednesday, the groups are reversed. On Friday the teacher meets the entire class for evaluation purposes, follow-up studies of the week's activities, and the use of audio-visual aids.

On Tuesday and Thursday, the teacher schedules a conference with each student. Some teachers utilize the 3×3 for individual book reports and humanizing teacher rapport with students.

Another schedule which is very popular is the large group, small group, and middle group schedule. Some teachers who teach two or more classes at the same grade level find this structure very effective. For example, a teacher who has as part of his assignment two tenth grade English classes with a total of 60 to 65 students might use this schedule:

DIAGRAM 3

Monday	Tuesday	Wednesday	Thursday	Friday
Small Group 1 (3 modules)		Small Group 3 (3 modules)	Middle Groups 1, 2 (4 modules)	Middle Groups 3, 4 (4 modules)
Small Group 2 (3 modules)	Large Group (all groups combined) (2 modules)	Small Group 4 (3 modules)		

The structure, whether designated by modules or hours, should be flexible. It should rely on teacher strengths rather than weaknesses, and it should also allow for the individual growth of students through the individualization of learning.

TEACHER–STUDENT CONFERENCES

Individualization in a flexibly scheduled school must also promote conferring. An English program reaches its efficiency level when students, teachers, and administrators recognize the meritorious effects of conferences. By conferences, one does not mean a ten-minute session after school but designated times throughout the students' and teachers' school day. Participants can sit down, relax, and use an effective scheduling tool for self-discovery and sensitivity to self. Too often, teachers, not having time for conference periods, allow students to discuss anything they like whenever the teacher runs out of material to teacher them. The conference period gives the student a chance to speak freely about academic problems which might be influenced by social problems or which might have been influenced by family problems outside the classroom. In this conference teachers respect the power of listening. Some discussions which have taken place during the conference give the teacher enough feedback material to evaluate his teaching style and methods.

The student sees another aspect of a teacher's manner in a one-to-one conference period. Individual instruction permeates the conference period. Composition correction in the student's presence helps a student to realize his poor writing style and the corrections are made immediately. Book reports given in a conference period aids the teacher in asking individual questions which may be relevant to the student's life and interest. When the small group discussion is so involved that more time is needed, students may use the conference period to further the discussion.

Overall, in a flexibly scheduled school the conference period becomes an integral part of individualized instruction. Teachers of English need additional time for in-service training and conferring among themselves or with other staff members. The added time allotted to the teacher gives him an opportunity to enhance his teaching role.

DIFFERENTIATED FACILITIES

Differentiated facilities will generate additional enthusiasm for the teaching of English. The large group or lecture room, the small group room, the teacher's office, the reading clinic, and the English Resource Center are fundamental facilities for promoting good instruction. The purpose of these rooms will vary. The large group or lecture room is used primarily for lectures, demonstrations, showing of films, playing of records, dramatic presentations, student panels, teacher panels, and talks by outside resource people.

The Large Group. Generally speaking, the large group facility seats from 100 to 300 students. Team teaching demonstrates the best use of the room. In a three-man team, teachers meet once a week during their unstructured (free) time to plan the large group lecture. Each teacher contributes to making the lecture interesting. After deciding that a 20-minute or one-module lecture is not enough time and that a 60-minute or three-module lecture is too much time, the team may decide on a 40-minute or two-module lecture. Questions posed by the team members consist of:

1. How much background material will I have to present for the understanding of the unit?
2. What visual activities could be used?
3. Will the lecture represent a continuum of a large unit?
4. How much student participation can we utilize?
5. How will we divide up the time? Shall one of us take the entire lecture, or should we split it up in different parts?
6. Who will make sure all the equipment is working?
7. Who will take roll? (Preferably a teacher aide.)
8. What will happen in the next three lectures?
9. What about unity?

Any team of teachers or individual teacher needs to develop and to evaluate continually present and new curricula for effective large group presentations. In the final conference stage for a large group lecture, the most difficult task faces the teacher. The question of *why large groups* becomes the major concern.

Many times a teacher in a traditional school program may have to repeat the same material during one school day. Pity the poor teacher who has to read the fight scene in Gibson's *The Miracle Worker*. Pity the students enrolled in that teacher's last-period class! In a large group presentation repetition is resolved. The teacher-lecturer's energy is concentrated on just one reading of the play. Students who miss the presentation may hear the recording of the lecture during their independent study time in the resource center or teacher-office area. Another feature germane to large group instruction is its flexibility. Teachers may show a short film, play a recording, or participate in a panel discussion in one lecture instead of many classes.

The Small Group. What takes place in the small group indicates the growing concern for the indivdualizing of instruction. The small group in a flexibly scheduled school is student-centered, not teacher-dominated; the teacher becomes a resource person. The following answers were volunteered by students when asked to what questions a small group teacher should address himself. They were:

1. Am I a good listener?
2. Am I willing to allow a discussion to take shape before I introduce my objectives?
3. Am I willing to be challenged or criticized by students?
4. Am I spontaneous in my responses to my students and just as eager as they?
5. Do I know how to steer objectively a discussion back on the right track?
6. Do I hide behind the textbook response or answers and not have any opinions of my own?
7. Can I ask questions that will stimulate thought?
8. Am I observant?
9. Can I handle shy students or obnoxious students without destroying the continuity of the group?
10. What kind of person am I? Do I communicate effectively with my peers? administration? my family?
11. Can I admit that there may be another interpretation contrary to mine to a question I pose which may also be correct?
12. Do I have a sense of humor?

The teacher involved with small group teaching must be willing to consider flexibility and individualization of learning as prerequisites for effective teaching. The small group will not only be relevant to the students' lives, it will also become an integral part of the learning process. In small groups, students become aware of individual differences among themselves. Because they sit in small circles rather than in rows, students learn to listen carefully, to observe and deal with behavior effectively, and to speak clearly and concisely. They become sensitive to each other.

PROGRAM DESIGN: A SEQUENTIAL LEARNING UNIT

The following chart is an example of a sequential learning unit demonstrating the use of the large group lecture, middle group lab situation, and small group discussion.

Subject: Arthur Miller, Witchcraft, and The Crucible

    Grade 11
    Number of students 400
    Number of teachers (team)   3
    Number of large groups ...   3 (two modules each week)
    Number of middle groups ..   4 (three modules each week)
    Number of small groups ..   8 (three modules each week)
    Length of unit ....   3 weeks

Resource persons for large group:

1. Rev. J. Strathern, Assistant, Congregational Church
   Lecture title: Witchcraft and the Puritans
2. Don Freuchte, Drama teacher
   Lecture-demonstration: "A director interprets Arthur Miller"
3. Mrs. Anne Waggonner, team member
   Lecture title: McCarthyism and *The Crucible*
4. Karla Bell, Mike Berman, students
   Dramatic presentation of several scenes from the play

MIDDLE GROUP LAB—RELATED ACTIVITIES—30 STUDENTS EACH

1. Follow-up discussion of the play.
2. Discussion of the lectures (question-and-answer period).
3. Introduction of vocabulary words from the play.
4. Writing practice using the play for topics.
5. Rehearsal for student presentation.
6. Listen to a taped interview with Arthur Miller.
7. Schedule appointments for individual composition instruction.
8. Assign independent research for presentation in middle group.
9. Help students develop various individualized projects.

SMALL GROUP—STUDENT-LED DISCUSSION—15 STUDENTS EACH

1. Discuss questions and issues raised in middle group and large group.
2. Present and discuss independent work previously assigned.

Much of what is discussed depends on what the student has learned during independent study. Teachers suggest supplementary material which is found in the English Resource Center and the library.

THE ENGLISH RESOURCE CENTER

    Located in an area easily accessible to students and conducive to independent study, the English Resource Center promulgates individual learning. Multiple copies of novels, plays, essays, and periodicals are available for the student's use. Although the teacher's assignments for independent work are given to students during their middle group experience, the same assignments will be found on a bulletin board in the Center. For example:

Teacher: Waggoner
Grade 11—Large Group Lecture Oct. 29

The Crucible

Middle Group Section 1-4
1. Readings: Acts II, III *Crucible*
   Bantam edition pp. 20-43
2. Writing:
   Be prepared to write a comparison of two characters from the play.
3. Supplementary reading (closed reserve in the ERC)
   Chapter 1 "The Paragraph"
   Harbrace Writing Course

Small Group

Discussion Leaders Over Critical Materials
   Pat Albrect—Sect. 1
   Pam Alden—Sect. 2
   Shelly Schonfield—Sect. 3
   Bruce Hod—Sect. 4

Conferences

Students who have conferences with me on Thurs. 9–11:30 I will meet you in the ERC and not my office.

Sect. 4

Richard White: See me as soon as possible.

In addition to finding related material covering a specific unit of learning, many self-teaching aids are available to the students: Programmed instruction in grammar, spelling, and reading helps to individualize instruction.

When a teacher discovers specific problems in a student's writing, the student is directed to the English Resource Center for additional help. The teacher may make assignments in a programmed text or supplementary material for the correction of the student's writing errors. During independent study, the student goes to the English Resource Center to fulfill the assignments. When the student feels he has corrected his writing errors, he makes an appointment with his teacher for a re-evaluation of what he has independently learned about his writing style.

Selected supplementary material and critical material is found in the library. Rather than using this center as a study hall, the library becomes an integral part of the student's learning. The library serves as a media center; the librarian, a media specialist. During the teacher's initial planning stage for a specific unit of study, the librarian is informed of the unit and helps with the presentation of the unit. In the unit Witchcraft, Arthur Miller, and *The Crucible,* the librarian provides a media package. She will prepare a bibliography of supplemental materials, provide a list of reference materials, and suggest film strips and recordings available to support the unit. Because the librarian has helped to plan this unit, she strengthens the learning experience.

The emphasis on individual learning in a flexibly scheduled school reaches maximum effectiveness when students, teachers, administrators, and staff members realize that the total school is a learning center. The concept that a boxed-in school, teacher, or curriculum will produce a boxed-in mind must be alleviated. Scheduling with an emphasis on individualized learning attempts to overcome this.

THE HUMANITIES AND INDIVIDUALIZED INSTRUCTION

6

This chapter covers what happens to humanities courses and humanities students in individualized programs. In order to see the relationships more clearly, what is meant by "humanities" must be determined. This term has been bantered about quite a bit by educators. When "humanities" is used here, it means human aspirations regulated by human values expressed in language and art forms which symbolize the spirit of man in any age. This stipulative definition of humanities can and should become an educational norm for all subject areas. As a norm, it needs a good methodological framework. One aspect of that framework is flexible scheduling.

In developing a humanities curriculum the ultimate aim is to offer the student general and specialized studies in humanities and, at the same time, to emphasize and interrelate the humanistic endeavor that transcends all educational progress. Normally, humanities courses as such are infrequently offered at the high school level. Special offerings to honor students that touch on selections from world literature is the fare, at best, for most high schools. Recent trends are moving toward intergating art, music, drama, and literature as a basis for studying man and his achievements within a value context; but, one wonders if this is what students and teachers are seeking in a humanities program.

Consider a college-level humanities course for a moment. Here we find a great deal of consistency and conformity. Essentially, these courses endeavor to give the student a concentrated study of classic works of art, religion, philosophy, literature, and history. The approach is often chronological, seeking to interlace the studies with a historical continuum. Frequently, weekly seminars with each faculty member involved are scheduled. Generally, this measures up to being a good humanities course but seldom achieves sufficient dialogue between faculty and students, particularly in the area of bridging educational and human values.

There are a variety of reasons why humanities courses have not been prevalent in the high school curriculum. They are "luxury" courses not open to every student. They frequently take the form of lengthy syllabi with copious reading assignments and tedious examinations. The students are inundated with the literary "jewels" of the past, but when the course is over, one questions whether they have experienced some configuration, some synthesis of man's nature and identity. This is not to say that flexible scheduling or any other approach to individualizing instruction can change all this; however, high schools that are using flexible scheduling are making traditional courses more effective and are introducing new courses that have more meaning and more relevance to the life and times of the student. Humanities is certainly one such area of study.

Offering courses in the humanities now is becoming more popular among educators. Everyone seems to be agreed on the need for dealing with the imaginary or real gap between the techno-scientific and the humanistic values of education. This may be said also of the need to place more emphasis on studies based on an interdisciplinary approach. The passage, in 1965, of the National Foundation for the Arts and Humanities Act represented the effort of educators to invest in humanistic studies as well as in theoretical and scientific studies. The meaning intended here, however, should not be misconstrued. Science is as humanistic as any other human endeavor. Courses of study do not have to be labeled "humanities" to be humanistic, and this is a justifiable indictment of educational practice at any time— namely, to segregate, specialize, and compartmentalize courses of study and so deprive them of a holistic integration of creative human values.

From where comes, then, the individuation process of evolving self-awareness, self-esteem, and meaningful human goals in education? In this book, many pages are devoted to the organizational and leadership aspects of the individualization of learning *via* flexible scheduling and other innovative techniques. It is now time to turn to the appraisal of a humanities program within this context.

The humanities program might include the following courses: (1) Humanities I, a seminar on the study of man and the human situation; (2) The History of World Religions; and (3) Philosophy. It should be said at the outset that it is to the credit of flexible scheduling that these courses, like numerous other electives, can be offered. This is not a definitive program in the humanities but, at the same time, it will be seen that they are courses that deal with questions that are of deep concern to the students. Moreover, these courses are also desirable for and desired by the students. They may well be given "required" status in programs of the future.

HUMANITIES I: AN INTERDISCIPLINARY APPROACH

This is an interdisciplinary team approach to the humanities. It is a one-year elective course taught by five teachers who attempt to explore with the students significant areas of literature, art, religion, music, science, mathematics, philosophy, history, and language. Disciplines of such a substantive nature as these require a valid presupposition for revealing their interrelatedness. Therefore, themes of the human ethos "set the stage" for the exploration of these disciplines. There are many themes and they vary from year to year. Thus, apart from asking the question central to the course, "Who am I?" the themes of freedom, aloneness, and happiness have been used as "vehicular carriers" for viewing the more substantive disciplines of the course material.

It can be seen that the aim of the seminars is to go beyond the mere study of names and places and of other data of history. Rather, the interest has been in what makes literature, art, music, or any subject valuable to an individual for other than its essential or usual value. To accomplish this the course is developed from the point of view of the student as he discovers for himself the what and the why of these areas of life, as he speculates about himself in relation to these areas, as he evaluates these areas as to their worth and meaning to himself and his generation. Hopefully, the course will aid the student in arriving at a realization of himself as he relates to the rest of humanity.

There are certain "indispensables" that reinforce the point of view of studies. There is the need for cooperation among the "experts" from the various disciplines. There is a common allegiance to common objectives which hopefully assures an internal coherence regarding the themes. At the same time that universality is sought, uniformity is not insisted upon. The students are assured that the studies will adhere to contemporary interpretations but will not be cut off from the voices of history and man's gifts to mankind.

That this is a unique approach to the humanistic theme in education may perhaps best be seen in the desired behavioral or performatory objectives of the course. For example, when self-realization and self-worth are called behavioral objectives of the course, this means that the course is a drama and the student is not a spectator but is on the playing field. More than that, he is not only a player but has the leading role. Increasingly, the burden of generating the conceptualized experiences of the course is placed upon each individual student. The staff produces only what the students themselves cannot produce.

Another objective is freedom. This means freedom of the mind and the imagination. Students are urged to look for their own possibilities of being and becoming, and, at the same time, to attempt to see the possibilities for mankind. Out of this particular emphasis on freedom, students realize that a human education is a basic norm for the human situation in general and for various disciplines of learning in particular.

Still another sought-after outcome is the existential quality of commitment. By this is meant a quality of personal awareness that projects concern: a concern for excellence in its form rather than its content; a concern for personal integrity of being; and a concern for ideas. Commitment at these levels of behavior, it is felt, cultivates the interrelatedness of human endeavor both at the personal and at the subject field level. In summation, the following might be considered viable goals for the student:

1. Creativity within the context of a disciplined imagination.
2. A synoptic point of view for a pluralistic society.

3. Discernment of values and their interrelation.
4. Recognition and respect for human diversity.

PROGRAM DESIGN: HUMANITIES TEAM IN ACTION

At this point it would be useful to explicate more specifically the previous statement of philosophy and goals by outlining a semester's presentation of the humanities team in action. Following this, the logistics of the operational aspects of the course as flexibly scheduled can be presented with greater clarity.

Semester's Theme: "Man, The Hero With Many Faces." Utilizing this central theme, a clearer awareness of our identity and of the forces that shape our being is sought. When arriving at the end of the study, there will be agreement and disagreement regarding the conclusions. But out of it all, the feeling of a certain heroic struggle will be there. Perhaps the heroic is as close as it is possible to come to knowing what is truly man's nature. If this is true, then it is also true that each person is, to a degree, a hero but a hero with many faces—not a romantic, national knight in shining armor, but a struggling, unknown, and committed human being.

We ask: "What kind of a world do we have? What is our present condition?" This is only another way of asking: "What lies ahead for our hero?" These are basic questions that will be asked during this study experience. Below, the are worded thematically as they tie into the large group lectures and small group seminars (discussions). For clarification, instead of indicating teacher names, their particular field of study is substituted. Primary themes generally use large group instruction, while seminar themes generally are small group discussions.

	Primary Theme
English	"Is Man Fated?"
	Seminar Themes
Math/Science	"Are We Stuck With Math?"
Philosophy/Religion ..	"Let's Search For Absolutes"
Fine Arts	"Is Art Universal?"
English	"Are We Encapsulated by Linguistics?"
Industrial Arts	"Do We Want What Technology Gives?"
	Primary Theme
Fine Arts	"What Is Man's Joy?"

Seminar Themes

Math/Science	"Where is the Beauty In Science?"
Philosophy/Religion . .	"Who is the Happiest Man?"
English	"Why Do We Laugh? Why Do We Cry?"
Fine Arts	"What Is Lovely and Un-Lovely In Art?"
Industrial Arts	"Selling Joy Through Gadgetry and Creature Comforts"

Primary Theme

Math/Science	"Is Man Alone?"

Seminar Themes

Math/Science	"Is Mathematics Above Man?"
Philosophy/Religion . .	"Is There A Creator?"
English	"What Separates Man From Man?"
Fine Arts	"How Individual Is Art?"
Industrial Arts	"What Is Destructive About Technology?"

Primary Theme

Industrial Arts	"Is Man Safe?"

Seminar Theme

Math/Science	"Two Cultures: The Fed and Unfed"
Fine Arts	"How Do the Practical Arts Contribute to A Better Life?"
Philosophy/Religion . .	"What Is the Nature of War, Violence, and Destruction?"
English	"The Place of Criticism and Censorship In Literature"
Industrial Arts	"How Does Man Place Reasonable Limits On Technology?"

Primary Theme

Philosophy/Religion . .	"Is Man Really Free?"

Seminar Theme

Math/Science	"Is Science Leading Us?"
Fine Arts	"Does Art Need A Framework to be Art?"
English	"How Does Literature Liberate Man?"
Philosophy/Religion . .	"What Is the Nature of Anarchy?"
Industrial Arts	"What Is the Construction Engineer's Primary Commitment?"

No doubt the reader is now wondering how the above outline is implemented within a flexibly scheduled structure. Humanities I is experimental, therefore, two operational plans could be explored. Perhaps the reader will decide which plan he prefers. For the first plan, Plan A, the following restrictions are placed on the course organization:

1. Enrollment is limited to 150 students in order to safeguard a maximum of 150 in the large group lecture and a maximum of 15 in the small group seminars. These numbers are based on a team complement of five. Thus, each teacher will be assigned at any given phase of time, two groups of 15 students.
2. No time-phase should exceed seven weeks if each teacher is to receive all 150 students in his small group sections by the end of the year.
3. Following the above procedure the maximum length of stay for a small group with any one teacher is seven weeks, which fits into a total of 35 teaching weeks in the school year.
4. It also follows that only five major themes may be assigned to the five teaching phases of seven weeks each.

The course scheduling as such is based on a time assignment of six modules per week. (A twenty-minute module is used in this school program.) In Plan A, a two-phase structure is used which includes two modules once a week for large group presentations and two modules twice a week for small group seminars. To illustrate, each team member's block time schedule would be integrated with the scheduled time of both students and the other members of the teaching team (see Figure 6.1).

All teacher-student time slots must be tied to the same day and modules for large groups and small groups. When this is accomplished, there is maximum interchange of all students with all teachers at any given moment of the course.

To coordinate the salient features of the course's interchange, each teacher is given four large group assignments for presentation of his subject-field approach to the theme under study. The remaining three weeks are also his to fill with special media presentations, outside lecturers, student presentations, and so on. The small groups are primarily in the hands of the students. The four teachers not having assignments for the large group presentation do attend, however, in order to coordinate their particular subject field to their small group meetings. At the end of seven

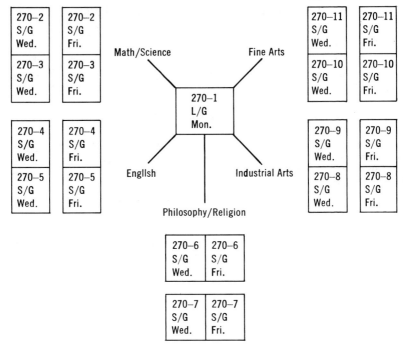

FIGURE 6.1
Humanities I (270) Large Group–Small Group Time Schedule in a Flexibly Scheduled Structure

weeks a new theme is launched, a different team member is assigned to the large group presentations, students for small groups are reassigned to a different teacher, and the entire process is repeated for another seven-week period.

OUTCOMES AND CONCLUSIONS

In brief, the outcomes of this plan are:

1. Five thematic teaching units are developed within an interdisciplinary approach.
2. Each student will study with a different teacher at seven-week intervals.
3. Large group presentations will allow for lectures, guest speakers, multimedia, student presentations, symposia, and field trips.
4. Alternate options to course content and method may always be introduced.

Most of the features of Plan A are also utilized in the second plan, Plan B. The major difference is that in Plan B the students assigned to each teacher at the beginning of the year *remain* with that teacher for the entire year. Thus, to implement the interchange of students, the teachers exchange classes with each other at designated times and usually for only one meeting a week. The advantage claimed for this plan is that it allows the students and teacher to remain with each other long enough to develop featured motivational and carrier goals of the course. At the same time, students do experience interaction with the other members of the teaching team and their particular field approach to the theme under study.

During the two years in which this course has been offered, much evaluation has been carried on with students. Their often-repeated suggestions have been: "Don't structure the course too much; let us explore." Only give us information when we need it." After using both Plans A and B, it is this writer's feeling that Plan A does more for the individual needs and interests of the student and allows them more of the sheer enjoyment of conversation with each other and with the teachers. The price paid for this free-dom is a tendency to lose continuity of study. Plan B definitely affords more stability and continuity but reduces interaction with other students and teachers. Both plans allow for a great deal of personalization and indivdualization of educational goals and values.

THE HISTORY OF WORLD RELIGIONS

This writer's major contribution to humanistic studies at this particular high school are courses in religion and in philosophy, both introduced into the curriculum in 1964. Why religion and philosophy? Religion studies in the high school curriculum justifies the term "break-through" to characterize its presence. It took 126 years, namely from 1837, when Horace Mann was Secretary of the Board of Education in the State of Massachusetts and the public schools feared religious sectarian teachings, to 1963, when Mr. Chief Justice Clark (*Abington School District vs. Schempp*, 374 U.S. 203) created a new legal climate, making public school studies in religion not only admissible but virtually required if one's education were to be considered complete. Philosophy has a valuable place in the American high school in this writer's opinion primarily because students want to study philosophy and also because fuller development of students' minds calls for philosophical inquiry at ages sixteen and seventeen. Both religion and philosophy are indispensable to the goals of the humanistic studies outlined in this chapter.

In contrast to the Humanities I described previously, History of World Religions is certainly more content- or subject-matter oriented. Moreover, if religion, as Humanities I, is to incorporate certain indispensables, the most important would be that it retain its historical methodology. Because it is a course in the study of religion, it cannot, in a public domain, brook any theological, philosophical, or valuational approach. At the same time, three lectures a week of historicizing over a period of one year is too demanding even for the most disciplined student. It is precisely at this point that flexible scheduling can offer some solutions.

Program Design: What Is Religion? The History of World Religions is a one-year course of study. As an elective open to juniors and seniors, it meets for two modules three times a week. Sessions are characterized by lectures, discussions, visiting lecturers, field trips, and the use of visual media. This is a one-teacher, self-contained course, but variability of lecture, seminar, reading, and research is obtained by scheduling for large group and small group instruction. Also, because flexible scheduling does create scattered periods of unscheduled time for the student's independent study, a course such as the History of World Religions can claim some of this independent study time and "teacher-schedule" it as part of the course requirement. This is accomplished with the utilization of instructional resource centers and open labs. It should be noted, however, that this use of student time is optional and relative to student needs and interests. For this particular course, the arrangements described below seems to be the most effective.

The course is structured to allow for:

1. Two modules of large group lecture each week dealing with the facts, data, and phenomena of various religions.
2. An "in-class" reading tutorial where assigned readings are discussed and clarified as to meanings. This is a small group session.

3. Another small group seminar of two modules duration each week devoted exclusively to discussion and student interaction.
4. An additional two modules of "out-of-class" reading in the Humanities Resource Center.

Performance objectives (or broad course objectives) are prescribed for the student as follows: objective research, tutorial reading, lecture notation, student data services, symposia, and functional examinations. The course syllabus contains seven learning units. Performance objectives will be integrated into each unit, which will terminate with a six-module performance paper based on research, reading, lecture notes, and student data services. All of the above activities will take place in the classroom, which will also serve as a resource center.

Within each unit, which will be a self-contained learning performance, the following experiences are afforded:

1. Lectures containing the facts, data, and phenomena of the learning unit will be presented on Mondays. Students will keep notes on lecture data. Comprehensive and carefully delineated reading lists will be given to the students in printed form every Monday.
2. In-class tutorials based on reading lists will take place every Wednesday. The instructor will clarify and supplement questions raised on the material. Students will keep a reading log containing facts and data. In-class tutorials will be extended two modules per week in the form of supplementary reading during the student's independent study time.
3. Student data services are integral to the research performance papers and symposia. For each learning unit, seven to ten primary segments of the substantive material will be assigned to students on the basis of three to five students per segment. In researching these segments in depth, these students will also be responsible for providing the other students with their data findings when requested. These findings are available to all students in an "open book" format during the writing of performance papers as well as during the conducting of symposia.
4. The symposia will be held once toward the conclusion of each seven-week learning unit. The intent here is to allow the students to perform as "experts" in an interaction of knowledge fields.
5. The functional examinations afford the student an opportunity to bring to bear all the aspects of learning he has experienced in the seven-week unit. This examination will be conducted in "open book" format as a research performance lasting for a period of six modules. These terminating experiences are called *Performance Examination As Research* (PEAR).

Unit I, then is seen as typical of the learning units of the course. The primary question under study is: "What is religion?" The main segments for lecturing, tutorial reading, outside reading, and student data services are:

1. The nature of religion defined.
2. The characteristics of normative religion.
3. Theories regarding the origin of religion.
4. Questions that concern students about religion.
5. Methods of studying religion.

Unit four is typical of the units that contain the descriptive data of the religions as such. The primary object of research and study is: "The Religions of India" and the main segments include:

1. Indus Valley civilization and religion.
2. The Aryan invasion and civilization.
3. Religion of the Vedas.
4. Religion of the Upanishads.
5. Contemporary Hinduism and recent developments.
6. The life and teachings of Gautama Buddha.
7. Theravada Buddhism.
8. Mahayana Buddhism.
9. Tantric Buddhism.

It is felt by this writer that the future of the teaching of religions in the American high school is more apt to be assured when flexible scheduling is employed which allows for a wider and more numerous selection of courses and when the course can be structured with a variety of time-slots which emphasize the objective and performatory aspects of being students of religion. As mentioned earlier, this particular religion course is clearly committed to a subject-matter content approach as compared to Humanities I, which has a more subjective and inter-related approach. In looking at a course in philosophy, below, it is again found preferable, as in Humanities I, to allow for more dialogue.

PHILOSOPHY

As with religion, philosophy should be introduced in the high school program to fill a void now generally present in the American high school curriculum. The reader should not be left with the impression that when flexible scheduling is adopted in any school program it automatically brings courses in religion and philosophy.

These courses can and should be present whether or not flexible scheduling or any other innovative technique is implemented into a school's program. However, this book has been dedicated to the conviction that more flexible school schedules can enhance the individualized character of instruction for many courses, and this is certainly true of philosophy.

Though not commonly taught in the American high school, in many other countries philosophy is generally a part of the student's program during his final year and often it is a required subject. This has not been the tradition in the American high school due, perhaps, to the lack of emphasis on classical and humanistic studies. Philosophy has a natural, if not necessary, function in a humanities program, and it also affords the student with an excellent opportunity to investigate and deal with questions about life that are of great concern to him. To carry such investigations into "dialogue" with dead and living philosophers and at the same time to discuss and write philosophy in a deeply personal style is to perfect and extend the cognitive powers of the mind and further to stimulate the natural tendency to know truth.

Our philosophy course is a one-year elective open to juniors and seniors. This is not a watered-down attempt to deal with philosophical studies. We read a "hard-core" of philosophers. But again, this is not simply the history of philosophy; neither do lectures make up the classtime fare. Student experience centers around performing the philosophical tasks: reading, discussing, debating, and writing philosophy. There are no examinations in the conventional sense. Students are required to write short and long papers adhering strictly to philosophical style. In the classroom, more often a lively discussion ensues among the students, with the teacher taking only a peripheral role.

When a course of this type is flexibly scheduled, features favoring student interest as well as the individualization of learning and involvement are enhanced considerably. Experimentation presenting viable options for the improvement of learning is always possible. For example, during the first two years of the course's unfolding, there was a strong student tendency to dominate class time in discussion. This is not to be scorned, but it did create an imbalance with the teacher's time, leaving insufficient lecture periods. The following year a request for a two-phase course structure with large group and small group instruction permitted one large group slot for lectures and two small groups meeting twice a week for discussion.

This structure was later broadened to three small groups and one combined lecture. Student numbers in the small groups were reduced to eight and ten, affording a marvelous opportunity to personalize and individualize the course for the student. A further demonstration of accommodation of student needs was evident when, in some instances, students could be cross-sectioned into two separate small groups. If one recurring value of flexible scheduling were emphasized, it would be that it accommodates an insatiable desire of the students for interaction and discussion of philosophical issues in small groups, while also allowing the instructor to present basic material to as many as 150 students in one lecture if desired.

CONCLUSION

This book contains a basic inquiry concerning the individualization of instructional methods and it makes some claims relevant to that inquiry. One aspect of this thematic material is flexible scheduling. The question is raised: What is the overall learning yield when a new methodology such as flexible scheduling is put into the course structure? There is a general assumption that all students, regardless of subject matter, are in a position to make optimum progress because of the flexibility of course scheduling. Therefore, flexible scheduling ideally aims at matching total student performance with total administrative and teacher output. Philosophically, this is not an innovation. Educators constantly aspire to achieve the "tailor-made" educational program for each student. The fact that prominent undergraduate colleges across the country continue to explore and establish individualized study programs for their students provides ample testimony to the appeal of such course structuring to educators. The American high school is now a part of this programming.

High school principals and curriculum coordinators do not need to be told that some subject areas require flexible scheduling more than others, but these administrators also realize that the restrictive patterns of the past have seriously limited attempts to improve courses of study. Flexible scheduling, by contrast, accomplishes one very important thing: It opens the way to greater adaptation to students' needs and interests. In the hands of competent administrators and teachers, it allows for maximum exploration of all subject matter in the interest of effective learning geared to a variety of learning styles and learning strategies. There is one other accomplishment the authors are looking for in flexible scheduling: Creating a climate for developing optimum individuation and humanization processes in the experiences of the student.

These accomplishment claims are not realized at the expense of either traditional values or contact hours with students in a subject field. On the contrary, the educational goals are more difficult than ever to achieve, requiring more understanding and skill from the teacher, more response from the student, and generally a longer school day.

In this chapter, Humanities I could be considered a prototype for the optimum in utilization of variable instruction open to the teacher and his students. Within a Humanities Department, philosophy and religion present options of a more specialized and concentrated nature to the Humanities I student who has, hopefully, become more aware of the deeper modes of his own humanity. But at any and all levels of the program the teacher addresses himself to his task as both a mentor to students and as a human to human beings. It is in this conceptualized form that an entire high school curriculum may be said to be humanities-oriented.

THE ART PROGRAM AND THE
INDIVIDUALIZATION OF INSTRUCTION

7

FLEXIBLE SCHEDULING AS A VEHICLE FOR CHANGE

The central question of this chapter asks: How can more individualized art programs be developed by employing a flexible schedule? One way to answer this question is to look first at the conditions the art teacher finds disturbing in a traditional schedule and then to see if the flexible schedule might improve on the existing problems. In the visual arts program, most schools have a number of problems in common.

1. The length of a traditionally scheduled class period usually is not long enough for real student involvement in the problems of art. By the time materials are distributed, class organization takes place, and clean-up is finished at the end of the period, little time remains for constructive learning activities.
2. Generally speaking, there is a smaller percentage of college preparatory students in art classes than in the school as a whole. Most art teachers suffer a marked "dumping grounds" depression.
3. The classes are often too large to be easily manageable in the kind of setting that demands more physical freedom. Thirty or forty students in an art class places very severe restrictions on the kind of work that can be accomplished. Often the activities of the class seem to be limited to mechanical, how-to-do-it projects for this very reason.
4. Because of the restrictions of time and class size, there is little opportunity for teachers to work closely with individual students and thereby accommodate individual differences.
5. In a traditional schedule there is little or no time between classes to make the necessary physical preparations for each class. Thus, a good part of teaching time is devoted to the management of materials,

the setting-up of demonstrations, and the reorganizing of the room as demanded by changes in class composition.
6. There is no provision for the fact that different tasks require different amounts of time to complete. At times, 45 or 50 minutes is too much instructional time and at other times it is not nearly enough.

Flexible scheduling is by no means a panacea for the solution of all art problems when attempting to individualize instruction. However, it has proven to be effective in some areas of the art program when developed by an imaginative staff. The easiest problem to solve, for which flexible scheduling was designed, is that of the length of class meeting times. The basic difference between the traditional schedule and the flexible one is the *variation in instructional time.* Before determining the length of class time, a number of questions must be considered which deal with the nature of the class, with the use of instructional materials, and with the student composition and their previous experience in art and in a flexible schedule. Generally speaking, the less experience students have had with variable time patterns and the less experience they have had with art, the less successfully they will be able to use long, unbroken time periods.

The next most important factor in determining the length of class time is the nature of each individual course. For example, how much time is necessary for the organization and clean-up of the materials used? If the course is a general art course, this will vary from project to project as students use different materials, but if it is a specialized course, there may be considerable differences from course to course. A class in ceramics will probably require much more time for clean-up than a class in drawing.

The method of instruction is also a major consideration in determining the length and structure of the meeting times for a given course. In a traditional schedule, when a teacher must spend from 10 to 20 minutes each class period stating simple facts and outlining simple procedures, from one-fifth to one-half of the class time is taken up with such trivia. Surely there is a more efficient way of organizing these kinds of learning tasks.

One solution is to set aside one short period each week for assignments and discussion of problems with clear instruction on the necessary room procedures. The remaining class time during the week can then be spent in actual work, with no general announcements made at all. If general procedures are established early in the year, studio or lab time can be all work time. The teacher has a great deal more time for individual contact with students, and the students have a great deal more uninterrupted time for work. The students learn to understand that in one kind of setting they are expected to come into the room, get materials, and get to work; in a different setting they are expected to be seated and wait for directions, discussion, or films.

Such a seemingly simple factor as determining the length of time for a given class activity may not be so easy. Reflecting on this makes one wonder how secondary schools arrived at the present solution of having all classes meet for uniform time patterns through the school week. The difficulties encountered in attempting to reach more academically oriented students is equally complex. Part of the problem lies in the attitudes of colleges and universities concerning the preparation demanded of entering freshmen, in misconceptions concerning these attitudes, and in the national attitude of indifference to the arts.

GREATER STUDENT PARTICIPATION

Flexible scheduling is no solution for national indifference, but experience in art is. The flexible schedule can provide the opportunity for college preparatory students to participate in an art program without endangering their college entrance requirements. This can only occur, of course, when the entire curriculum is carefully scrutinized and an accurate assessment of time needed for the accomplishment of the goals of *all* courses is made. When the assessment of time-needs is honestly made, it is possible for students to be involved in six, seven, eight, or even nine courses, and one of these courses can be art. In the first year of flexible scheduling at Claremont High School in California, the number of college preparatory students in art increased so greatly that a plan for requiring a fine arts course for graduation was dropped since it became apparent that virtually every student in the school would at some time be enrolled in an art, music, or drama course.

The opportunity for bringing a wider range of students into

the art program is enhanced when the program is organized with the greatest amount of scheduling freedom. Because the general procedures and problems for a class can be outlined in a short period once each week, and because students can accomplish so much in studio or lab periods when they are free from interruptions, it is possible to schedule lab activities in a very open manner and with overlapping of both time and students. Students enrolled in different classes can still work in a lab at the same time. Their schedules can overlap so that the greatest possible number of students may enroll in art courses with their time in art interspersed between other classes.

Labs can be structured, with specific students appearing at specific times, or "open," with students appearing during their unscheduled (independent study) time. This utilization of a flexible schedule involves a number of difficult decisions concerning planning, preparation, and organization of course content. It also carries with it a number of risks, both real and imagined, depending on the nature of the community, the students, and the teachers. However, it also allows the possibility of involving many more students in art. Most art teachers agree that some experience in art is important for all students through high school, but with the present competition of academic and technologically aimed courses this is a virtual impossibility in the traditional school program. It seems reasonable to assume that art will have the greatest impact on the whole society if those who will be society's leaders have had some art experience. At present, it is these potential leaders, the college preparatory students, who, with their crowded academic schedules, are being eliminated almost entirely from art programs. The more flexibility that can be achieved in the scheduling of art classes, the greater the possibility of exposing these students to art concepts.

CLASS SIZE AND TIME RELATED TO INSTRUCTIONAL TASK

Class size is one of those pervasive problems that plagues all teachers, whether art or academic. If the period each week devoted to explanations and assignments is for large group instruction, then extra time has been afforded the schedule by combining smaller instructional groups together for general instructions. This additional time can be used to make other class groups smaller. This may appear to make the course of study more rigid than desired, but if the material presented in the large group is broad enough and if the method of presentation is varied, it can be an effective means of allowing more flexibility in the smaller classes.

Related to the size of the class is the question of providing different amounts of time for the completion of different tasks. On one level this can be thought of only in terms of the content of the course. On another level, however, it should be thought of in terms of what each individual student is doing in the course. On what problem is he working? What are his aims? What did he enter the class to learn? Here the concept of individualization of instruction begins to emerge. If we are to take into account the varieties of individuals, then we must begin by recognizing that different individuals require different amounts of time to perform the same task. All students do not want or need to do the same tasks. Furthermore, some students *need* to be in class longer than others, and some students *want* to be in class longer than others. If such allowances for individual differences can be made, the issue of class size diminishes in importance. In an open lab organization, there are some times when many students are in the studio working and other times when only a few are there.

Not only can variability of time structures help to solve the problem of class size, but it also provides an opportunity for individual student-teacher conferences which are virtually impossible in the conventional, overcrowded art classes. By scheduling large groups for general presentations and middle groups for work activities, it is possible to establish very small groups of students for more individualized activities. In these labs as few as five or six students may be found.

The use of teacher time in flexible scheduling opens many new possibilities. The prospect of having long unbroken blocks of unscheduled time is an inviting feature, particularly if the school administration recognizes that to professionalize education teachers need time to pursue professional activities beyond the correcting of papers or the preparation of clay for tomorrow's class. In some cases this may mean doing research or writing. In the case of the art teacher it may mean producing works of art during school hours in his own studio or in school facilities. If an art teacher is truly to involve students in art, he must be involved in art and serve as a model to the students.

In brief, flexible scheduling can solve some of the dilemmas which are characteristic complaints of many art programs. The schedule, however, is only one of several factors affecting the whole process of education. Changes in the structure of the schedule or in the curriculum are not guarantees that fundamental problems will be solved. Usually, when these changes are undertaken, other problems—new problems—arise. Least cynics and critics leap too quickly to the conclusion that flexible scheduling is no solution at all, it must be pointed out that the real issue is not whether flexible scheduling is good or bad. Rather, have the questions concerning what is education or what is learning ever been faced in the conventional secondary school? It seems evident that the traditional approach to scheduling and to teaching are solutions to unreal problems; we may be "educating" people for reasons that do not exist outside of the structure of the school. Thus, the dramatic changes that flexible scheduling, or any other innovative technique for individualizing instruction, brings to the school serve not to create new problems but simply to uncover facts that have always existed but that have been buried beneath the monumental and nearly impenetrable fortress of secondary education as it has existed for so long in this country.

THE PROBLEM: WHAT IS LEARNING?

During the late 1950s and the 1960s, we were concerned with two major issues in the schools: (1) What shall we teach? (2) How shall we teach it? A vigorous argument raged immediately after the first space orbit and continues to rise occasionally from the tangle of concern about programmed instruction, sensitivity groups, and the whole milieu of contemporary concerns in education. The argument is centered around the importance of subject matter versus the importance of method of teaching. The simplistics maintain that how the teacher teaches matters little so long as he knows the subject matter well; or, conversely, that if a teacher teaches well, he can teach anything. It is, in fact, probably impossible to try to separate the two; stated simply as questions of teaching, however, it is as sensible to separate subject content from teaching method as it is to separate the whole area of teaching from that of learning. This is what the content–method argument does.

The concentration of effort and interest over the years on subject matter and teaching is not surprising. Man has been passing on information and knowledge to his children since his very beginning. Earlier, this passing on of knowledge centered around the very practical goal of staying alive; but as man became more sophisticated and his living patterns became more complex, the living patterns themselves became an important part of the "curriculum." The rites and rituals, myths and magic of the group had to be learned by every member so he could take his place in the group. Still, most of the things to be learned were necessary for survival, and most of the methods of learning were by imitation. Up to a point, every youngster was a good student because his very life depended on it.

The development of writing as a means of storing and transferring information, together with consistent victories in the survival battle, formalized—perhaps ossified is a more apt term—the whole process of education. No longer did the youngster learn by imitating his elders in order to survive in a difficult world. This, of course, took hundreds or thousands of years and, stated this way, brings us too quickly to the challenge of secondary education today. But, it does serve to point out three essential ideas. First, when the young Neolithic boy watched and then imitated an older male throwing a spear, he knew that success on the hunt was imperative. He had a reason for doing it. Second, when he threw the spear at a deer or a boar, he knew immediately whether or not he had done it well. And finally, if he had done it well, the prize was at hand. All of the elements necessary for learning were present: *strong personal motivation, immediate feedback* about the results of his effort, and *strong positive reinforcement* when he was successful.

As man becomes further removed from the immediate contingencies of survival, and as education becomes more abstracted from the "real world," the motivation to learn changes. The contiguity between action and result is weakened and reinforcement for correct responses becomes less frequent. It is not surprising that it took so long for man, the hunter, to learn that he could get food by putting seeds in the ground, letting them grow, and thus, make a new creature of himself—man, the farmer. The hunter was reinforced immediately for success. The farmer had to wait weeks or months for feedback and reinforcement. In a sense, our educational system is putting students in the same position as man, the hunter, learning to become man, the farmer. The "seed," in the form of textbook, lecture, or assignment, is planted. The reward for proper care and nurture is postponed until after a test is taken, an assignment is corrected, comparisons with others made, and, finally, a grade is given. A long-term gathering of grades (over a period of twelve years in public schools today) results in the final harvest—graduation from high school and, in some cases, entering college for more of the same.

A growing problem of compulsory schooling in the world Marshall McLuhan has called "The Global Village" is that a significant number of youngsters have decided they do not want to be part of the tribe.[1] Not only are they unable to tell if they are throwing the spear straight, they do not wish to be hunters. Not only does no one tell them whether the seed has been watered, they do not like the taste of the fruit it produces. This has really been true of education ever since it became centered around the acquisition of abstract information as contrasted with pragmatic survival problems. But, prior to compulsory education, a young person could take it or leave it as he chose. Probably a large number of those students who help make art classes "dumping grounds" in many schools would leave it if they had any choice in the matter. This is not to say that these students should not be in the art class or in school but rather to emphasize the fact that school, as it is presently structured, affords little motivation or reinforcement for many students.

ART ACTIVITY AS A PARADIGM FOR LEARNING

Significantly, many students who do poorly in "academic" subjects do well in art. Studies in the nature of intelligence in recent years have indicated that this may be the result of the fact that most academic courses are based on verbal and symbolic manipulation abilities which represent only a portion of the

---

[1] Marshall McLuhan, Quention Fiore, and Jerome Agel, *War and Peace in the Global Village* (New York: Bantam Books, 1968).

spectrum of our intelligence. But, there may be another important reason for the success of the poor academic student in the art class which lies in the nature of studio activity in art. The class most commonly used to place students of poor academic ability is the crafts class. Together with the school shop and the homemaking class, the crafts class is the place where the youngster with reading, writing, and arithmetic difficulties may be able to do something.

What do these classes have in common? A very important characteristic which is much more complex than simply "working with their hands." In all of these classes students normally develop projects which stand as tangible results of their efforts. Not only are they tangible; frequently they are useful as well. They serve a purpose or fill a need. The student can look at the result and say, "There! I made that! I can eat it! (Or sit on it, or wear it, or drink out of it.) There was really a reason for doing it." Of course, if "it" was something selected by the teacher for him to do, the likelihood of his saying this with great enthusiasm may be diminished, but it is still there. He is once again man, the hunter, with a real purpose for his actions.

Additionally, most projects in such classes have opportunities for feedback built into them. This piece fits that, or it does not. Those two fit the next, and so on. And, when all is done, the student may wait expectantly for a grade, but he can usually tell without any help whether or not he was really successful. So, planned or not, the important characteristics of a good learning situation are present: motivation, contiguity of reward to action, and feedback. Perhaps most important is the fact that the concepts used in the performance of crafts activities can be formed by the student as he works and observes the results of his efforts. This is the greatest difference between traditional approaches to academic subject matter and "hand work." An academic procedure has the teacher stating concepts more or less directly to the student and then telling him to use the concept to solve problems in an abstract, usually verbal, manner. In a crafts class the instructor may also state the concept, but, by working directly on a project, the student, consciously or not, reformulates the concept in his own terms as he seeks a concrete solution in the form of a successful project.

SYSTEMS MODEL APPLIED TO THE LEARNING PROCESS

The new urgency in education to be more effective has changed conditions so that research in learning is now beginning to find its way to school. One development which has found much use in computer technology and has been adapted for analyzing learning, education, curriculum, and, in fact, almost every operation or organization with which we work is the systems model (systems approach or systems analysis). At the University of Utah Asahel Woodruff has worked for several years on developing practical uses of a systems approach in the curriculum structure in schools.[2] His work with the National Art Education Association in 1968 and 1969 brought the use of this approach to the heartland of art education, which formerly had been almost totally based on developmental psychology.

The systems approach is essentially a tool for looking with greater clarity at what actually happens in any learning experience. It is ironic that John Dewey, who has come to stand for extreme permissiveness and chaos in the minds of his critics, in 1896 had proposed the concept of the reflex-arc in learning, which is essentially what is called a "feedback loop" in a system. The learning theory, which is part of what Hilgard calls functional psychology and which Dewey was instrumental in establishing, is readily adaptable to the systems model; and, when it has been adapted the approach to curriculum becomes clearer.[3]

Simply, an industrial or technological system is one in which raw material, energy, or data (input) is fed into a treatment process, and a product, work, or information (output) results. The treatment process consists of an application and of a comparison of the results of that treatment with what was intended. It would not do to put in pistons, gears, a drive shaft, and fenders for an automobile process and end up with an output of rocking chairs or teacups. Nor would the prospective consumer be satisfied if,

---

[2] Asahel D. Woodruff, *First Steps in Building a New School Program* (Salt Lake City, Utah: Bureau of Educational Research, University of Utah, 1967).

[3] Ernest R. Hilgard and Gordon H. Bower, *Theories of Learning* (New York: Appleton-Century-Crofts, 1966).

with all the parts together, the product only looked like an automobile but acted like a horse. So, the system requires a table of specifications to determine the adequacy of the product. If a comparison between actual product and specifications for the product reveals that something is wrong, the information is fed back into the system and alterations in the treatment are made until the product meets specifications. A simple system is illustrated in Figure 7.1.

When the system is altered as in Figure 7.2 and 7.3, it becomes a quality control system. This means simply that the system has a built-in feedback loop so that the product or output is checked against the specifications and changes can be made in the system if necessary. By changing the diagram slightly, as in Figure 7.4, the model is applied to a learning cycle. Note that in the case of learning an antecedent condition—call it "need, or want, or stimulus"—is present, and that a conclusion in the form of satisfaction with the response or the attainment of a goal is reached or can be reached. This really does not differ from an industrial system in which a product is desired and in which the

FIGURE 7.1
A Simple System

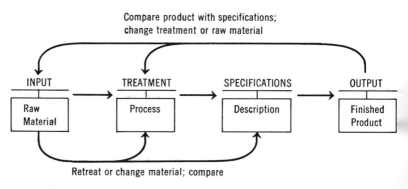

FIGURE 7.2
A Quality Control System

attainment of the product results in stabilization of the process or treatment, at least for the production of that particular product.

If we return to our stone age hunter, we can see the quality control system at work. The hunter needs food to stay alive. He perceives that the plunging of a sharp weapon into the body of a deer will satisfy the need. He makes several attempts, each time adjusting his aim so as to come closer to his goal. When his spear brings the deer down, his goal has, at least for now, been attained.

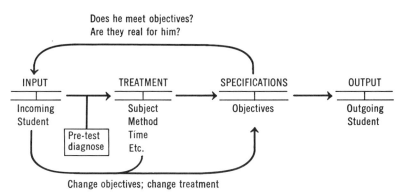

FIGURE 7.3
A Quality Control System Applied to an Educational Environment

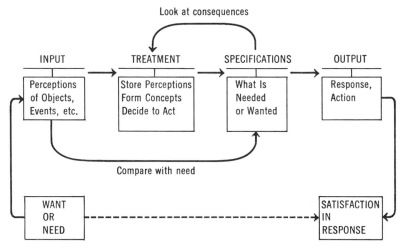

FIGURE 7.4
The Learning Cycle

Each time he is faced with the need to bring down a deer to satisfy his hunger, he repeats the process. If he is at all perceptive, or has a good teacher, and is endowed with the necessary physical apparatus for good spear-throwing, each time he repeats the cycle it will be a bit easier. The circumstances of the hunt will vary, but with perception he will be able to form the concepts necessary to adapt his actions to the change. If his perceptions are faulty, hopefully his teacher can guide him to their formation. If not, they will both perish of hunger.

So it is with the learning process. The function of the school is to provide the setting for learning to take place, and the function of the teacher is to guide the formation of concepts once the materials for perception have been provided. A major difficulty in school over the years is that the perceptions have been made by someone other than the student, and the concepts, in an abstract written or spoken form, have simply been handed to the student for memorization. This pattern is being broken through a variety of devices, but until teachers really understand the basis for change the devices are likely to remain merely gimmicks, many of them expensive ones at that. The application of the systems model to the learning process helps clarify where change should occur.

TABLE OF SPECIFICATIONS—OBJECTIVES AND DESIRED BEHAVIOR

As indicated in the diagram of the quality control system (Figure 7.2, p. 118), a basic component is the table of specifications. If there is no indication of what the product is to be, there is no way to tell that it has been produced. In the public schools, the product is a high school graduate. But just what kind of high school graduate? An educated graduate? Are they all the same? Should they all be the same? Should they differ? How will we know, how do we know when a young person is "educated"? These are all questions that schools should be able to answer in order to determine the effectiveness of the educational system. Some of these issues are now centers of controversy as young people take larger roles in the life-process of the nation.

One thing most schools specify is that a graduate is a good citizen. However, it is not enough to say that an objective of public schooling is the production of good citizens. We must know what a good citizen is and how one acts in order to judge whether our process is geared to their production. If it turns out that we are not producing good citizens, we must turn to an analysis of the process itself to discover the weakness. It may be that the materials for perception (content, subject, method, etc.) are faulty. Perhaps we are placing raw materials (students) with too great a difference in qualities into the same system and the same process. And perhaps our means of comparing results with the specifications is not measuring what we intend. If the product is intended to have particular kinds of feelings, we must devise a way to get those feelings into some observable form. By observing the behavior of the student, we must be able to tell whether or not he has those concepts in his repertoire which will cause him to act like a good citizen. If we accept the premise that learning involves change from one state to another, we may realize that many students come to us already behaving like good citizens and have no need for the production treatment through which we put them. Others may require an entirely different kind of treatment.

Until the specifications for the expected behavior are clearly stated, there is no way to tell whether they have been met, nor is there any way of telling whether the treatment process is really necessary. In this regard the National Art Education Association, in its publication "The Essentials of A Quality School Art Program," has adopted the following statement:

> Art in the school is both a body of knowledge and a series of activities which the teacher organizes to provide experiences related to specific goals. The sequence and depth of these experiences are determined by the nature of the art discipline, the objectives desired, and by the interests, abilities and need of children at different levels of growth. As a result of the art program, each pupil should demonstrate, to the extent that he can, his capacity to: (1) have intense involvement in and response to personal visual experiences; (2) perceive and understand visual relationships in the environment; (3) think, feel and act creatively with visual art materials; (4) increase manipulative and organizational skills in art performance appropriate to his abilities; (5) acquire a knowledge of man's visual art heritage; (6) use art knowledge and skills in his personal and community life; (7) make intelligent visual judgments suited to his experience and maturity; and (8) understand the nature of art and the creative process.[4]

---

[4] "The Essentials of A Quality School Art Program," A Position Statement by the National Art Education Association, Washington, D.C., 1968.

This is really an excellent statement of the aims of art education in the broadest sense. The qualification, "each pupil should demonstrate, *to the extent that he can* . . ." opens wide the door to practicality. The difficulty with most instructional programs is that the objectives are too often stated in vague terms, for example, "*understand* the nature of art and the creative process." When we modify this by stating that the student will "demonstrate, to the extent that he can, his *capacity* to understand the nature of art . . ." at least a start has been made in providing for differences in raw material input (individual differences). More important, we have called for demonstration of a capacity. We can say that if the student does not demonstrate this particular capacity either he or the program has failed.

A major problem remains, however. Just how does he go about demonstrating that he "understands"? Of what does understanding consist? How does a person act when he understands the nature of art? This is complicated by the fact that artists themselves disagree about the nature of art, at least when they try to state it verbally.

In order to use this objective in the design of a school program, it will be necessary to come to some conclusions about the nature of art and then to specify what constitutes understanding. People like Robert Mager have pointed out that terms such as "to understand," "to appreciate," "to express," are really much too vague to allow for any kind of measurement to take place.[5] The whole area of writing educational objectives and the attacks behaviorists make on those that have been written may seem at first like nit-picking with little purpose.[6] However, we can only reiterate that, if the educational institution sets out to accomplish a task, the task must be specified and some means of checking on its completion must exist. In art particularly we have been guilty of stating our objectives in terms that allow no known method of checking. It is not surprising that art so often finds itself regarded as a frill.

---

[5] Robert Mager, *Preparing Instructional Objectives* (San Francisco: Fearon Publishers, 1962).

[6] See Chapter 3 for a discussion and definition of behavioral or instructional objectives and their application in developing individualized instructional materials.

We set impossible goals and have no way of proving that they have been attained.

There is a need to state our educational or instructional objectives in behavioral terms so that evaluation may take place. The evaluation necessary is not only for the purpose of measuring student progress but also for measuring the effectiveness of the whole instructional process. However, even if the objectives are clearly and behaviorally stated and evaluation takes place with precision, little will be accomplished if the activities, concepts, and goals are confined to the classroom. This is perhaps the most frightening problem we face today. We have only to look at the countless examples of urban decay, polluted rivers and streams, and collections of refuse in once-lovely landscapes—not to mention gaudy dime-store knick-knacks, ticky-tacky housing tracts, and crowded, ugly, confusing commercial areas—to realize that man's quest for beauty has had little effect outside the art room.

Despite efforts to teach design fundamentals, form-follows-function principles, and man's need for personal expression, it would seem that the desire for beauty in our environment has remained pretty much inside the art room. In the same way, it would appear that the need for healthy bodies has stayed in the gym, that the necessity of being an active participant in the democratic process stops at the door of the government class, and that the desire to read and understand fine literature ended with the last book report or critical analysis in the English class. Figures on the physical condition of draftees, on voter registration and turnout, on library use and book sales would seem to indicate that carry-over of our objectives is somehow lacking in the world outside the school. There is no one simple reason for this condition. More likely, it is a complex of problems created in part by a state of confusion as a result of the information explosion and audiovisual technology.

If we go back to the discussion of the learning system and the analogy of the stone age hunter, we will find one important clue to help solve the problem. It lies in the thing which starts the whole cycle of behavior and learning into motion. We can call it need or drive or stimulus or motivation or any term we choose. It may be any or all of these things. Whatever it is, its function is to make the learner behave. The hunter is driven by hunger or stimulated by food or need to survive, and so he begins the cycle of satisfying that goal. This is the clue which we must use to help today's students in reaching their goals.

RELEVANCY AND THE ART CURRICULUM

What does a sixteen-year-old art student need or want? Knowledge of the terminology of the Bauhaus design principles? Not very likely. Ability to make a linear, value, or chromatic analysis of a fifteenth-century fresco? Extremely doubtful. While he may find that such knowledge and ability will make him more visually perceptive, he must first feel a need to be more perceptive. The need must come from him, not from a teacher or a textbook. The teacher can talk, preach, assert, exhort, assign, or stand on a soapbox and scream from now until doomsday, "You need to know how to analyze the values in 'Guernica.'" However, until this desire comes from the student his actions will only be based on the need to comply with the teacher's request.

There has been a tendency for the educational system to become a system unto itself, with little meaning outside the schoolroom, just as there has been a tendency to teach art for art's sake with no real importance in the lives of individuals or societies. One solution is to use the life needs of individuals as the basis for instructional units. Of course, a kind of life-centered approach has been tried and is still being used in many schools. The difficulty with most existing programs is that they are organized not around needs as felt by students but on social needs as discerned through governmental and economic organizations. The familiar "visit to the fire station" unit in first or second grade is an example. The unit is usually set up on the premise that the youngster needs to "appreciate" and "understand" how important the friendly fireman is. What the youngster really wants to know, especially once he visits the station, is how the water gets pumped, what makes the siren work, and so on.

So it is with art. If the student feels a need to paint a picture of a tree, that need can be utilized to guide him to make perceptions and form concepts about balance and composition. But when we begin with the study of composition as such, even in a high school art class we are probably doomed to a high percentage of failure unless the class is made up of students with a wealth of experience and perceptions which has made them feel the need to understand more about a highly abstract subject area.

Much has been written recently about the need for relevance in schools. The term has been used so often that it is almost a cliché. Before discounting it as a whim of unruly university students or minority groups on the rise, it would be well to look at relevance in terms of the learning cycle. Of course, school is not relevant if the things it teaches have no bearing on life experience. If all our intellectual abstractions have any basis in reality, then it should be possible to use reality—the real world—to guide learning of the concepts derived from that reality. If concepts of balance and form are vital aspects of art, it should be possible to build concepts of them while working with and perceiving art objects. If, however, the art object in question has little value for the student, it is unlikely that he will form any concepts of balance while working with the object. Thus, if no concepts are formed, there will be no carry-over into his life experience. With no carry-over he will hardly feel that the experience has been relevant.

How can we help students develop concepts that will have staying power and value outside of school? One way is to develop instructional units around the things they feel a need to do. Joe wants to paint a picture for his Aunt Minnie's sitting room. Fine. Let's decide what sort of picture to paint. Will it be a landscape, a still life? Will it be a red, purple, or green painting? Will it be square, rectangular, or round? Will it be an oil painting, a water color, an acrylic? What are the qualities the student would like the painting to have? When these questions have been answered, it is possible, by working within this framework, to determine other qualities that the teacher feels the painting should have and to arrive at an agreement between student and teacher as to the acceptable conclusion of the project. In determining the characteristics necessary, it is possible to sneak in at least some of the things that will help build the concepts we are after.

The astonishing challenges of our technology and the mushrooming "information explosion" make the art program of the past an unlikely prospect for the future. Not only does it seem likely that teachers will continue to be responsible for more students, but, if they continue teaching in the present mode, teachers will have to be veritable store houses of information concerning all manner of materials, techniques, and approaches.

THE INSTRUCTIONAL PROCESS AND HUMANISTIC ENDEAVOR

A dilemma which is part of the whole question of behavior-izing instruction, of presenting material in large groups, of pre-test-ing and post-testing, is that all this seems to negate the human individual. Is he an object to be organized in large numbers, to be analyzed like rock samples, to be treated like a chemical compound and changed into something different, something somehow more desirable? The question of just what is desirable is difficult and frightening. The possibility of a student changing into some other kind of person than he was when he entered a program or a school is unsettling. What type of person will he be? Is it not inhuman to determine so exactly what people should be? Why would we want to make everyone behave in the same manner?

These questions reveal a basic attitude about education. In spite of our laudable words and our exemplary philosophies of past and present, we apparently do not really expect to reach the goals we have set. And since the goals are, in reality, out of reach, it is safe to have them as goals. In other words, because we do not actually expect learning to occur, the goals are not something about which we must worry. When, however, it is suggested that by analyzing and re-stating the goals we may be able to develop teach-ing stategies to allow us to reach them, we become uneasy. We are uneasy about who sets the goals and how they are stated. We are uneasy about the impersonality of the procedures used to reach them. We are uneasy about having students treated as though they are commodities to be processed. Yet, for a long time in the United States we have said that all youngsters must undergo the "process of education" until a given age. To fall back at this point on some kind of argument about the stating of objectives and the attainment of them concerning the individuality of students is to be blind to the present, if not downright dishonest.

The concern about treating humans like numbers in the organ-ization of large group instruction is to ignore a fact of modern life. Our problem is not how to ignore the fact but how to deal with it. How do we reconcile the necessity of numbers with a human intimacy? One visualizes a sea of students seated anonymously in an auditorium, self-checking answer sheets in hand, dutifully following an equally anonymous instructor or team of teachers through a lecture-demonstration. Or bland-faced youngsters replete with headsets, talking typewriters, push-button computors, all lined up beneath a shroud of blue florescence and white sound with no teacher at all. Is this the direction we are taking?

Probably not, because that is only part of the picture. Teachers generally do not question the importance played by attention to individuals. Most would agree that they seldom "reach" more than a small percentage of the students they have. This is especially true in high school where, even on traditional time patterns, a teacher's load is rarely less than 100 students. Yet, the most exciting secondary art programs are those with the most exciting teachers—the warm, radiant people who inspire a constant flow of excellent work from nearly all of their students. If this is the case, why not model our programs in all schools from the obviously successful ones; why recommend moving toward the impersonal, the dehumanized?

Let it first be noted that dehumanization is not the recommendation here. To look at a student or to analyze the learning process in terms of quality control cycles, behavioral objectives, or large group instruction does not rob that student of his humanness any more than the art historian's discussion of the relation of the religiosity of fifteenth-century Florence or the painter's analysis of the use of foreshortening robbed Michelangelo of his greatness. They add dimension and another understanding to what already exists. To relegate the role of the teacher to that of a technician making adjustments in a mechanical process similar to the manufacturing of puppets is to miss the point.

What we are saying is that both are necessary. We need both the empathetic, exciting attitude that the good teacher can provide, and the systematic, scientific approach to curriculum that is possible through the behaviorizing of objectives. Without the empathy, the sincerity, without what Carl Rogers terms "a helping relationship," very little learning takes place.[7] The student's major project will remain simply to get along in that par-

---

[7] Carl Rogers, *On Becoming A Person* (New York: Houghton Mifflin Co., 1961).

ticular room with that particular teacher. What happens when he leaves the room? Much the same thing that happens to the rats and pigeons of the behavioral psychology experiment with extinction. If no amount of the learned behavior, be it bar-pushing or color-mixing, brings about reinforcement, whether in the form of a food pellet or a grade, the behavior will not be practiced. Not until the behavior itself is reinforcing to the student will that behavior become part of his repertoire.

BEHAVIORAL OBJECTIVES

It is suggested that two primary ways of reinforcing desired behavior are available to teachers now. The first way of internalizing the student's will to learn is to analyze the curriculum in terms of behavioral objectives. This necessitates a curriculum based on individual student-selected projects through which these objectives may be reached. The second method is to provide a supporting learning environment to include teachers, materials, and tools, as well as other students, that will encourage each student to become responsible and self-reliant for learning. None of the techniques of large group instruction, programmed learning, small group discussion, and independent study are important except as they help attain these goals. Large group instruction and programmed instructional techniques are essentially devices which can free the teacher for the kind of relationship needed for the supportive learning environment. When the teacher's energy is required for the kind of teaching that can be more effectively accomplished through self-teaching techniques, then little energy or time remains to be devoted to the necessary empathetic, individualized relationships with students.

Large group instruction buys time; self-instructional methods buy energy. These are the two commodities most elusive to teachers. There never seems to be sufficient time to reach all the students and to work individually with them.

When an art experience is teacher-centered, as most are, with problems handed out like so many arithmetic sums to be discovered, is it really very different from having the teacher work on the product to insure its safe completion? But this situation will continue until teachers have the resources to allow students to select and develop their own problems. The resources include ways to deal with the myriad of problems or projects students will select if allowed to work individually.

The only way to build a program around the individual needs of students in art or in anything is to know in behavioral terms what is ultimately necessary for the student to be able to do in order to achieve his goal. With relevant, personally selected projects specified in behavioral terms, it will be possible to individualize the entire curriculum. It will be possible to provide self-teaching techniques, even programmed teaching, to handle those areas which now take such a large part of the art teacher's time. Color theory, basic design, even visual perception can be taught with these devices, not to mention the more purely mechanical but none the less time-consuming elements of an art program.

When all of these things are taught so impersonally, it is feared that students will emerge more conformist than ever from the formal educational experience. This is not necessary if the teacher finds the new role an exciting one. The poetry, the magic, the majesty of art can then be his concerns. Only when the burden of simple dissemination of information is lifted can the art teacher help his students confront the heart of the mystery—the who am I question to which visual art is a partial answer. The private discussion, the small group encounters, the personal searches will be the business of the teacher. The questions of what is the function of art in this youngster's life and in the life of man can become the central ones. In the vernacular of today's youngster, the art teacher will be working with his students "where it's at." Difficult as it is to prophesy, we can speculate that the age of how-to-do-it is past and the teacher with his students is face-to-face with an age of why-to-do-it.

> The hypothesis upon which he (the teacher) would build is that students who are in real contact with life problems wish to learn, want to grow, seek to find out, hope to master, desire to create. He would see his function as that of developing such a personal relationship with his student, and such a climate in his classroom, that these natural tendencies could come to their fruition.[8]

---

[8] *Ibid.*

THE ART CURRICULUM:
A SYSTEMS APPROACH

8

INTRODUCTION: PROGRAM OBJECTIVES AND SPECIFICATIONS

In this chapter we will analyze the art curriculum with the aid of a simplified systems approach. The objectives set forth by the National Art Education Association will provide the general specifications for this analysis. These objectives have been established so that they apply to all youngsters, since the association "takes the position that . . . (2) *all* children and youth must be offered a carefully planned program in art from kindergarten through high school."[1]

In those high schools where art is offered in the curriculum, the percentage of the student body enrolled is generally not more than ten to twelve percent. Of those students enrolled in art, or who have taken art at some time in high school, the number who have attained the NAEA objectives, even with the extenuating phrase "demonstrate, to the extent that he can, his capacity to . . . ," must be very few. Certainly, there is little demonstration that former public school art students "use art knowledges and skills . . . in community life," if the state of our urban centers and littered landscapes is any evidence. Thus, the entire list of objectives can be balanced in this way against the facts of contemporary life, and most artists and art teachers would agree that

---

[1] "The Essentials of A Quality School Art Program," A Position Statement by the National Art Education Association, Washington, D.C., 1968.

the evidence is strong that few adults have attained any of these objectives, even in terms of their own capacities.

Why are these objectives not being attained?

1. The possibility of participating in an art program, even when one is offered, is not available to enough high school students.
2. Most of the programs that are available fail to take into account: (a) the variabilities of students, and (b) the nature of the learning cycle itself and its relation to the different possibilities of treatment that could be used with these students.

Clearly, flexible scheduling brings more students into the art program. The more openly the program is scheduled, the more students are able to participate. And, the more the student is offered a choice about what he takes, the more likely he is to enter the program voluntarily, thus adding more students and, to an extent, solving the first problem of the learning cycle—that of personal desire. As flexible scheduling brings more students, how will we deal with them to attain our objectives? Certainly not as we have in the past, for if we do we are ignoring point two—the nature of the students and the nature of learning.

Art is a complex subject. It involves wrestling with difficult philosophical concepts as well as with concrete materials. It is bound up with making acute visual perceptions, organizing ideas and media, making judgments intuitively and abstractly, and a thousand other skills and capacities hardly even identified despite the thousands of artifacts and the millions of words about art that man has created over the centuries. Although men die feeling they have only begun to understand this complex subject, most high school art programs attempt to teach all things to all students, with the result that most students come away with little understanding of any of it and feeling that they know most of it. In addition, most art teachers are expected to teach all facets of the subject.

Consider the usual high school art program. Art I, Art II, Art III, and Art IV are often the course titles. The format usually follows one of two plans. In one, *all* art courses are general art courses. The student works each year on drawing, painting, sculpture (or modeling), lettering, and poster-making, with a "crafts project" or two thrown in for good measure. Each year the problems are, in theory at least, slightly more difficult than the year before. In the second plan, these problems are divided by media. Art I is usually an introductory general course, Art II may be design and commercial art, Art III drawing and painting, and Art IV sculpture and crafts.

In the programs where all the art courses are general courses, everyone, student and teacher alike, suffers because it is impossible to gain any real understanding of fundamental art concepts when one is constantly flitting from one material to the next. In the second type of program some opportunity does exist for students to become involved in media or approaches long enough to begin to understand how to use them, but there is another difficulty. If painting is not offered until Art III, the student who would like to paint, but who dislikes lettering, may never take Art III because he may not want to take Art II. Another student who wants to paint may not be able to because other requirements allow him to take only one or two years of art. He does not have the time in his schedule to take Art III.

Unfortunately, art programs have been conditioning students to believe that art is a series of off-hand dabbles in a variety of media, while the best opportunities for teaching—those in which the student is personally motivated by interest—slip away as the aspiring painter is required first to make travel posters and the aspiring sculptor to illustrate an adventure story with pen and ink sketches.

In developing a new approach to art curriculum, it will probably become necessary to design a generalized, prerequisite art course for initial exposure by the novice, the incoming student. The purpose of this course would be to fill in the gaps in students' backgrounds concerning the media available to them. If a good sequence in art existed in the elementary and junior high school, this course might be eliminated so that students could select drawing, painting, or jewelry-making just as they select French or Spanish or German without first taking Language I as a prerequisite. However, one of the problems encountered when a school embarks into new curriculum development is that rarely are all the students entering the school prepared to meet the demands of the new approach. Thus, one purpose of an introductory course is to bridge the gap between previous experiences and new expectations. In addition, a prerequisite course could serve to explain to many students the basic art concepts about which they have faulty or hazy understandings.

Of course, one of the factors necessary for the success of any system is diagnosis—deciding what the students need and what they already know. This need for diagnosis extends beyond determining who shall enter, or not enter, a prerequisite course. It is required at every step throughout the whole secondary art curriculum. It should be used to determine who enters any of the courses, and it should be used to determine what each student does while he is in the course. If a student is simply repeating problems and procedures with which he is already familiar and at which he does well, the experience has very little educational value for him. A close look at the students in high school art programs reveals several general groups with whom it is necessary to deal.

1. Students with little clear understanding of the foundations of art.
2. Students with little experience in the "new curriculum" or with all that flexible scheduling implies.
3. Students with emotional and intellectual difficulties.
4. Students with a great deal of background and understanding in art.
5. Students with highly specialized interests in specific areas of art.
6. Students with average or moderate interest, ability, and background in art. These are, by far, the largest number of students in the program.

THE ART CURRICULUM AS A SYSTEM—TREATMENT VARIABLES

The broad generalizations in the introduction will serve now to give direction in determining the "treatment process" phases of our "Art Curriculum System." Thus, in this section we will discuss the development of this curriculum and its administration. What are the best sequences and types of courses and, more particularly, the most adequate methods for attaining the stated objectives with a heterogeneous group of students. The number of variables possible within our treatment process is limitless; however, some of the directions that have been explored and found encouraging will be developed briefly. These treatment variables in the development of our "new art curriculum" will include the following: (1) the use of specialized, in-depth courses; (2) the variability of instructional time and student deployment; (3) the variability of course structures, for example, the open lab; (4) the variability of teacher time; and (5) the individualization of student assignments.

SPECIALIZED, IN-DEPTH COURSES

We hinted earlier at dissatisfaction with the usual approach to high school art courses as being too broad generally for the existing body of knowledge. One of the keys to a successful learning enterprise, is that the task to be undertaken, the goals to be attained, and the things to be learned must seem possible to the would-be learner. Yet, all too frequently we confront students with an array of materials that would confound the most adventurous professional artist. Even Picasso, virtuoso that he is in contemporary art, does not attempt to learn to throw the pots he decorates or weld the steel or pour the bronze for his sculptures. He is, first of all, a draftsman, as Moore is a sculptor and DeKooning a painter. A lifetime of activity in their various media has hardly been enough for these men; yet, we have been expecting fifteen-, sixteen-, and seventeen-year-old youngsters to come to understand "the nature of art and the creative process" when they are scarcely allowed the time to understand that red and yellow, when mixed together under certain circumstances, will make orange.[2]

Only when the student is allowed the time to become familiar with some of the fundamental characteristics of a medium can he begin to "think, feel and act creatively with visual art materials."[3] This simply cannot happen in a two-week or a six-week unit, followed by a two- or a six-week unit in another medium with another approach. Therefore, the basis for the high school curriculum should be the specialized, in-depth course.

An in-depth course is one which deals with one basic material or approach. What courses will be offered is probably dependent on the interests and abilities of the teachers available to the program. These courses could include drawing, painting, sculpture, ceramics, and so on. The infamous "crafts" class in particular is far too general for any real understanding or skill development. In ceramics, for example, it is only after several pots are built, decorated, fired, and discarded that the student really begins to de-

---

2 *Ibid.*
3 *Ibid.*

velop the respect for his material, the acuteness of perception, and the firmness of hand that bring him close to the goal he personally seeks in taking the class—making good art objects. To expect him to come close to the goal when ceramics is one unit of a multitude in a crafts class is to expect the impossible.

In a specialized course, especially if the student has the opportunity to work in it for more than one year, he has greater hope of attaining his personal goals and the program has greater hope of attaining one of its major objectives—"increased manipulative and organizational skills in art performance appropriate to his abilities."[4] He will have the opportunity to become involved. Far from narrowing students to a limited range of information, as some art teachers fear, this approach will lead to broader, more in-depth interest. As third- and fourth-year ceramics students become increasingly critical of the relation between form and glaze on their pots, they also become more interested in the problems of the young printmakers in the next room as they attempt to translate a wash drawing into aquatint and of the difficulties encountered in the chemistry lab when attempting to reconcile the results of a complex experiment. This cross-disciplinary perception does not happen spontaneously, but if we are really clear about our objectives in the whole program, we can teach them through the devices of any material with which the student feels comfortable.

VARIABILITY OF INSTRUCTIONAL TIME AND STUDENT DEPLOYMENT

If a curriculum were truly individualized and if an environment and the materials necessary for free learning to occur were a reality, a discussion of the organization of time would be superfluous. But until this ideal can occur in the secondary school, it is necessary to plan clearly how student, teacher, and room time will be used most effectively. In the flexible schedule, the breaking of traditional time patterns has in itself brought about new ways of looking at curriculum; however, these time patterns should evolve from the demands of the instructional program, not the other way around. Initially, teachers hesitate to give up time from their programs until they observe how capable students are when working independently. Given a good learning climate, teachers

---

4 *Ibid.*

will see that time given up from a conventional schedule in a self-contained classroom is not necessarily a loss to the program, but for most students it is, in fact, an advantage.

Within the art program provisions have been made for several different student groupings. Each of these can operate on slightly different time patterns or arrangements and within each group there are variations as well. The first group is made up of those students new to the program and the flexible schedule—particularly features such as independent study, unscheduled time, variable time patterns, large group—small group instruction, and so on. These students, who enter the program via the prerequisite course, begin the year with the class meeting for one short and two long periods each week. The short session, perhaps two modules in length, is used initially for assignments, explaining procedures, seeing films, hearing guest speakers, and so on. It is scheduled as a large group with all students meeting together at the same time. As the year progresses, however, the large group meeting will be held only once every three or four weeks and perhaps not even that often. Instead, the teachers will use the two modules to meet with smaller groups or special interest groups, or to give special presentations to some students who are still weak on basic concepts. The students not required to meet in the large group must spend an equivalent amount of time in an open lab during the week, do work at home, or undertake an independent study project.

The two longer class periods are scheduled as one phase so that the same students meet together at the same hour of the day on two separate days. In this way students have a greater feeling of belonging to a particular group; this allows a certain sense of security that is necessary for most younger students. As the year progresses and the large group meets less frequently, the students are introduced to the idea of working independently in open labs for at least some time during the week.

The next group are students who, due to emotional, mental, or aesthetic immaturity, are unable to cope with the demands for independence made by flexible scheduling. They are placed in a special class which provides greater supervision for the student with less self-discipline. This class meets on a more regular schedule, four or five times each week at the same time for about 45 minutes. Its structure is similar to the traditional class in a traditional schedule. These students seem to need the clarity offered by specific hours and a specific group of people around them in class. The process of encouraging students to work independently is carried out within more structured time patterns and is aimed at attitudes and work capabilities within the class rather than involving the organization of time as in other classes.

A third group of students are those who have demonstrated skills and understandings in a single area and are capable of digging even deeper into the subject. Students in these advanced classes show interests and competency for greater involvement and independent work. The function of the advanced classes is somewhat like that of a seminar: problems are discussed, evaluation takes place, information is presented. Few, if any, group assignments are given and all of the students are together because they are working on an advanced level in the same general area. The class meets together only once each week and the remainder of the student's time is spent in labs, resource centers, or working on independent projects outside of school. These students are also utilized as teaching assistants in labs so that these facilities can be available for longer periods of time without cutting heavily into teacher preparation or conference time.

The fourth group of students in art are those who wish to make in-depth studies in one or more areas or who have demonstrated exceptional ability in some way and wish to undertake special projects outside the confines of the mainstream of the curriculum. An art honors seminar which meets once each week for museum excursions, group critiques, and visits with artists is one possibility for these students. Another is the contract, a work agreement between student and teacher without any special meeting time. Another possibility is the temporary scheduling of a small group of students who are involved in similar enterprises. This can be done during some of the open lab time or during conference time.

Finally, there are those students, the majority, who have successfully demonstrated their understanding of fundamental art concepts and are ready to work in depth in specific areas. These are the students in the in-depth portion of the curriculum at the "beginning" or "intermediate" levels. Whether to maintain these levels as rigidly separate classes, that is, as Drawing I, Drawing II,

Drawing III, and so on, is dependent on the amount of individualized instruction possible. If the classes are scheduled separately, then one of the aims of the flexible schedule—that of bringing more students into the program—will be sacrificed. When instruction is truly individualized, it is possible to have all students in a course such as drawing in the same "class," regardless of their level within the course.

VARIABILITY OF TIME WITHIN COURSES—THE OPEN LAB

The key to openness in the flexible schedule is the student's independent study time or unscheduled time. In the art program this factor is used in the organization of "lab" time. The open lab is the time when students work in the art facilities without being a part of an organized class. They work on the projects begun in class or on the independent projects they have contracted with the teacher, but they work individually without any general instructions, directions, or demonstrations being given. Students in the open lab are from several different classes. There may be first-year art students working on class projects, painting students involved in the oil painting begun in class, independent study youngsters working on a contract, and another group of three or four students planning or working on an idea generated in the seminar. The teacher is the resource agent and the room a resource center for individualized activity. The teacher may also be the supervisor of the room, but in no way similar to the traditional art teacher who is directing and controlling all activities in the classroom. Students may come into the open lab either at prescheduled times or during the free times in their schedules on a volunteer basis.

The greatest advantage of the open lab is that it transfers much of the responsibility for learning to the student. It does not necessarily relieve the teacher of his responsibilities, but the function of the lab is to provide opportunities for students to work independently and to develop the abilities to make choices and to take responsibility for learning.

The ratio of scheduled time to open or unscheduled time for any particular student may vary throughout the school year. Students with only half of the expected art time scheduled initially can be required, under certain circumstances, to appear at certain times on a regular basis for labs. If a group of students from different classes are all having the same difficulties, they can be scheduled as a special group meeting at a common time for special work. This can also be done if students are working on problems not commonly shared by other members of their class. Some students may have difficulty organizing their time because of previous training or experience; although they should probably be rescheduled into a more structured class, this may not be possible and they may need to be placed on a more restrictive schedule.

The idea of having students coming and going in an unstructured manner, as is the case in open lab situations, is frightening to many teachers. This is true, in part, because teachers feel that the problems of room clean-up and of attendance will be overwhelming. But, if the proper environment is provided, youngsters are capable of determining when and how to learn. If it is not possible for students to learn the relatively simple tasks of clean-up and organization, then the problem-solving and creative thinking abilities in our objectives are completely out of reach. If room organization and care are a vital part of the subject, then a method must be found to make it relevant to the students and to develop the necessary strategies for teaching. Since most students have been trained to only clean up when they are told to do so or when they have been appointed "monitor", a good deal of retraining and learning has to be done in these areas.

VARIABILITY OF TEACHER TIME

When most students are free to plan a good part of their own use of facilities and instructional time, how does the teacher design a working schedule for himself? One absolute necessity for the teacher is a portion of uninterrupted time each week for planning and preparation. This should be flexible for, with teachers as well as with students, some opportunity must exist for choices to be made. The first demand on teacher time, of course, is that made by assigned classes. In as much as classes do not generally meet each day and many classes meet only once a week, not more than half of the teacher's time will be given to specifically assigned groups. If a particular teacher teaches only first-year art students and/or the general arts course for "problem" youngsters, the time taken by regular classes may be slightly higher. If the teacher teaches only advanced courses, the time assigned to these classes may be as little as ten or fifteen percent of the school week.

In addition to time assigned in scheduled classes, part of the week is spent in labs. The amount of time in lab will depend mainly on the structure of the lab system; that is, whether they are open or structured and whether there is a limit to the number of students who may be in the lab at a given time. The remainder of the teacher's time will be spent working with individuals and small groups. For the art teacher, much of this activity can often be accomplished during lab times. Thus, the art room can be open for a limited number of students although the teacher is in fact conferring with one or more individuals.

In scheduling teachers, a reasonable rule to follow is to allow a maximum of fifty to sixty percent of the teacher's total time for organized student contact either in regular classes or labs. Fifteen to twenty percent of the teacher's time should be scheduled for uninterrupted planning and preparation, and the remainder of the time for work with individuals and small groups. The more flexibly this time can be scheduled by the individual teacher, the more beneficial it will be for both teacher and student.

INDIVIDUALIZED STUDENT ASSIGNMENTS—THE CARRIER PROJECT[5]

An in-depth approach to subject matter is in itself a means of individualizing instruction, because it offers the student a choice of subject areas in which to study. Within each course still other provisions for differential interests and abilities must be made. To a large extent the secondary art program has an advantage it does not always use. "Dumping grounds" philosophy or not, most students take art because they want to take it. We should be able to build an exciting curriculum on that kind of interest and one which will allow teachers to attain the larger goals we have set. Here the format devised by Ashael Woodruff for organizing and analyzing what he calls a "carrier project" is invaluable.[6] A carrier project is an activity that a student really wants to do

---

[5] The "Carrier Project" is similar in many respects to UNIPAC or other individualized learning materials, as discussed in Chapter 3.

[6] Asahel D. Woodruff, *First Steps in Building A New School Program* (Salt Lake City, Utah: Bureau of Educational Research, University of Utah, 1967).

(an individualized project), not one which is assigned to a whole class of youngsters and which everyone has to do.

For example, take Stan, a senior boy in a ceramics class. Why is he taking ceramics? What does he want to do in a ceramics class? He knows that ceramics has to do with making functional objects of clay. Perhaps he has taken the class mainly because it looks like fun and he would like to make a set of mugs—maybe even beer mugs. If such a project is accepted by the teacher—without too much moralizing about beer drinking—as a valid ceramics project, how can it be used to help attain the major goals? To begin, the minimal acceptable qualities that the set of mugs should have should be listed. These qualities should be acceptable to both Stan and the teacher, and, if Stan is just beginning in ceramics, special care should be taken that these standards are not out of the realm of possibility for him.

PROJECT: A SET OF BEER MUGS
Minimal Acceptable Qualities

Specified by the student:
1. They will hold 12 ounces of liquid.
2. They will have a shiny blue glaze.
3. There will be four mugs.
4. They will be built with the coil method.

Specified by the teacher:
1. All four mugs will be the same size, shape, and color.
2. The handles will be pulled.
3. The handles, rims, feet, and general form will be functional according to mutually agreed-upon criteria.

After determining the minimal acceptable characteristics for the mugs, it is necessary to see what understandings, skills, concepts, and general knowledge Stan needs in order to successfully complete this project.

1. He needs to know how to prepare clay. This may include mixing, wedging, and storing, or it may simply be where to locate the clay in the lab.
2. He needs to know how to roll coils of clay and how to build shapes with coils by attaching them properly.
3. He needs to know how to control the shape as he builds it.
4. He needs to know that clay shrinks as it dries, and how this affects the size of his mugs as well as the problems it causes in construction.
5. He needs to know what function is and how to determine what a functional shape for a drinking mug could be.

6. He needs to know how to pull and attach handles.
7. He needs to know how to dry his mugs and the procedures or the process of bisque firing after drying.
8. He needs to know what a glaze is, how to prepare it for use, how to apply it, and the procedures or process for the final firing. He may need to know how to obtain a blue glaze.

Having analyzed in a general way the things Stan must know or be able to do in order to make his set of mugs, the components of each of the above points can now be specified in a more explicit way. Each item on the list must be analyzed carefully to clarify exactly what concept must be learned in order to perform the task. This clarification, in turn, will help determine teaching strategies.

Preparing clay may be simply an item of information if all the student needs to know is where to find the clay in the room. But in establishing a learning environment which is expected to reach beyond the classroom, a high school student will need to know where to obtain clay for making pottery outside of the classroom. At this point he may also need to know how to prepare the specific clay body used generally in class; if so, we are talking about a process. This process will include:

1. Knowing what ingredients to use.
2. Knowing what amounts of each ingredient to use.
3. Knowing how to measure the ingredients.
4. Knowing how to mix the ingredients initially and how to bring them to a workable state.
5. Knowing how to care for the clay once it is ready for use.

Each of the steps in the process is in turn made up of one or more concepts which may be structural in nature, or concepts of the consequences of an act, or a variety of other types of concepts. For example, the ingredients of the clay body are objects or materials which must be identified properly and the ingredients may have to be weighed on a scale which operates on certain principles. So the student must have concepts concerning the ingredients (structural) and scale use (act-consequence). Each step in the process of mixing clay is a complex of concepts, and by failing to understand any one of them, the student may be unable to perform consistently the whole process adequately.

One of the greatest weaknesses in the whole process of

education, especially in art education, is our failure to determine consistently and adequately just what it is that students need to know to "understand" art. If, in the case of these mugs, one of the criterion should be stated as "The mugs will have beautiful, flowing lines," then we must be prepared to define this statement and to offer some means for the student to demonstrate that he has an adequate concept of "beautiful, flowing lines." If the material has been analyzed in this manner, we are much more likely to identify all of the necessary concepts required for learning the material. The task analysis ultimately allows us to see the interrelationships between all types of materials. When the activities to be learned have been scrutinized and the objectives and concepts have been stated in a specific manner, it becomes much easier to see what kinds of teaching strategies and devices can be used to aid the student in forming the concepts.

As more "carrier projects" are developed in ceramics and in other areas of art, it becomes apparent that there are many overlapping concepts; this is, of course, what is implied by stating the general objectives of the course. It is a very difficult task to determine just where and how concepts should be learned when we simply state concepts *per se*. Vital ideas may be overlooked because something is taken for granted that was not part of the student's conceptual framework. Only when projects are analyzed and designed in terms of concepts and specific competencies can this be seen. One ceramics class, where students were having difficulty understanding and using the process of wax-resist decoration, provides an example. After the process had been analyzed properly, it became apparent that some students had not understood the principle of stencils and blockouts, while others were unclear about the principle of "resist." Once the problems were seen in this light, teaching strategies were worked out to deal with those two concepts and other approaches with these concepts were brought into the first-year art curriculum so that students would have a background on which to build when they entered ceramics.

Often in art we present projects which have little meaning for students. One reason for this lack of meaning may be that we have assumed that the ideas presented are so simple; we have simply overlooked the gaps in understanding of major concepts or at least the concepts major to the work the student is being asked to do. We need to be able to spot the gaps before beginning the projects. Before that can be done, identification of all the necessary concepts is paramount. As in the case of the wax-resist problem, it can turn out that thorough analysis of a few specialized projects in advanced areas can reveal a whole battery of material which needs to be worked on at earlier levels. In fact, the whole conceptual framework for a curriculum can develop from such analysis. Instead of beginning with concepts and then trying to fit projects to them, it is possible to begin with projects that have meaning for the students and to identify the conceps that make them up. Then we will be better able to organize an orderly sequence of concepts through the projects and through the curriculum.

The best way to develop an individualized curriculum based on the real-life interests of students is to begin with the point of view "What is it that the student really wants to do?" Then, the students and the teacher together should develop the criteria that the particular project needs to meet. From that point on, it is up to the teacher to develop the materials and strategies best suited for the student's learning. In this way it is possible to individualize instruction and make it more meaningful in a number of ways and on several levels.

Each time a new project occurs the teacher may have to develop a new set of teaching aids for use with it. But, as more projects are developed and as the conceptual areas are seen to overlap, this exhausting work will become more simple. The approach that an individual teacher takes in developing materials will vary. As discussed in Chapter 3, several formats are being tried in schools across the country and are available as guides to teachers developing individualized instructional materials.

The point of using a carrier project is the same as the point of allowing the student the choice of what art course he takes. It places the learning environment and the teaching strategies at the proper point in the learning cycle. Motivation is supplied by the student. He will undertake the project because he wants to, not because he is told to or forced to take it. Only when he recognizes the problem or feels the need will any learning take place.

MEASUREMENT AND EVALUATION

In order to measure and evaluate we must know what it is we are measuring. Here, we are trying to measure whether or not art learning has taken place. If we accept as a starting point that learning is change from one state to another a beginning is made. If that change can be said to be behavioral in nature we will be helped along further. Woodruff defines learning as "a permanent alteration in behavior while the behavior is going on."[7] This is quite a challenge, specifying, as it does, not only change but *permanent* change in *ongoing* behavior. According to this definition, one reason for the failure of the lecture as a learning environment is that the only ongoing behavior of which we can be sure in students is *sitting.* This is the trap that a large group approach can easily fall into unless the student is engaged in some observable behavior. This is another advantage that the studio or lab approach in art provides. The student is engaged in behavior while he is learning and the behavior is visible.

BEHAVIORAL OBJECTIVES IN ART[8]

Because learning is behavioral change our objectives must be stated in such a way that the behavior we are talking about is clearly understood. If we intend to measure behavior change, as we must if we are to know whether the objectives are being attained, then that behavior must be a living, acting behavior, an overt behavior, in short, an ongoing behavior. If objectives are stated in a global way in abstract terms descriptive of thoughts, feelings, or attitudes, we have no way of determing whether learning has taken place. By examining a ceramics program we can determine what objectives the program should have and we can keep in mind that the objectives must be stated in terms of measurable, life-functioning behaviors.

When a student takes ceramics he does so because he wants to make pots. This in itself is a life-functioning behavior. But, if

---

7 *Ibid.*

8 The reader is referred, again, to Chapter 3 for a discussion and definition of behavioral objectives.

we were to set as the objective of the course that "the student will be able to make pots," we have neither defined nor established a very sound goal. We would like to have him "think, feel, and act creatively with visual art materials," the material being, in this case, clay. We want him to "perceive and understand visual relationships in the environment," in this case, three-dimensional form and relationships between volume and surface decoration. We want him to be able to "use art knowledges and skills in his personal and community life," particularly his knowledge of form and function relationships. These are general areas with which we are concerned in this specific course. We want him to learn about the nature of clay so that he can act creatively with it. However, if we say to the student "now you are going to learn about the nature of clay," we most probably will lose that student because that is not why he took the course. In addition, we have said nothing to indicate how we will know or how the student will be able to show us that he does know something about the nature of clay.

But we can state, "Given a variety of eight materials (or six or ten or whatever), the student will correctly identify within five minutes (or thirty seconds or what is reasonable) the materials which are plastic and those which are non-plastic." Thus, this objective reveals whether the student knows one of the basic concepts concerning the nature of clay. It may be that it is a concept that should be developed at an earlier stage in the student's progression through the art program. If so, the objective in ceramics will be even more to the point. "Given samples of stoneware clay, porcelain clay, and raku clay, the student will be able to arrange the samples on a scale from 'most plastic' to 'least plastic'." Having stated the objective in this way we can now see clearly whether it has been reached and we can develop some teaching strategies and materials to help the student discover and form the concept of clay as a plastic material.

Only by stating explicit objectives can we determine whether they have been met and whether the student knows when they have been met. Only in this manner can we identify the competencies, the concepts, and the capabilities students need to complete a course or a unit of learning. The behavioral objective serves two purposes: (1) at the end of any given unit it gives us a gradient to discover whether the student has successfully completed the material, and (2) it can be used at the beginning of a unit to determine through which learning processes the student needs to go. If we use the behavioral objective as a means of ascertaining whether the student needs the unit or some part of the unit, we can make pretesting or diagnostic devices for the unit. We may then discover that the student already knows most of the material included. He can then go on to a different unit or skip parts of a unit rather than waste time and interest in going over material which he already understands. The procedure of using behavioral objectives as a means of evaluating the program itself is a radical departure from tradition. Evaluations are supposed to be of *students*, not programs. If we do not evaluate students how can we assign grades and grant units of credit toward graduation requirements?

GRADES AND CREDIT IN ART

Traditionally, the granting of credit is tied to time spent in the classroom. In most schools art receives half the amount of credit as other courses having equal time in class. Grading is normally handled by requiring the same work in the same quantity from each student and generally in a highly subjective manner, attaching a point or letter value to each product turned out. An average of these values gives a semester grade.

The student who consistently works at an advanced level, who is obviously creative and able, and who does voluminous amounts of work receives an "A" at the end of the semester for the number of credits the whole class is worth. The student at the other end of the scale, who vegetates through the class and attempts little learning, may receive a failing grade for his lack of enthusiasm, ability, and effort, but more often he is allowed the lowest passing grade (after all, how can anyone fail art?). He then receives the same amount of credit as anyone else in the class.

The complaint from high school students—that they do not take art because they can only get a "B" or "C" as they are not very good at it—is justifiable. Those students who are college-bound are pressured to get as many "A's" as possible, and to do so means avoiding classes which may not yield this precious token. If we are going to the effort of establishing an art program of flexibility in order to allow more students into the program and of individualizing instruction to ensure their learning, we must also give some concern and concentrated thought to one of the pervasive issues which is part of conventional school systems today.

It seems apparent that traditional units of credit are no real indicator of amount or quality of work accomplished. Grades received do not serve as real indicators of learning. A flexible schedule compounds the credit problem because it does away with almost all time comparisons for classes. An English class may meet for twelve modules of time per week, an art class for six, and a history class for ten. In addition, the student in the art class may spend most of his time in labs and not in regular classes. Do all of these labs and classes receive the same amount of credit? Specifically, how do we handle the individualized lab portion of the class?

Initially, the solution would appear to be that credit should be allowed in proportion to time spent in class. This is the easiest method of treating the problem, especially in terms of clerical work. Thus, the English class receives twelve units, the art class six, and the history class ten. Unfortunately, the amount of time spent in the classroom is no measure of activity in education. Through the use of independent study, open or structured labs, seminars and flexibility in the use of scheduled time, students vary widely in the amount of time spent in "class."

What, then, is the solution? Since we are tied to the task of giving credit it can be done on the basis of work completed. This work might be assigned or it might be in terms of the projects the student has selected. If the awarding of credit is important, then it is important that the projects be specific. If they are not, who will determine when credit has been earned? How can the student know whether requirements have been fulfilled? How can the teacher tell whether the student is working in a meaningful direction? Another purpose for a behavioral objective is that its attainment represents an increment of credit in the course.

Credit is intended to be an indication of quantity and grade is intended to be an indication of quality. Just as the awarding of credit on the basis of attendance is no indication of educational involvement, so the awarding of a grade is little indication of amount earned. Since grades are arranged on a value scale, the implication is that either the material to be covered may be only partially learned or that there are expected levels of learning within the assignment. But if learning is permanent change it cannot be partial, and to say that the levels of learning within an assignment are worth different values is to imply that all students come to a given project or unit with equal background, ability, and motivation, which is certainly not the case. In art, particularly, the grade is too often tied, whether by accident or by design, to some kind of inexplicable entity which we call talent within the student. This entity, or lack of it, is the greatest deterrant to most students enrolling in art. Students feel that if they are not "talented" in art, they cannot possibly attain good grades in art.

This points to the great weakness in the whole philosophy of grading. By the time a student reaches secondary school he is likely to choose to take those courses which will offer the greatest possibility of his receiving good grades. Those courses are most likely the ones in which he has already demonstrated that he is capable or talented. As time goes on he tends to avoid all courses which may not result in good grades, or he finds that what he really learns matters very little to the teacher or to the grade he will get and he concludes that good grades are out of reach anyway. This, of course, is an oversimplification, but it carries the essence of the grading dilemma. The goundwork has been prepared at a early age so that, by the time a student reaches high school, he is pretty much convinced that he is "good" at some things and "not so good" at others. His choice of elective courses in high school is based on this conviction, regardless of his developing interests.

When grades are thought of as being rewards for doing things in school, what do we expect will happen when the youngster leaves school? An axiom in behavioral psychology is that to cause extinction of any learned behavior it is only necessary to remove the reinforcement so that, regardless of how often the organism exhibits the behavior, no reward is received. If this is applied to school it should be expected that when the student leaves the art room and receives no grade (reinforcement or reward) for behaving in an "art" manner, he will soon cease to exhibit the art-like behavior. A look at our urban and suburban surroundings and our littered landscapes may be convincing evidence that this is the case. If we move to the other end of the psychological spectrum to analyze the expected results of grading, we will arrive at the same conclusion. Whether we are talking about gestalt insights or "self-actualizing" persons, no reality is attached to any experience, no perception can occur unless it is felt from within the person. External judgments of work by a teacher is not real, and, as it is not real, it can have no effect on the behavior of the student that can be said to be permanent. So, in either case—the almost mechanical conditions of operant conditioning or the very personal experience of actualization—the grade remains a totally ineffectual means of promoting lasting learning.

CERAMICS: A PARADIGM FOR INDIVIDUALIZING INSTRUCTION

9

RATIONALE FOR THE COURSE

By now it has become apparent that the flexible schedule offers more to art programs than simply structural changes and variations in time patterns. A more thorough introduction to individualizing art programs will be gained by looking at a specific course. Any course would help the reader gain clearer insights into the program and the schedule, but ceramics will be used since it is the course with which the authors have had the greatest experience. It is also representative of what is termed an "in-depth approach."

The first question to be answered is: "Why teach ceramics at all?" Clay is a responsive material relatively easy to manipulate and it allows a great deal of experimentation and experience to be bought cheaply. The nature of clay demands a kind of spontaneity which makes it an appropriate medium for the often-impetuous adolescent. Two other characteristics which make clay a good vehicle for learning about art are the immediacy with which one knows the results of his efforts and its relative freedom from the demands of recognizable imagery.

The immediacy of clay gives it a psychological learning advantage in that the reward for success is constantly available. The student sees and, equally important, feels the results of his efforts. Without the intermediary of a teacher or a grade, he has direct knowledge of what he is doing. The pot stands or it does not; the handle stays on or it does not; the clay is centered or it is not. The student is in direct contact with the material as well as with himself. This is as close to experiencing creation as is possible in a physical sense. No tools or machines, however primitive, need stand between the student and his work.

The second characteristic which makes ceramics a good learning device is one that is shared with other craft media. Since the intent of a craft object is to function usefully and visually, students gain satisfaction without having to commit themselves to points of view with which they have little experience or feeling of involvement. The problems in ceramics center around gaining physical mastery of a material and developing sharper visual perceptions. Both are conceptual areas basic to the understanding of art. In addition, the whole activity is close to the life desires of most young people. They are creating objects for use; they are somehow being of service to themselves and others by providing for physical needs.

The nature of the material itself and its relative freedom from the complexities of emotional communication, together with the need-serving qualities of applied ceramics, make it an excellent choice for a high school art course. It is also a good vehicle for learning about the nature of three-dimensional form as well as for learning about the development of art and its relation to society throughout man's history. Contemporary trends in particular point out the changing emphasis on individuality in personal expression as contrasted with the more anonymous pottery of the past.

The pacing of activities, which is so important in working with clay, lends itself to the philosophy of flexible scheduling. In working with slabs, for example, or on very large pieces, there is a time factor which is difficult to deal with in a traditional schedule. The clay needs to "rest"; only so much can be done; then time must elapse before more clay can be added or trimmed. Weather alone makes a difference in what may be done in an hour or in a day. When students are free to determine their own use of time they can make good use of this knowledge to become truly independent learners.

GENERAL OBJECTIVES

Consistent with the rationale for offering ceramics as a high school art course, what kinds of objectives will the program have? Since we earlier accepted the aims of the National Art Education Association as the general objectives for the entire art program, how will they fit a program as specific as ceramics?

As a result of the art program, each pupil should demonstrate to the extent that he can, his capacity to:

1. Have intense involvement in and response to personal visual experiences:
   a. by voluntarily attending ceramics classes and labs an average of three hours a week for at least one semester.
   b. by voluntarily attending an exhibit, display, or studio of ceramic work and discussing it with others.
2. Perceive and understand visual relationships in the environment:
   a. by being able to describe the relationship between foot, belly, neck, and rim in any given ceramic pot.
   b. by being able to identify and discuss examples of good form/function relationships in objects of everyday use.
3. Think, feel, and act creatively with visual art materials; by voluntarily making ceramic objects of his own design.
4. Increase manipulative and organizational skills in art performance appropriate to his abilities:
   a. by being able to prepare and care for clay and objects of clay from construction through the final firing.
   b. by being able to properly construct unique objects of clay.
5. Acquire a knowledge of man's visual art heritage:
   a. by being able to describe generally the differences in the construction of pottery from basketmaker to the wheel, and the general relationship of these methods to the culture of the times.
   b. by being able to distinguish and discuss the differences between the pottery of the American Indian, the Helenic Greek, the medieval Japanese, and the contemporary American.
6. Use art knowledges and skills in his personal and community life:
   a. by voluntarily purchasing or trading his own for a piece of pottery for himself or for someone else.
   b. by voluntarily sharing his points of view about the existing examples of ceramics in his community with others.
7. Make intelligent visual judgments suited to his experience and maturity:
   a. by being able to discuss, on the basis of judgments formed while taking this class, what are examples of good pottery from a group of given examples.
   b. by making objective critiques of the relationship between form and material in his own and the pottery of others.
   c. by keeping that work of his own which is good and by voluntarily destroying that which fails to meet the criteria which he has set for good pottery.

8. Understand the nature of art and the creative process:
   a. by voluntarily attempting projects that are unique to him.
   b. by voluntarily discussing with others events or objects which seem both unique and important to him.

SPECIFIC OBJECTIVES

It is possible now to list the more specific objectives of the course. They should be based on the instructor's knowledge of ceramics as he perceives them from his own experience. But because the student takes ceramics to accomplish some specific objectives of his own, let us look at a project to see what objectives might be attained by allowing some student choice. When an individual project is looked at carefully and all the skills and concepts necessary for the accomplishment of the task are listed, it incorporates many of the skills and concepts we hope to attain in the ceramics program. To return to the project of the four shiny blue mugs described in Chapter 8, each of the points listed as necessary for the completion of the project has within it skills and concepts which become part of the student's whole understanding of ceramics. For example, there are a number of things a student must see, understand, and be able to do in order to make a coil pot. In this project the goal is to make a set of mugs, but to do so requires that understanding and skill in making coils first must be demonstrated. In addition, each of the points in the task analysis has inherent in it a variety of directions and levels on which the student can work. Mixing, wedging, and storing clay might be done by the teacher so that the only learning we really are after is that the student know where clay is kept in the room and how he can obtain it. But on another level a student might be locating, digging, and processing his own clay for use. The same is true of preparing glazes or engobes. For one student it is simply a matter of learning about the equipment necessary and about the recommended consistency for use of the material, while for another the step might be a study of glaze formulation. Analysis of one carrier project that is selected by a student because he wants to do it will help to develop a set of objectives which covers nearly all of the things to be learned in ceramics.[1] A comparison of the

---

[1] See Chapter 8; also see Asahel D. Woodruff, *First Steps in A New School Program* (Salt Lake City, Utah: Bureau of Educational Research, University of Utah, 1967).

objectives of the project with the general objectives will make this more apparent.

Specific Objective	*General Objective*
1. Mixing clay	
2. Wedging clay	Increase manipulative and organizational skills
3. Storing clay	
4. Rolling coils	
5. Building a coil pot	Think, feel, and act creatively with visual art materials
6. Deciding about shapes	Use art knowledge and skills in personal life; make intelligent visual judgments suited to experience and maturity
7. Making handles	Increase manipulative skills
8. Deciding about handles	(As in number 6)
9. Clay shrinkage	Increase manipulative skills
10. Preparing engobes	Increase manipulative skills
11. Applying engobes	Increase manipulative skills; make intelligent visual judgments
12. Preparing glazes	Increase manipulative skills
13. Applying glazes	Increase manipulative skills, make intelligent visual judgments, use art knowledges and skills, etc.
14. Drying and bisque-firing pots	Increase manipulative skills
15. Glaze-firing pots	Increase manipulative skills

In this project, as in all beginning projects, the main emphasis is on learning about the nature of the material. As the student works along he becomes more aware of the possibilities and the restrictions of clay, and more emphasis is placed in other areas as he works on more projects. Each of the objectives is met by the student working through a lesson dealing with that objective or by his passing a pre-test which shows that he already knows the material in that lesson. In this project it would be possible to organize the learning unit so that the student did not have to learn the material in objectives 1, 2, 3, 9, 10, 12, 13, 14, and 15. These objectives could be replaced by simple instructions on where to find the materials already prepared. In a high school in-depth course, however, being able to work with the media on one's own is fundamental. The first of the general objectives, which deals with being able to be involved in the experience and with potential as a learner, is an inherent objective in all of the student's learning activities.

When each of the major general objectives is stated behaviorally and when the components of each general objective is made specific in terms of overt behavior, the course becomes even more clear.

1. Preparation and care of clay. (These are first three points in the task analysis.)

   Given the proper formula, the student will be able to mix ten pounds of clay from dry materials and slurry in fifteen minutes, observing all the restrictions and safety precautions regarding the equipment use.

   The student will be able to describe how to store clay properly so that it loses none of its working qualities over a period of several days.

   The student will be able to wedge five pounds of freshly mixed clay into an homogenous mass in ten minutes.

   The student will be able to identify plastic clay, leatherhard clay, and bone-dry clay from a group of twenty samples in a period of ten minutes.

2. Construction of pottery (points four, five, and six).

   The student will be able to name three major methods of forming pottery by hand.

   The student will be able to construct at least two pots by using one of the methods listed within a period of three weeks. Each of the two pots will be at least ten inches high and at least five inches in diameter at its widest point, and may be of any shape the student desires.

   The student will be able to construct one pot of a pre-determined shape using the same method as above in a period of no more than two weeks.

   The student will be able to describe the processes necessary for attaching two pieces of clay permanently together.

3. Form (points six and eight).

   Given an example of a functional ceramic vessel, the student will be able to list three or more necessary elements of its function that will, to some degree, dictate its form.

   The student will be able to identify from a list those properties which are critical to the relationship between form and function and to explain the reasons for his choice in objective terms.

4. Handles.

> The student will be able to list three methods of making handles.
>
> The student will be able to make and attach at least three handles to a pot or to three different pots using one of the three methods listed.
>
> The student will be able to list three properties necessary for a functional handle.

5. Clay shrinkage.

> The student will be able to discuss how shrinkage affects the building of pots.
>
> The student will be able to complete a pot of a given finished size by compensating for clay shrinkage.

6. Engobes.

> The student will be able to define an engobe.
>
> The student will be able to prepare a colored engobe for use.
>
> The student will be able to list three methods for applying an engobe.
>
> The student will be able to apply an engobe using one of the three methods he has listed.

7. Drying and firing.

> The student will be able to define bone-dry clay.
>
> The student will be able to define bisque-fired clay.
>
> The student will be able to identify both bone-dry and bisque-fired clay samples in a group of fifteen miscellaneous examples within five minutes.
>
> The student will be able to describe the changes undergone by clay in the processes of drying and of firing.

8. Glazes and glazing.

> The student will be able to define a glaze.
>
> The student will be able to list three reasons for using glazes on pottery.
>
> The student will be able to prepare a glaze for use.
>
> The student will be able to list three methods of applying an even glaze on a pot.
>
> The student will be able to apply an even glaze coat to a pot using one of the three methods he has listed.
>
> The student will be able to prepare his pot for placement in the glaze kiln.

These are the most important of the behavioral objectives related to each of the areas in the sample project. The student must demonstrate his ability to use each of these behaviors as he moves along toward his own objective of producing a set of four shiny, blue twelve-ounce drinking mugs. Other projects for other students will reveal more objectives and, taken together, they form the basis of the ceramics course of study. Since all of the individual objectives relate to the major objectives, all students will meet the major objectives of the course.

The objectives themselves suggest teaching strategies. For example, the lessons on drying and firing might call for the student to construct several samples for experimentation. Changes in weight and size could be recorded or even photographed as the samples dry to give the student his own evidence of the changes undergone by clay during the drying. One of the samples could then be bisque-fired and again the change noted. If the student places a bisqued sample and a bone-dry sample in water for a few minutes, he will gather more evidence about the metamorphosis of clay in ceramics. As we learn more about the nature of learning, and more about how perceptions are translated into concepts, better alternatives will be offered as teaching strategies.

Some students are able to perceive the importance of these changes in clay on the basis of verbal information alone. Still others will be able to form the necessary concepts by observing teacher demonstrations, slides, or films on the subject. Yet others must work through problems which make it possible for them to see and to use the characteristics in the context of a real problem in order that their perceptions, and thus their concepts, become clear. The numbers of students in each of these categories is difficult to anticipate, but the differences are apparent with each of the concepts necessary for any given project. The students who can exhibit the behavior called for in our first objective in clay preparation after only verbal information may not be the same as those who need only verbal information to perform the second behavior. Some students need to work each area through in a physical way to form their concepts while others, because of differing background, experience, and visual acuity, are able to form most of the necessary concepts from verbal information. It is as wrong to expect the student with little verbal skill to learn the concept when the only material presented is verbal as it is to force the student with strong verbal capabilities to work physically through each concept when he may be able to demonstrate quickly

his understanding in another way. The structure of the course—
even a ceramics course—must allow for these differences.

CERAMICS COURSE STRUCTURE AND ORGANIZATION

The time structure of the ceramics course uses a large group meeting once each week for a period of about forty-five minutes. The
purpose of this meeting is to present material of a general but
basic nature in order to allow students to form some ideas about
ceramics as quickly as possible. The materials of the presentation
follow a sequence which is closely related to the needs of the
total group of students in the course. In reality this is an impossibility, but the use of post-testing for diagnosis during the
large group meeting and of follow-up activities with those who
need them during classes or labs help make it more feasible. When
the objectives of the course are stated behaviorally, construction
of testing devices for diagnosis and evaluation is made quite
simple. The objective itself is very nearly a test item in most
cases.

The sequence for the large group presentations for the first
semester is listed below. It is based on the objectives found in the
student projects which, in turn, are based on the general objectives of the course. The sequence concerning construction has
been expanded in order to give students a background from which
to select methods, and the question of the relation of surface
decoration to form is larger for the same reason.

 1. Introduction to procedures; pre-test for course; clay mixing
 2. Building pots by coil, slab, and wheel
 3. Etching clay together; storage of unfinished greenware; changes
    in clay from plastic to leatherhard
 4. Metamorphosis of clay from wet through bisque state
 5. Slab building expanded; how, why, history
 6. Coil building expanded; how, why, history
 7. Wheel building; how, why, history
 8. Glaze preparation and application
 9. Form and volume; structural problems
10. Decoration and form; use of impressed and incised texture
11. Decoration and form; use of applique
12. Form and function; general
13. Form and function; handles
14. Form and function; lids

15. Form and function; spouts and lips
16. Engobes; contrasted with glazes, basic uses
17. Engobes; preparation and application
18. Post-test and review

In connection with some of the presentations, assignments of a general nature are made to the entire group. For example, following the first presentation each student must prepare ten pounds of clay for his own use. Following the second lecture each student must make a commitment about the first project on which he wants to work and about the method he will use. As each student enters the large group he receives a guide sheet to help him work through the presentation and an answer sheet for the diagnostic post-test given at the end of the session. The guide sheet he keeps for reference, but the answer sheet is turned in as he leaves the large group meeting. The test at the end of the presentation is given not as a grading device but for diagnosis to determine which students have not mastered the concepts which were the basis of the presentation. It also serves to diagnose the presentation itself.

The test is checked by the students so that they know the results immediately and can schedule themselves into the ceramics room at the proper time to work further if the test indicates this need. This procedure is feasible because a student gains very little by cheating on this kind of test. Because all of the work in the class is organized with behavioral objectives in mind and because the purpose of the large group is to cover information he will have to know in order to proceed, it is to his advantage to learn it there. If he does not, he will have to learn it at some later time in order to complete his projects. For example, if the student passes the test on clay mixing he can move ahead to mix his clay. But if he does not know this material, he still will have to go through it before he is able to mix clay. He will save time by learning the information during the large group presentation and he will not have learned it if he cheats on the post-test.

The test itself is presented on an overhead projector transparency, partly to save time and paper and partly to prevent the test becoming an item for trade. As students leave the room they receive a packet of information concerning the presentation for the following week. In a school which still must rely on units of credit for graduation, successful completion of the work in the large group results in one unit of credit.

In addition to being in the large group, which may have as many as 200 students, each student is scheduled into a smaller class with from 20 to 25 other students which meets once each week for at least one hour (three modules). Labs are also available and they are considered a part of the student's program, although they are not put into his schedule as such. Initially at least, each student may select the time from his unscheduled independent study time to attend labs as he needs them. Following the large group meeting the students use their time in one of the following ways:

1. If the diagnostic test reveals unclear understanding of the concepts being discussed, during the regular class meeting the student will be grouped with other members of the class who have the same problems. More intensive activities are conducted with this group in an attempt to bring about concept formation. The work is done in a problem-solving context in areas of the student's interest and, if it is not possible to arrive at the necessary behavior in this session, the student is scheduled into labs for further work. He must be able to exhibit the behavior within a given period of time. Some of the concepts are more complex than others but if it appears that he is not at all capable of attaining them, he is either rescheduled into the General Art course or dropped from the class—at least temporarily—until he can develop the competencies necessary for completion of his project.

2. If the student does demonstrate adequate understanding of the material, he may use either lab or class time to work on projects of his choice or on a class assignment if one was given. However, he must not only demonstrate understanding of the concepts being developed in the large group but he must also demonstrate his competencies in each part of the project on which he works. The number and the length of the lab periods in which he works are left to him with the following exceptions: (1) If he appears unable to manage adequately the use of his time despite his demonstrated competency he may be assigned to regular lab periods. (2) His interests may coincide with students from other classes and it would be to their mutual advantage to form a group which meets reularly to consider similar interests.

Each of the large group presentations represents a single "lesson." Some of these lessons are a necessary part of every unit of work or project a student would choose to do in ceramics. The concepts presented must become part of each student's repertoire of behaviors if he is to achieve any of his goals in the course. Some of the large group activities will be part of a student's project only if he and the teacher choose to include them, but they are included in the sequence of presentations in order to make the student aware of their existence in the mainstream of ceramics. These concepts should be part of his background even though he may not use them in his own work.

The nature of the large group requires that diagnosis (pre-test and post-test) be primarily verbal, although techniques such as making identifications from samples on slides or films make up a large part of the material as well. The packet of materials the student receives for each large group session includes a pre-test on the material, printed materials, charts, and so on to help him form the necessary concepts. A study sheet which is used during the large group presentation and an answer form for the post-test are included. Even after the student successfully completes the post-test for the large group, he is required to demonstrate his understanding when he has to apply the concepts in a project. The large group test is primarily verbal, but the pre-test for the lessons in his unit or project include both verbal and motor competencies.

STUDENT PROGRESS RECORDS

In order to keep a clear record of the student's progress with minimal clerical work for the teacher, the form shown in Figure 9.1 is used. When a student completes the post-test for the large group lesson satisfactorily, a vertical mark is entered in the box for that lesson as shown in boxes one through six. When he is not successful, no entry is made until he is. When he begins a project calling for that concept, a diagonal is entered as in boxes 1 through 6, 42, 44, and 46. If the project is completed successfully, another diagonal is entered which crosses the first, as shown in boxes 1, 2, 3, and 42. A record of the units attempted with the numbers of the component lessons are recorded.

When the unit is completed, the credit earned is recorded. The student is not given credit for doing a project in which he

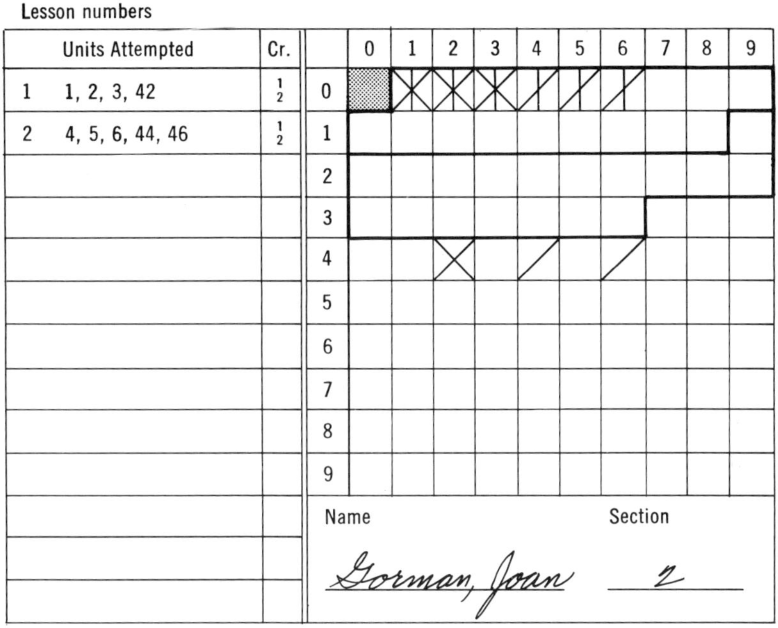

Lesson numbers

Units Attempted		Cr.		0	1	2	3	4	5	6	7	8	9
1	1, 2, 3, 42	½	0	▓	X	X	X	/	/	/			
2	4, 5, 6, 44, 46	½	1										
			2										
			3										
			4			X		/		/			
			5										
			6										
			7										
			8										
			9										

Name	Section
Gorman, Joan	*2*

Key: Vertical mark—Post-test completed (boxes 1–6)
One diagonal—Concept development (boxes 1–6, 42, 44, 46)
Two diagonals—Project completed (boxes 1, 2, 3, 42)

FIGURE 9.1
Student Progress Report (Individualized Instruction)

has already demonstrated total competency. Only by adding new skills or concepts to the project is it educationally acceptable. In beginning ceramics this might mean simply thinner walls, different blaze, or control of brushwork, but it is a new skill. Note that the first 18 boxes and the second set of boxes (19-36) are heavily lined. This indicates that these are basic lessons which must be covered by students to receive credit for the large group sessions.

Another helpful record-keeping technique is film. By photographing student progress, a good visual record is constantly available and helps remind the students of their own progress in a way that lesson numbers and marks in boxes do not. A permanent setting for photographing work is set up in the room, complete with floodlights and clearly legible name tags. Work in progress is photographed at critical points in the execution of the unit or at regular intervals and remains a permanent record of what has been accomplished. The photographs and the record of units are also used to keep each student's counselor informed of his progress.

The amount of learning accomplished by each individual student varies considerably and so does the amount of credit received for the course. Because the class activities are organized on behavioral principles, the grade received is the same for all students. If the objective for the lesson or the unit is accomplished, there is no quibbling over a rating scale. If the objective is not reached, work continues until it is. Thus, there is no penalty for a student who begins slowly but develops rapidly as he builds a repertoire of concepts, or for the student who gets off to a fast start but slides away into other areas of interest. They each receive the quality grade for the work completed and no grade at all for work not finished. Since students who fail in high school usually have a record of failure, they are often surprised and spurred by their own capabilities when they find that they will get a positive and concrete result in terms of a grade for whatever they do accomplish. The outstanding student who "wings his way along" above the crowd will get the same grade, but perhaps more credit.

Because of the large enrollment in ceramics and the use of the large group, there is always the danger of students feeling anonymous and unimportant. When the method in the large group is seen by students to be freeing them to be able to do more competent work of their own choice, this feeling begins to vanish. The study sheets used in the large group are designed as much as possible like self-instructional techniques so the student is aware that he has learned concepts that he can use immediately. The presentations are made as clear and interesting as possible through the use of various devices such as 8mm films, slides, and transparencies. These materials are available to students for review and also are used as the basis for some of the self-teaching instructional materials in lessons.

FACILITY UTILIZATION

The students have a feeling of belonging to the ceramics room which is enhanced by their personal storage areas that are clearly labeled with their names and are open for all to see. Some students turn these into personal display cases while others use them strictly as utilitarian devices. Having his own spot and having it open and unprotected is intended to help students learn responsibility not only for their own things but for those of others as well. Clay is handled on an individual basis for the same reason; there would always be hard feelings if students were assigned to prepare clay for others to use. Also, clay mixing and supervision can take almost all of the instructor's time if the students do not learn responsibility for preparing it themselves. The same is true of other tasks such as glaze preparation and kiln loading. If concepts about the necessity of certain procedures are not made part of the behavioral repertoire of students, then we are left with those situations in which the teacher is also a janitor and students feel no responsibility for general work unless they are ordered to do it.

Ideally, the ceramics facility is open throughout the entire school day for student use. This is another factor which makes students feel responsible for the room. They know they are always welcome there. In practice, however, some limitations must be imposed. The room can only hold so many people and there is only so much equipment available. Unfortunately, some restrictions regarding the use of the potter's wheels must be made. If students enter the ceramics lab while another regularly scheduled class is meeting, then they must understand that the people assigned there have priority on space and equipment. Other restrictions on room use may be made when the teacher or teacher aide is not available to offer adult supervision. Nevertheless, students need to feel free to use the ceramics room just as they need the experience of deciding when they will use it. The results of individualized projects and student-initiated activities is resounding proof that students can and do learn independently.

TEACHER SCHEDULES

The schedules of two teachers involved in the ceramics program are illustrated in Table 9.1 along with a schedule for the ceramics lab (Table 9.2). Both illustrations indicate the types of activities that may be undertaken. The course is taught by a team approach inasmuch as both teachers are involved in planning and in presenting the large group lessons. Each teacher has two sections of 25 students that meet once each week. Both teachers also supervise and work with students in labs, although teacher "B", because of his commitments in another class, has much less time in the ceramics lab than teacher "A".

CONCLUSION

The ceramics class, an in-depth course, makes use of what we know about the cycle of learning. In addition, through the use of carrier projects, behavioral objectives, the independent use of lab

TABLE 9.1

Ceramics Teacher "A"—Weekly Program in a Flexible Schedule

Modules[a]	Monday	Tuesday	Wednesday	Thursday	Friday
1		Conf			
2		Conf			
3		Conf	Prep	Prep	Prep
4		Prep			
5		Prep			
6	Conf	Lab	Cerm Lab		Cerm Lab
7	Conf	Lab	Cerm Lab	Adv Ceram	Cerm Lab
8	Prep	Lab	Cerm Lab	Adv Ceram	Cerm Lab
9	Ceram LG	Lab	Cerm Lab	Conf	Cerm Lab
10	Ceram LG	Lab	Ceram MG	Conf	Cerm Lab
11	Prep.	Lunch	Ceram MG	Lunch	Lunch
12	Lunch	Lunch	Ceram MG	Lunch	Lunch
13	Lunch	Ceram Lab	Lunch	Cerm Lab	Conf
14	Ceram MG	Ceram Lab	Lunch	Cerm Lab	Conf
15	Ceram MG	Ceram Lab		Cerm Lab	Conf
16	Ceram MG	Ceram Lab		Cerm Lab	Prep
17	Conf		Conf	Conf	Prep
18	Conf		Conf	Conf	Prep
19					
20					

[a] Periods of time—20 minutes in length

time by students, relevant large group sessions, and requested small group meetings, this organizational approach has made a beginning in truly individualizing instruction without sacrificing what appears to be the major goals of an art program. It is, admittedly, only a beginning. If all activities were individualized and placed in the context of life-functioning behaviors, the function of any grouping at all—even in terms of subject matter —would be unnecessary. Indeed, this is a distinct possibility. Cross-disciplinary courses such as Humanities I (discussed in Chapter 6) and some of the team approaches to art and industrial arts,

TABLE 9.1 (cont.)

Ceramics Teacher "B"—Weekly Program in a Flexible Schedule

Modules[a]	Monday	Tuesday	Wednesday	Thursday	Friday
1					Conf
2					Conf
3					Cerm Lab
4	Prep	Prep	Prep		Cerm Lab
5	Prep	Ceram MG			
6		Ceram MG			
7		Ceram MG		Prep	
8	Prep	Conf			Lab
9	Ceram LG	Ceram MG			Lab
10	Ceram LG	Ceram MG	Conf		Lab
11	Prep	Ceram MG	Conf		Conf
12	Lunch	Cerm Lab	Lunch		Conf
13	Lunch	Cerm Lab	Lunch		Conf
14		Lunch		Lunch	Lunch
15		Lunch		Lunch	Lunch
16	Conf	Prep	Conf	Conf	Conf
17	Conf		Conf	Conf	Conf
18	Conf		Conf	Conf	Conf
19					
20					

[a] Periods of time—20 minutes in length.

TABLE 9.2

Ceramics Lab Schedule

Modules[a]	Monday	Tuesday	Wednesday	Thursday	Friday
1					Open Lab
2					Open Lab
3					Open Lab
4	Open Lab				Cerm Lab
5	Open Lab	Ceram C1	Cerm Lab		Cerm Lab
6	Open Lab	Ceram C1	Cerm Lab		Cerm Lab
7	Open Lab	Ceram C1	Cerm Lab	Open Lab	Cerm Lab
8		Open Lab	Cerm Lab	Open Lab	Cerm Lab
9		Ceram C1	Cerm Lab	Open Lab	Cerm Lab
10		Ceram C1	Open Lab	Open Lab	Cerm Lab
11		Cerm Lab	Open Lab		
12			Open Lab		
13		Cerm Lab		Ceram Lab	Open Lab
14	Ceram C1	Cerm Lab		Cerm Lab	Open Lab
15	Ceram C1	Cerm Lab	Open Lab	Cerm Lab	Open Lab
16	Ceram C1	Cerm Lab	Open Lab	Open Lab	Open Lab
17			Open Lab	Open Lab	Open Lab
18			Open Lab		Open Lab
19					
20					

[a] Periods of time—20 minutes in length

or art and music, point out the difficulties encountered when we persist in compartmentalizing subject matter in neat categories. We find it difficult to think in terms of the unifying relationships between subjects. Furthermore, these programs are based on philosophic approach which allows a certain amount of time for art, so much for music, so much for history, and so on.

Task analyses made on the model that Woodruff has presented or some other model yet to be developed will help break down what are really artificial barriers between subjects—barriers which continue to keep life out of the school.[2] Perhaps what is needed is an approach to the whole problem of education based on the concepts developed by A. H. Maslow's Holistic-Dynamic Theory in the study of personality.[3] If such a condition were to occur the school could, in fact, become a "classless society." It is not outside the realm of immediate possibility to think in these terms within the art program, although setting up the program will take a good deal more organization than presently exists in the programs of most art teachers. Even on a flexible schedule, with an added load of students many teachers feel tremendously overburdened, primarily because their teaching approach is still a traditional one. In his visionary chapters dealing with education in A.D. 2001, Leonard talks about "educators" rather than "teachers" and describes their function as that of devising "learning environments" in which children come to learn as they wish.[4] An art program could be devised along these lines even with the primitive information and facilities we now have. Other disciplines may find it more difficult to enter into a totally individualized instructional program because our knowledge of how abstract learning takes place is still so limited and because the construction of the basic curriculum is therefore felt to be more difficult. Whether this is true is open to question, but, nevertheless, the nature of the activities in art lend themselves quite readily to the development of a more open curriculum.

A disadvantage emphasized by many critics of the idea of a classless school is that it will destroy the opportunities for social interchange and, more important, for intellectual stimulation from others. This need not be true if opportunity exists to get students together for discussion and work and if the atmosphere in the learning environment is such that it encourages exchange. The ability to exchange ideas and information and to gain from the experience of others is a learned one, and there seems to be no reson why that cannot be part of the built-in requirement of the learning environment of a school.

[2] *Ibid.*

[3] Abraham H. Maslow, *Motivation and Personality* (New York: Harper and Row, Publishers, 1954).

[4] George B. Leonard, *Education and Ecstasy* (New York: Delacorte Press, 1968).

Even where open curriculums have been tried in art (as in schools on flexible schedules), most of the teachers have been left in the traditional position of giving assignments and checking and grading completed work. Not until a complete battery of well-developed "carrier projects" based on behavioral objectives (or other techniques for individualizing curriculum content) is available can a whole curriculum be developed in the "unstructured" manner suggested here. Unless art teachers make greater efforts to prove the worth of their subject than they have done until now, such an effort will certainly come, but it will likely occur in the "basic education" areas of the curriculum such as language and mathematics rather than in art.

THE STUDENT AND
THE EDUCATIONAL SYSTEM

Part III of this book emphasizes several inter-related activities other than instructional which have a major impact upon the student as an individual and as a human being within the school as a complex social system. The major underlying theme of this section is simply that many traditional schools—schools in which all youngsters by law must spend a good part of their waking lives—are sterile, and dehumanizing institutions. Designed around a mid-Victorian philosophy concerning the youngster's lack of responsibility and need for control and conformity, most schools have created organizational constraints to individuality and petty humiliations to which students, with few exceptions, must submit in order to survive.

Students are seldom afforded opportunities for individual autonomy which will enhance the development of self-confidence, self-assurance, or responsibility of individual behavior. Free expression of ideas or legitimate and authentic interchange between students and school faculties are often limited or unnecessarily constrained. In general, the personal dignity of the student as a human being, as a member of a social institution that above all should value and respect individuality and human worth, is lacking. In many conventional school programs the student might legitimately say: "We are treated like second-class citizens in a school program that barely tolerates our existence."

Public schools and public school educators who are genuinely interested in developing more individualized educational systems must be cognizant of the clients whom the institution was designed to serve. Human individuality and personal dignity are the essential underlying considerations that require greater emphasis if schools, public or private, in this country are to create more humanizing and stimulating environments—environments designed for active, not passive, participation of youngsters in the school's program.

Several independent, yet interrelated, topics which in one way or another are oriented around the theme of creating greater student dignity and more humanizing as well as individualized school programs have been chosen for Part III of this book. In general the major concern is with the overall environment of the school from the perspective of the student as an individual and the effect of the school upon the student. Chapter 10 explores alternative strategies for allowing teenagers greater opportunities for schoolwide participation and the development of individual expression and responsibility. Most conventional secondary school characteristics such as homework, letter grades, and dress requirements have had considerable influence upon the conditioning and socialization of youth in our society. Unfortunately, we continue to perpetuate the importance of these myths in our schools year after year without analyzing their effect upon the learning process or without suggesting more appropriate alternatives. Chapter 10 also presents an alternative approach to the conventional guidance and counseling program found in most secondary schools, particularly as this has relevance to the individualization of student needs in order to provide services for those who require greater specialization. It is a major supposition of this section that the interpersonal relations between students and counselors in many conventional schools is viewed by the student as being contrived or unauthentic (in the student vernacular, "phony" behavior), and a reorganization of guidance and counseling functions can do a great deal to enhance better understanding and alleviate the frustrations, anxieties, and conflicts that prevail in many student bodies vis-à-vis the school and society in general.

Chapter 11 presents an empirical analysis of high school environment. Data from a typical suburban high school are reported by utilizing a broad-base socio-psychological instrument for assessing high school climate. This student-oriented questionnaire has proven to be an extremely useful tool in determining what students really feel about school life, the general school environment, and related school activities. It is also useful as a predictive device for analyzing many of the social and environmental problems experienced today in secondary schools due to hostile and anxious students reacting to a general social climate of frustration and unrest.

THE STUDENT: HUMANIZING
THE SCHOOL PROGRAM

10

Today we face the paradox of a confused, generally affluent, sometimes violent society condemning a [younger] generation for being confused, generally affluent and sometimes violent.[1]

Most conventional secondary schools are basically quite inhospitable places. Their atmospheres are more reminiscent, it seems, of some penal institutions than a place ostensibly devoted to learning and to the creative process. The cell-like self-contained classroom works to the detriment of both teacher and student in that it does not provide an atmosphere conducive to self-expression and authentic interaction. While there has been some progress in providing students and staff with a more hospitable environment in a few scattered secondary schools in this country, most high schools today are organized and function little different than those of a century ago. Essentially, the proposition in this chapter is quite simple: It is of little value for a school staff to expend considerable energy and effort in changing conventional school structures or to create more unique instructional programs without also devoting equal effort to changing conditions concerning student participation and involvement in the development of these programs.

Several pertinent questions may be asked in relation to this proposition: What is the typical secondary school really like from the perspective of the student? Does the conventional school organization impede the development of creative skills and individuality? Does the typical school environment provide for the student's needs in meeting the demands of a complex, rapidly changing society? It has been suggested by several critics of present-day

---

[1] Quoted from John E. Corbally, Jr., chancellor of Syracuse University, in a speech given to the Maxwell Review students, n.d.

school programs that there is a mismatching between the school's curriculum and the adolescent's life. The student, blocked from responsibility and productivity, is confined to a world of leisure, play, and academic consumption. He needs to have the opportunity for responsibility and authority, which would make academic achievements more relevant. But, if this change occurred, the school's present curriculum would still be inappropriate. It contributes to his irresponsibility by keeping him in a passive and subject-oriented status at a time when he needs to develop his capacity for responsible action.[2]

American culture has always been organized around active mastery rather than passive acceptance. Its peculiar genius is the development of manipulative skills rather than contemplative processes. Paradoxically, however, our contemporary society prizes creativity and those who possess it, even though we reserve our greatest admiration for the glories of mass production.

The conflict between more humane and liberalizing pursuits of man and the many dehumanizing aspects of our technological society is now one of education's most pressing concerns. Educators and the learning systems they design must account for both the quality of the human endeavor, as well as quantitative factors in our environment; for not merely man's production, but for the production of men who are free to create new images of freedom. The present conditions in most secondary schools denies the existence of this freedom. Students are bound to the arbitrary masters of time, control, and supervision. We channel students into archaic mazes that impede rather than expand their individuality and, consequently, their initiative and potential for creativity.

---

[2] For example, more recent critics of the American school system which offer excellent insights into the nature and treatment of adolescents in our schools are: Edgar Z. Friedenberg, *The Dignity of Youth and Other Atavisms* (Boston: Beacon Press, 1965); Edgar Z. Friedenberg, *The Vanishing Adolescent* (New York: Dell Publishing Co., 1959); A. S. Neill, *Summerhill* (New York: Hart Publishing Co., 1960). Norman Friedman, "The Schools and the Defeat of the Child" (unpublished article, n.d.).

The reader should also be aware of the following: Philip W. Jackson, *Life in Classrooms* (New York: Holt, Rinehart and Winston, Inc., 1968); Neil Postman and Charles Weingartner, *Teaching As A Subversive Activity* (New York: Delacorte Press, 1969); and Ryland W. Crary, *Humanizing the School: Curriculum Development and Theory* (New York: Alfred A. Knopf, 1969).

Students are pigeon-holed and categorized, ear-marked and compartmentalized into curricula and programs which offer few inherent opportunities for the development of significant inter-personal relations. To individualize and humanize the participation of students, schools must emphasize greater degrees of variation and flexibility, accommodating adolescent interests and competen-cies.

The majority of secondary schools are not oriented toward individualizing instruction or creating open avenues for student participation, although many of them claim to do so. The students act and react collectively; they are effectively conditioned to their environment and societal norms. The teacher may be the only real learner in the typical secondary school because he is often the only real active participant. Because of overly bureaucratized organizational structures, students, assigned as groups rather than as individuals, must conform to these patterned procedures so that—at least ostensibly—the majority can benefit. As a result, students become passive agents within the learning process.

Instructional materials are also not written to accommodate the individual in most schools. They are designed around the normative dimensions of the school in terms of accommodation to groups of students, uniform time patterns, and an undiffer-entiated teaching staff. Essentially, the total school system is a monolithic administrative convenience. For example:

> What kind of human individual experience does the school provide for a student who lacks an adequate reading background? Most commonly, the school structures him into a remedial reading course, which he often finds as defeating as any other course be-cause he still must compete for grades when he really lacks the training and encouragement necessary for real advancement. The argument is not with the tremendous current efforts of teachers but with the structure of the system. A remedial reading student in his remedial reading course still carries around his reading handi-cap with him to all his other classes. How do we justify our actions as human? How can we say we are freeing the student from his deficiency? The curriculum is not designed around the individual's needs. We only make the curriculum cumulative by adding on course after course to "enrich" or compensate for gaps in the already over-burdened structure.[3]

---

[3] Dwight W. Allen, "A New Approach to Individualizing Instruction," (unpublished paper, Stanford University, Stanford, California).

It is imperative that the organizational structure of the school not be anti-individually or anti-humanistically oriented. If the concepts of human recognition and individuality are important to our thinking in public schools, then the individual must not be lost in the instructional process and each student's integrity, uniqueness, and personal dignity must be recognized in the design of our educational systems. The student must be allowed the opportunity to develop certain levels of decision about his own education and his activities within the program of the school without needless coercion or threat from peer or adult.

THE STUDENT AS A CO-PARTICIPANT IN THE EDUCATIONAL ENTERPRISE

Typically, students in most secondary schools in this country have nothing to say about what they will learn, who will help them learn it, where they will work, or what materials they will use. The most important and crucial decisions about learning are made for the student by others. He is given little or no opportunity to participate in the instructional process. The development of any responsibility, even shared responsibility, by the adolescent for his own education is almost nonexistent in most school programs. The student is a passive agent and he is allowed very little opportunity to emerge as an active participant in the instructional or learning process.

The purpose of this section is to suggest briefly several interrelated themes and subsequent activities that may be undertaken in secondary schools for allowing teenagers greater participation in the instructional decision-making process. Consequently, we are intent upon finding alternative strategies which will provide teenagers with greater involvement in school-related functions and activities. These strategies must allow students some participation in educational decision-making and, therefore, provide situations for developing responsiiblity and self-initiative. It is assumed that opportunities for student self-expression and creativity will exist as instruction becomes more individually conceived and the atmosphere of the school is created with more open, anabolic climates. Alternatives must be developed to the arbitrary limitations conditioned by most traditionally oriented school programs.

DEVELOPMENT OF STUDENT RESPONSIBILITY

One objective of many schools in designing more flexible class schedules and concomitant independent study programs is to inculcate in each student a greater sense of responsibility for his own education. This is accomplished in part by creating a school situation where each student has some unscheduled or free time during the school day. With the implementation of these independent study programs, students are no longer supervised all day by teachers or other school officials; instead, they are given a good deal of freedom outside of the traditional classroom for making appropriate choices concerning activities and interests related to the school program.

Consequently, more varied school study facilities are developed along with a definitive independent study program so that most students can find some degree of success and achievement. The student is faced each school day with making decisions about the proper use of his time and the proper use of specialized study facilities which have been designed for independent and individualized use.

There are some decided advantages to this type of school organization in addition to the opportunity for allowing students self-initiated activities: (1) During their unscheduled time students may complete out-of-class assignments (homework) in appropriately designed school facilities and with the individual help of teachers. (2) Students may initiate unique interactions with other school personnel, for example, counselors, administrators, or the school psychologist, as well as developing informal activities with peers or teachers. (3) Greater opportunities are afforded for meaningful student-teacher contacts. The teacher can truly "individualize" instruction on a one-to-one teaching basis.

The accessibility and use of specialized, uniquely designed school facilities are essential in this type of program; the school library, instructional resource centers, open laboratories, teacher office and planning areas, and other unique study and student interaction areas are prerequisite to a successful involvement of the student in the school program.

In developing programs which allow students greater freedom for developing responsibility, the role of the teacher must change considerably. For complete success in independent study programs the teacher must be committed to the concept and willing to guide and direct the student when necessary. Initially, it will be necessary for the teacher to play a dominant, almost aggressive, role with students. Even though an opportunity is provided through independent study for teacher and student to meet frequently in a one-to-one relationship, this may not take place as often as it should unless the teacher provides direction for the student. It is generally recognized that many high school-age youngsters are often reticent to meet with teachers, particularly when help is needed. This is partly due to the fact that we have placed a negative connotation on the interaction between student and teacher in most conventional schools. When students meet with the teacher (generally after school), the inference has been that the student is in "trouble" or that some type of disciplinary action is necessary. Therefore, teachers must help students develop positive attitudes in respect to the proper use of independent study and the correct utilization of teachers. Initially, the teacher will direct the student in the independent study process; later, the student will assume the majority of the responsibility.

In schools designed for independent study and greater student involvement and participation, the anachronistic concept of "homework" must be conceived much differently by teachers, parents, and students than it is today in most schools. For those students who grasp the concept of individual responsibility and learn to utilize their unscheduled or independent study time wisely, it is possible for most of their homework (we prefer to call it out-of-class assignments) to be completed during the school day in study facilities designed for individualized work. Students are encouraged to do their out-of-class assignments at school where teachers, instructional resources, library, and other study facilities are at their immediate disposal. Parents who peruse the new math or other modern curricula will soon recognize that the traditional method of sending teenagers home with homework assignments is an archaic educational procedure.

Teachers must design their out-of-class activities differently than the traditional homework assignments given under conventional circumstances. These out-of-class assignments should be structured so that the student can make use of the school facilities designed for research and study. The whole concept of homework, as it is presently established in most traditional schools, needs close scrutiny by teachers and educators generally. Too often assignments are overly generalized rather than individualized; they are activities designed primarily for students to regurgitate information, copy redundant prose, or memorize unneccessary facts. Any useful out-of-class assignment, if it is really to be of value to the student's learning sequence, must be individually designed—an activity that helps him overcome some individual weakness or develop a needed skill. Unfortunately, most homework is actually teacher-contrived busy work. The rationale provided by many teachers when confronted with the purpose of homework is "that the student needs to develop good study habits in order to be better prepared for college." Unfortunately, the home is one of the least desirable places for developing significant study or learning habits, although this is seldom recognized by teachers in conventional school programs.

As school schedules become more open and flexible and as they become more capable of accommodating greater degrees of interaction among faculty and students, opportunities will emerge for professional staffs to evaluate and discard many of the anachronistic methods that permeate secondary schools. In turn, many assumptions held by the educational establishment concerning the ability of adolescents to accept responsibility for their own education and related learning processes will no longer be valid. If the school is to assist the student appreciably in the growth and maturation process, then it must find new and more appropriate methods of allowing students to exercise options for developing responsible behavior. Schools that have implemented independent study programs, have found that teenagers are capable and willing to accept greater initiative and responsibility for their education. They are capable of making significant decisions concerning learning activities and the instructional process.

THE STUDENT-FACULTY SENATE

The student-faculty senate or student-faculty board is another approach which has found some success in school programs in attempting to involve students in the learning process and to provide avenues for greater student participation. The purpose of this group is to generate open, frank discussion about concerns common to all participants—students and teachers—in the school. Initially, the senate is generally not a policymaking or governing body; it serves as an open forum for ideas, criticisms, and suggestions (involving any area of the school, instructional or noninstructional) and as a vehicle for conflict resolution among faculty, students, or other school groups. It can also serve as a viable mechanism for change in the instructional program of the school. Essentially, the student-faculty senate is an informal organizational mechanism. Its importance lies in its effort to foster communication between student and faculty at an organizational level. It can provide a functional and necessary link in the feedback network of the school as a complex social system. Thus, the senate provides not only necessary communication concerning issues and concerns vital to the well-being of the organization but also an opportunity for greater student participation and an open channel of interaction between student, professional staff, and school program.

In one school the student-faculty panel was composed of four students, one representing each class, and four faculty members, with representation distributed throughout various faculty groups. Any student in the school was eligible for membership on the student-faculty senate without developing any prior qualifications. Each class president was responsible for recommending one student to the panel and final responsibility for appointment rested with the student body president. Correspondingly, any faculty member was eligible for membership on the panel. Final selection was determined by a faculty election.

> It should be reemphasized that the Board is a "hang-loose" organization. Hopefully, it will be as flexible and informal as possible. The Board will not make formal policy; instead it will be a place for discussion and feedback. Matters such as the effects of the dress code, student behavior and attitudes, curriculum, large group lecture facilities, or the module system in general are just a few topics that could be discussed. The Student-Faculty Board's discussions, and any agreements or conclusions, will be made public. Perhaps action will be encouraged by some conclusions the Board may reach.[4]

---

[4] Claremont High School Faculty Handbook, 1968-69, Claremont, California.

The student-faculty senate is conceived initially as an informal, nonpolicymaking body. This does not preclude the possibility, with time and continued interaction and sophistication of the concept, that this group could be included in the formal decision-making structure of the school. At least the administrative and policymaking mechanism within the school should give considerable recognition to the suggestions and recommendations that come from this group.

Several activities were developed for student participation in one innovative high school intent upon creating as many functional opportunities as possible for student involvement in the instructional process and administration of the school. In this regard, the following is of interest:

> . . . The principal presented a summary of the involvement of students at different levels in school affairs. In addition to their taking part in student body affairs, there are eight students on the student-faculty board, . . . students on the instructional council, chief policy making body of the school; two students on the teacher evaluation committee; six groups of six students each on the pre-accreditation committee, and 25 students to be selected for the accreditation committee.
>
> Also, there are two students on the committee to draw up a profile for a new superintendent, two on the committee developing a family life and sex education program, a student school board observer and two students attending Parent-Faculty Association board meetings.
>
> Students are also involved in community affairs, in the Youth Commission which is serving in an advisory capacity to the city council, and in Youth Councils of the . . . Community Coordinating Council and the . . . Council of Churches.[5]

STUDENT PARTICIPATION IN INSTRUCTIONAL CHANGE

Much has been written recently concerning the pressing need for differentiated levels of decision-making opportunities in educational institutions. Most of this dialogue has been aimed at exploring the relationship of decision-making among the administration, the teaching staff, or, in a few cases, the community. In most instances, however, the student has not been included in this rhetoric.

Prudent and successful administrators would not consider

---

[5] Editorial, *The Claremont Courier* (October 25, 1969).

introducing a change proposal or instructional innovation into their schools without first consulting and carefully working out the details of the plan with their staffs in order to introduce and implement the change properly. Many would admit that any change would find little success if staff participation were not accomplished. Yet, we generally fail to include the students in our preparations, and this failure constitutes one of the major errors made in attempting to bring about significant organizational change in schools. We fail to allow for student participation in our planning, and then, when the innovation fails as many inevitably will, our invariable first tendency is to blame the students for this failure.

Schools entertaining organizational or instructional changes must be cognizant of the importance of allowing student participation and involvement during the critical stages of program development. Several activities can be undertaken with student groups in these situations. A few are suggested here:

1. Students should be included in the planning of any innovation or change in the school's program; in fact, representatives of the student body should be allowed to attend faculty discussions concerning the proposed change. The students invited to participate in the planning and discussions should also represent a full range of interests and abilities, from academic to non-academic. From this type of participation can come commitment, and, if any significant change to the school is to succeed, the students' commitment is as vital for success as the faculty's.

There exists a tendency in the "conventional wisdom" in education that a school should hide planning sessions from students. This stems in part from an idea that the inner workings of the school are none of the students' business or that students are not mature enough or sensible enough to provide significant input concerning the proposal under consideration. This is an unnecessary and extremely detrimental attitude if fostered by the "power structure" in any educational institution. Most teenagers are more mature and more capable of offering significant suggestions in enhancing and improving their school program than many administrators and teachers are willing to admit. Most people who work closely with students marvel at the degree of perception and insight they possess concerning school organization and instructional programs.

2. Some schools that have implemented such significant changes in their schools as flexible scheduling or team teaching programs have established student advisory councils (similar in nature to the student-faculty senate) that work closely with the professional staff during the planning period. This group, representing a cross-section of the student body, can provide meaningful input and feedback from the students concerning the change under consideration.

3. Once a decision is made to implement a specific instructional change, it is imperative that the professional staff include the students in planning for new skill developments that will be required in order for the program to succeed. In developing an independent study program, for example, it might be necessary for a staff to prepare the students with more sophisticated library or study skills prior to the implementation of the program.

4. In addition to the acquisition of some basic skills germane to the change about to be instituted is the necessity for student involvement and understanding relevant to significant behavioral and attitudinal changes. Again, one of the serious errors made by schools implementing independent study has been underestimating the amount of time it takes for these behavioral changes to take place.

The wise use of independent study time requires both a willingness to accept responsibility and a certain maturity in the student's outlook. After years of experience in an educational system which denies the student the opportunity for either, these will not come easily or quickly. It is not uncommon to hear a principal comment, after two or three months of experience with flexible scheduling or independent study, "I can't understand it. Our students are still wasting much of their time." In fact, it may take two or three years to undo what has been done in traditional schools for many years, in order for positive behavioral and attitudinal changes to manifest themselves as we would like to see them.

To provide the student a climate where he can become acquainted with responsibility and greater school participation, where he can truly begin to mature, requires that we grant him the right to make mistakes. This privilege, while frequently afforded the adult population in our society, is often considered taboo among the youth, particularly when it has to do with success at school. There is no better institution in our society for trial and error than the public secondary school. The individual student will never have as much supervision, and as much direction and assistance, again in his lifetime as he is given in the typical school. Why not provide students with the tremendous learning potential that can come from making mistakes and errors in their explorations throughout a school's program. Independent study and the opportunity it creates for developing individual responsibility is an unique experience in which the student can fail or experience degrees of failure in terms of his decisions about the use of time without suffering adverse consequences to his school program generally.

5. Maturity and responsibility cannot be taught to anyone; they can only be learned over a period of time and through trial and error experiences. Some traditional schools (often prior to the implementation of a flexible schedule) have given their students an advance taste of responsibility by issuing honor passes while their traditional schedule was still in effect. Or, a school that may never adopt any type of innovation on a grand scale could still implement a limited independent study program for some of its students on certain days of the week in specific subject areas.

6. In terms of planning and participation, students can be and should be allowed greater opportunities to visit other schools where a given innovation or unique instructional practice is already being conducted. We see squads of teachers and administrators visiting from school to school, but seldom is the same opportunity afforded the student in order for him to gain a glimpse of the world outside of his classroom.

7. Schools entertaining a future implementation of flexible scheduling might experiment by shortening the periods of each school day during the last semester of traditional operation. If each period were cut by ten minutes, time would be gained which could be used at the end of the day to give the students an opportunity to study independently or to work with faculty members in small informal groups. This activity could be valuable both as an opportunity for teachers and students to talk about upcoming changes

and as an opportunity for the staff to explore student feelings about the change.

Whatever approaches are tried, it is vital that we not lose sight of the student in our planning and that we attempt to allow students as many opportunities as possible for participation on a substantive level in the operation and implementation of instructional programs. We have a far greater ally in our students when considering school-related changes than we have yet realized. Recognition of the student as an important human entity in an essentially humanizing institution can become an important factor in implementing strategies for change and program development.

STRATEGIES FOR STUDENT INVOLVEMENT IN SCHOOL PROGRAMS

Considered here will be two functions which are found in all high schools and in which significant changes can be made for providing greater student involvement and for creating a more humanistic school atmosphere. These functions are: (1) the traditional activities associated with the assigning of rewards and punishments in the form of letter grades, and (2) dress regulations and other artificial restrictions inflicted upon students. Inasmuch as these have been concerns to many high schools in recent years, it seems that they can serve as relevant strategies for inculcating a greater sense of student involvement and participation in the school's program. This assumes, of course, that the school is capable and willing to allow students the degree of latitude and flexibility necessary to function appropriately within these areas. This section will present programs and techniques which have been employed in a few innovative schools for providing greater latitude and freedom of expression in these areas of the school's program.

GRADING PROCEDURES—THE PASS–FAIL SYSTEM

One factor that is extremely important in the process of individualizing instructional programs is to use achievement, rather than time spent in class or in a specific course, as the criterion for educational progress and evaluation. One of the greatest concerns in any school that seriously considers the implementation of any type of individualized instruction is the assigning of grades. It immediately becomes apparent that the traditional and anachronistic method of letter grades (A, B, C, D, F), which are common practices in most school systems, is no longer applicable to a truly individualized form of instruction.

Present methods of evaluation and the assignment of letter grades leave too many unanswered questions about a student's learning development. "What skills are required by the time they graduate? How do secondary schools measure, besides the learning content of a course, a student's social develoment? What about his increasing ability to learn? What is the standard of value for measuring this elusive quality? How do secondary schools measure a student's ability to make decisions—one of the most important functions of a civilized man?"[6] Whatever concerns we may have, our preoccupation must be with student performance and the functional and operational methods for evaluating student performance. *Performance* is the execution of the functions required of a person and the exhibition of a skill or learned behavior. A *criterion* is the standard of judging and the measure or test of quality of performance expected. As discussed earlier in this text, performance criteria are essential to significant evaluation and measurement of student achievement and learning development. Establishing performance criteria for secondary schools is not necessarily just a curriculum problem but a problem involved in determining schoolwide objectives and in establishing more humanistic considerations.

Unfortunately, it is likely that secondary schools will continue for some time to place emphasis upon what the student knows—factual information and its attainment—in any given subject area and they will continue to grade the student accordingly. Grades will continue to determine the student's progress and advancement in school and in society generally. It is hoped that these grading practices would eventually attempt to evaluate and indicate individual performance. Actually, grades, as they are presently constituted in many school programs, are seen more as obstacles along the educational path than as a significant educational yardstick. If too many students fail, we lower our grading standards. Thus, the grading system becomes arbitrary and super-

---

[6] Allen, *op. cit.*

ficial and, too frequently, a meaningless criterion of student ability, performance, or achievement in any given subject area. Secondary schools need a grading system which is more conductive to individual student achievement and progression as determined through criteria of performance.

In lieu of a full-blown and completely developed system for evaluation and the measurement of individual student performance, many schools—secondary as well as universities and colleges —have turned to an interim technique which is proving to be successful. The remainder of this section will be devoted to the rationale and application of pass–fail grading systems which are being adopted in more progressive schools in an attempt to combat the problems associated with letter grades as they are presently employed.

Do letter grades produce pressure on students rather than encourage meaningful learning? In place of the present arbitrary hierarchical grading structure, is a pass–fail system more appropriate and an improvement to present-day school programs? Can we divert our emphasis from the acquisition of "good grades," almost for the sake of grades, and emphasize the more significant aspects of the learning process? Some schools have attempted to answer these and other questions related to traditional grading practices by adopting the pass–fail method of grading.

The teachers of these schools attempt to determine what attitudes toward learning students will develop once the pressure of grades is removed. It is not sufficient for students to master the fundamentals of mathematics and science; they must also organize these essentials so that they become tools in the solution of problems that will be encountered later in life. The ability to "apply" is seldom assessed through traditional grading schemes. It is not so much a matter of how many problems a student can solve in an hour-long examination, but whether he has the persistence and disciplined thinking that allows him to use the tools he has acquired in solving other problems later on. The problem is not the assessment of quantities of knowledge but the capability to assess qualitative factors and the student's ability to apply what he has learned. This measurement is difficult in secondary schools when the only yardstick available for evaluation is the typical A, B, C system of grading.

It has been suggested that the obsession with "good grades" has become a harmful classroom disease, and many educational institutions in this country are afflicted. In 1964 a team of professors from the University of Utah Medical School made a survey of doctors in which the following relationship between professional success and college grades was found:

> There is almost no relationship between the grades a student gets in medical school and his competence and success in medical practice. Poor medical students—that is poor grade-getters—may in some instances, become good doctors, while some who get high grades in school may become poor doctors.[7]

This information astounded the research team involved in the study. They considered it a "shocking finding" to a medical team who spent their professional lives selecting applicants for admission to medical school on the basis of grades. This caused the team to question seriously the adequacy of grades not only in selecting those who should be admitted but also in measuring a student's progress through the program.

A similar study was also conducted at Columbia University when 342 medical graduates were polled to determine their success several years after completing their diplomas:

> Those who had graduated from college with honors, who had won scholastic medals, who had been elected to Phi Beta Kappa, were more likely to be in the lower professional performance levels than in the top levels.

> . . . .

> Why should this be? For one thing, some subjects in both surveys undoubtedly were superior scholars but poor performers. They scored high in theory, but when they got out of school and sat at the table of real life and the chips were flung down they couldn't play the game very well.

> Besides these impractical academicists, however, it's certain that many had been brainwashed with that pernicious modern myth: the belief that school grades are of supreme importance. They had so devoted themselves to getting high marks (some students constantly scheme, cheat and argue with teachers to get them) that they didn't take enough interest in what they were studying.

> It's a sad fact that most parents and school people have placed mere grades instead of education upon a pedestal; and in the worship of these symbols education is forgotten and harmed by neglect.

---

[7] Richard Reynolds, "The Obsession with Good Grades Can Be A Harmful Classroom Disease," *The Los Angeles Times* (September 8, 1966).

The inadvertent brainwashing of children so that they will worship grades begins early and continues strongly in the home and school. Besides having his parents and everyone else he knows hammer the idea of grade-getting into him, a youngster finds the same overstress on grades in school.

John Holt, author of "Why Children Fail," who interrupted his teaching career to observe a classroom of 10-year-olds in action for one year, reached this conclusion: Current school methods destroy the love of learning by encouraging students to work for petty rewards—gold stars, or papers marked 100 pinned to the wall, or A's on report cards or names on honor rolls and dean's lists; in short, for "the ignoble satisfaction of feeling they are better than someone else."[8]

Parents who go to extremes in demanding high grades often put frightful pressures on their children. Some children crack under the pressure. Student suicides are not uncommon among students who cannot meet the demands expected of them. The grading pressure in college is carried over with devastating effect upon the high schools of this country, making the college preparatory programs even more stringent and arbitrary. And as the population explosion puts pressures on the colleges, admissions standards based on grades are raised higher and competition becomes more intense. It makes one wonder if the day is not near when all collegians will be scholastic robots, devoid of color, humor, and originality, trained for only one thing—obtaining high grades.

So far the greatest resistance to overemphasis on grades has come from the college student. A large segment of the college population is conscious of the ridiculousness of this idol worship; probably most of them have been subconsciously aware that grades are not nearly as important as parents, teachers, and other school leaders tend to believe. Many college students cope with the pressure of good grades by cheating on examinations. The publicity received by the Air Force Academy a few years ago is ample evidence of the extent to which students will go when required to obtain recognition through grade accomplishments. This indicates an inevitable reaction to the absurd worship of grades and the educational system that perpetuates them. In recent years many students have indicated the artificiality of this system and

---

[8] *Ibid.*

the dissatisfaction with it. The competition for grades and degrees leaves the student with little time for scholarship or learning for the sake of learning and enjoyment. One student protested: "I'm so sick of grades I'm ready to quit. I can no longer enjoy a good book. If it's not a book required in a course I'm taking, I don't have time to more than skim through it. If it's required reading I can't enjoy it because the back of my mind keeps trying to figure out what the instructor will ask in order to grade me."

Some schools and educators are attempting conscientiously to develop alternatives to the traditional approaches to grading and the consequences that they have created. Classroom tests and mid-term examinations may be given but there are no grades recorded as such. Instead, a final grade of "P" (pass) or "F" (fail) is given. One educator indicated that students often "maintain status and self-esteem in the form of high grade point averages, often to the extent that the grades, rather than learning, become a major preoccupation." Under a pass–fail grading program it is hoped that students will concentrate on their studies and not the external, artificial rewards given in the form of letter grades.

PASS–FAIL GRADING: A CASE STUDY

In most secondary schools students have many opportunities to enroll in courses that are not included in their required program or major area of interest. Frequently, these courses (generally referred to as electives) are not selected by the student because he is fearful of jeopardizing his scholastic record or he is concerned about the possible failure in an unfamiliar task. It is an unfortunate fact that many parents and educators have so emphasized the importance of high grades instead of educational achievement that significant processes of learning are often neglected. Because of this fact and other equally important educational concerns, several teachers in one large suburban high school became interested in teaching certain selected classes on an experimental basis completely disassociated from the external reward of the letter grade. An experimental pass–fail grading system was recommended to and adopted by the Board of Education in this school system in order to explore the possible alternatives in grading practices.

As an example of the possible activities that can be conducted in secondary schools, the following constitutes the regulations for this program and a list of courses that were included:

1. *Regulations for the Pass–Fail Program:*[9]

   a. This is an optional program for both student and teacher. No student is required to use the pass–fail grade unless he volunteers for the program. Also, no teacher is required to employ it unless he feels it will benefit his course of instruction. Thus, two separate grading systems will prevail concurrently:

     (1) The conventional A, B, C, D, F grading system, and

     (2) The optional pass–fail grading system.

   b. Students will be accepted for the pass–fail grading program on the following basis:

     (1) The course in which the pass–fail grade is elected cannot be required for graduation or college entrance. Thus, only those courses considered to be electives will be allowed to employ the pass-fail grade. The student and his counselor will determine the student's elective course or courses. It is possible that a math or foreign language course will be considered an elective for some students.

     (2) Students enrolled in six or more courses including PE may elect pass–fail in any or all elective courses over and above the fifth course:

        6 courses—1 pass–fail course

        7 courses—2 pass–fail courses

        8 courses—3 pass–fail courses

        9 courses—4 pass–fail courses[10]

     A student with only five courses may select one pass-fail course if he has the written approval of the Director of Guidance in addition to the other required signatures.

     (3) Some junior and senior students who are enrolled in fewer than six courses will be allowed to take more than one elective on a P–F basis if their graduation and college admission requirements have already been met.

     (4) The student must have approval from his teacher, counselor and parent. A pass–fail contract will be entered into by the

---

[9] Extracted in part from material describing a program developed in Claremont High School, Claremont, California during 1967-68. See also, John M. Haskell, "Pass-Fail? A System Worth Trying," *The Clearing House* (November, 1967).

[10] This high school had previously implemented a flexible schedule which allowed all students to be enrolled in at least seven or eight courses, and it was not uncommon to find students enrolled in as many as nine courses during any given semester.

student in which all signatures are required. The pass–fail contract may be obtained from any teacher participating in the P–F grading program.

(5) The student must indicate his decision to employ the pass–fail grade to his teacher by the end of the first week of the semester with the counselor and parent approvals to be obtained by the end of the third week.

c. In recording credit for the course in the student's records the following rules shall apply:

(1) Course title and grade received (either "P" or "F") are recorded.

(2) Neither the "P" or "F" grade will be computed in the student's grade point average.

(3) Full credit toward graduation is received for a "P" grade; no credit is received for an "F" grade, but the "F" grade will be entered in the student's records.

d. Approval for employing the pass–fail grade must be initiated by the student at the beginning of each semester. Approval from the teacher, counselor, or parent to use the pass–fail grade in any particular course during the Fall semester does not automatically guarantee approval for the same course during the Spring semester. At the end of each semester the student's progress under the pass–fail system will be evaluated and further approval granted for subsequent semesters based on the recommendation of teacher and counselor.

e. Students will have the option of changing the courses in which the pass–fail grade is employed from one semester to the next.

f. Students may participate in the pass–fail grading program only if they enroll in a course or courses that incorporate the P–F grading system (see section 2). Due to the extensiveness of scheduling, students will not be reprogrammed into courses employing the P–F grading system during the school year.

2. *Courses Incorporating the Pass–Fail Grading System:*

English	Journalism	English Literature
	Speech	Modern Literature
	Creative Writing	World Literature
	Corrective Writing and Speaking	Art of the Film
		Library Science
	Advanced Placement	
Social Sciences	History of World Religions	History of Africa
	Philosophy	History of Political Theory
	Humanities	Economics
	Directed Readings	Contemporary Affairs
	History of the Impact of the West on East Asia	

Mathematics	Division II Math	Advanced Senior Math
	Intermediate Algebra	Calculus
	Probability & Statistics	Logical & Critical
	Trig & Analytic	Thinking
	Geometry	Math Projects
	Consumer Math	(Individual)
		Computer Program-
		ming
Science	Biology ICM	
Art	All Art Courses	
Music	Girl's Glee	
	Mixed Chorus	
	Music Theory	CHS Band
	Music and Art	Stage Band
	Appreciation	Varsity Band
	String Orchestra	Orchestra
Drama	All Drama Courses	
Business Education	Typing I	Consumer Economics
	Intermediate Typing	Record Keeping
	Business Typing	Data Processing
	Shorthand I	General Business
	Driver Education	Bookkeeping I
	Work Education	Business Machines
Homemaking	All Homemaking Courses	
Industrial Education	All Industrial Education Courses	
Foreign Language	All Foreign Language Courses	

Teacher Evaluation and Recommendations. At the end of the first year an extensive evaluation was conducted by the teaching staff concerning the effectiveness of the pass–fail grading system. In reviewing the teachers' responses there was no question that all teachers involved in the initial pilot program were exceptionally positive concerning the success of the program and the educational potential of a pass–fail grading system. Several of the questions are given here with representative remarks from the participating teachers.

1. *Do students profit from participation in certain courses in which they are motivated to learn through means other than the conventional letter grade?*

   "Definitely Yes . . . particularly in courses designed to encourage creativity and innovation . . . where a 'grade' evaluation of a student's work could act as a discouraging element."

   "not certain courses but all courses."

   "Yes, because the motivation comes from a true desire other than a grade which is in reality an artificial motive. There is freedom to explore and widen the student's horizons."

2. *What are some techniques of motivating students to learn when the student is not striving for a conventional letter grade?*

Several teachers indicated that they employed the "same techniques as in the conventional grading system." Others particularly stressed:

"encouraging interest and pride in the student's work."

"imparting to student's your own enthusiasm for the subject."

"letting students see that areas of study are creative rather than competitive or required"

"have students realize that what they get out of a course is a result of their choice."

"touching on that personal motivation—the desire to know"

3. *What courses lend themselves to pass–fail grading (and what courses do not)?*

"all courses, unless there is a problem with college entrance"

"all electives—any course not required for college entrance"

"any and all courses—the hang-up is elsewhere (with records, colleges, etc.), as you know"

"courses which provide students with avenues of expression without fear of censure—courses which students now avoid through fear of failure."

"It's more the students who may or may not lend themselves to pass–fail than the course. I can't think of a course that wouldn't be appropriate as long as teachers and students have the right attitudes."

4. *From your experience this year, is it possible to have students in a course who are to be graded on a pass–fail basis while other students are working for a letter grade?*

5. *Can students be successfully included in courses when the student is participating purely out of interest or need and not eager to achieve a letter grade?*

To these two questions all responses from the participating teachers indicated that there was no problem whatsoever in having mixed groups. In many instances students who opted for the pass–fail grade were more highly motivated and accomplished better work than the letter-grade students. This indicates that self-motivation is after all the best method for stimulating students to achievement rather than external symbolic rewards.

6. *Has the inclusion of your particular course on the pass-fail system affected other courses in your department, or other departments in*

the school, which were not included in the pass–fail experiment this year?

From the teachers' responses, there is little to indicate that a pass–fail grading system in some courses or departments of the school greatly affected other curricular areas where there is as yet little enthusiasm for this program.

In summarizing the preceding evaluations from the teachers who experimented with the pass–fail system in this school the comments of one English teacher are offered as being indicative of the attitude of teachers concerning the necessity of finding alternative solutions to the conventional grading procedures.

The longer I teach the more aware I become of the basic cruelty and inaccuracy of grades. I have heard stories from many students which confirm this. Parents often give harsh punishment for low grades, lavish monetary rewards for high grades, all of which furthers the childs hate and distrust of prodding parents, judgmental teachers, and of the educational system which encourages such unfairness and superficiality. I have had students beg me, in tears, to raise their grades in order to avoid disciplinary action from parents. When I was unable, in good conscience, to do this, they began to regard me as another policeman rather than as an educator. Further, they would often refuse help rather than be branded as "dumb."

Another insidious result of grades is that they discourage free, independent, and creative thinking. Students soon learn what each teacher considers "right" and "wrong" and tells the teacher "what he wants to hear" rather than what the student really thinks or feels. The whole purpose of education is defeated here. So-called "bright students" are often merely memorizers and yes-men, "dull students" who are not bright enough or willing enough to play the game become hostile and distrustful. Thus, grades do not reflect the real abilities or interests of students.

My final point is that we are living in a society which inflicts on its members—adult and child—tremendous pressure to conform in order that they may reap its material rewards. Yet at what a cost! Children are pressured in grade school to learn and "get ahead" (get A's and B's) and be "well adjusted" ("fit in and don't cause trouble") so that they will get good grades in high school. In high school they must conform, study, keep quiet, and stick to the dress code so they can go to college. In college, though by this time the spirit has usually been crushed out of them, they study and cheat and cram so they can get a "good job." At no point in this robotized process have the student's feelings, interests or talents been mentioned, not to speak of any real *learning*. The prize at the end is money—not knowledge. It is for this that students are expected to slave quietly—beginning at six years of age! Colleges and graduate schools do not consider IQ, nor recommendations from teachers, nor test scores as gravely as they do grades. One has only to look at the face of a student as he scans his report cards or begins an exam to sense the degree of pressure he is under. School is universally hated by youth—liked only as a source of social contact. Why not? It has been associated with coercion and fear from the beginning.

Participating Students' Evaluation. A survey was also conducted by the students who participated in the pass–fail grading program. In addition to the grading experiment itself, one of the important "by-products" obtained from this exercise was the degree of student involvement and participation that was aroused in the general student body of the school. The student survey was initiated, developed and written, and conducted by the students with little direction from the professional staff of the school. The grading program was presented in such a way so that it became *their program,* as well as the teachers involved in it. Students were involved in all planning and implementation phases of the grading system, and, as much as possible, feedback concerning the effectiveness of the program from the perspective of the student was obtained. Essentially, it was a student experiment as well as a faculty experiment.

Responses in this survey polled from the students concerning the effectiveness of the grading system are given in the following data:

1. The percentages indicate the students' responses to the question concerning the number of courses a student should be allowed to take on a pass–fail basis.

0 courses	3.5%
1 course	5.7%
2 courses	21.0%
3 courses	8.0%
4 courses	6.0%
No limit	55.7%

2. Indications to the question concerning the amount of effort pass–fail students felt they were putting into their course as compared to the effort they thought they would have made under the conventional grading (A–F) system.
   They felt they worked:

Less	19.8%
Slightly less	17.3%

Same	60.5%
Slightly harder	2.7%
Harder	0.0%

Generally, students interpret "effort" as meaning "work accomplished" on assignments for a class. Hence, 37.1% of the pass–fail students felt they were doing fewer "normal" class assignments than they would have done under the conventional grading system. However, most students felt they had maintained comparable effort as they would have under the conventional grading system.

3. This represents responses from students concerning the value which pass–fail students felt they were deriving from their course as compared to the value they would have anticipated under the conventional grading system.

Less value	4.2%
Slightly less	1.4%
Same	62.5%
Slightly more	8.3%
More	23.6%

Thus, 31.9% of the pass–fail students felt they were receiving more from the course than they would have under a conventional grading system.

4. Responses to the question concerning the reasons why students decided to use the pass–fail option.

Student responses fell under three categories:
1. Wished to relieve the pressure of letter grades   43.8%
2. Felt they would enjoy the course more under pass–fail   35.6%
3. Were curious about pass–fail and its effects   11.0%

Finally, this survey also revealed that of the students who expressed opinions about the advantages and effectiveness of the pass–fail grading system, 90% of these students were positive in their attitudes regarding the potential benefit of this grading system.

STUDENT DRESS AND STUDENT BEHAVIOR

One of the most prevalent and insidious myths pervading the educational community to which many school administrators ascribe is the notion that standards of student dress and standards of student behavior and achievement have a close correspondence or are, indeed, synonymous. At this writing the author is unaware of any research studies or any other even superficial evidence which would support this pernicious contention. (We are so prone in secondary education to inflict adult value judgments in the name of "good" education upon teenagers.) Rather, there is considerable evidence from a few progressive schools and a few courageous educators to indicate, in fact, that the relationship between student dress and student behavior is indeed fallacious.

This section will report, summarily, the activities conducted in one high school when the traditional dress code was eliminated by the school administration and the creation and enforcement of dress standards were handed over to the student body through their elected officers for monitoring. This type of activity seems appropriate and consistent with the general theme of providing avenues by which students can gain greater involvement and participation in secondary school programs. In conducting an experiment of this nature it was not particularly surprising to this school administration and faculty to find that the students were completely competent and mature in their treatment of the dress code situation.

The students' statement of a rationale for change, the level of maturity in evidence in handling the problems and procedures for developing and implementing a new program, and the establishment of a student court, controlled and operated by students, for enforcing the new dress standards were ample evidence that they can be successfully included in the operational and decision-making levels of a school program.

The Students' Rationale for Change. Not long ago students won strong support in Grand Rapids, Michigan, when 250 teenagers walked out of class in protest against a ban on mustaches. Similar incidents have happened all over the country. This year (1967-68), administrators, parents, teachers, even youth itself, are split over where to draw the line on school dress and grooming. Accordingly, for values to remain relevant, they must be able to stand the test of challenge. The challenge is hereby presented, along with a workable alternative. It is not intended to be "the answer." Rather, an attempt is being made to express the feelings of those students who seriously question the relevance of the prevailing dress code. If the current values cannot meet this or any challenge, workable alternatives must be sought quickly.

Institutions are by nature conservative. They change more slowly than the conditions they serve. When this happens, pressures build up, changes are made to fit the new conditions, and a period of stability follows. Most high schools do this sort of thing almost annually. The dress code is reviewed and some changes may be made. Only, it is the "code" itself which is hopeless. It never closes the style gap; it is always a little behind. Moreover, there is never real stability. Constantly changing rules, in fact, tend to produce confusion and insecurity. Therefore, current conditions demand a change which will be wide enough to solve current problems and flexible enough to lend stability for a longer period of time.

Furthermore, the current dress code is very detailed. From head to toe it covers "acceptables" and "not acceptables." All of the "acceptables" and "not acceptables" tend to make one feel regimented and even alienated. In addition, detail is often its own destroyer as inherent inconsistencies arise.

Although the question of students' dress and grooming may appear to be trivial, the consequences to the students are not trivial. Acts of individualism often lead to physical and mental harassment, even when those acts are within the bounds set by the current code; furthermore, students are being threatened with suspension if they do not comply with the code. More and more, the dress code appears not only expedient but absurd.

Detailed, expedient codes are absurd because they are inconsistent with the goals of the school and education. A code needing constant revision and subjective detailing is only a form of expediency. It makes minor adjustments to please students, temporarily, but never does it hold relevance to students with an overall view of school and its place in education. Some students today are searching for true human values and sometimes arbitrary regulations obstruct this search. After all, these expressions of self-identity in the form of dress are important to the student and harmless to the world. By setting standards for "the proper atmosphere of education," the school has made certain people "acceptable" and certain people "unacceptable." The school then imposes upon students anything but true human values.

Non-essential things, absurd things, get in the way of education. Education is to overcome ignorance, narrow mindedness, and prejudice. It is to discover, understand, and communicate with people. This means, in a more specific sense, it is to overcome shallow symbols, such as clothes, that get attached to people. This, the clothes-symbol, is what has relevance to students.

In the context of education, freedom of dress and freedom of thought are interlocked. Freedom of dress is the outward manifestation of freedom of thought. Freedom of thought was hardly shown in the hair-cutting incident in the last school year. Instead, intolerance was expressed. It was an intolerance bred by the code and by our system of values. The school decides long-hairs are "not acceptable" because their appearance is "disruptive." At the same time some football players shave off all their hair and their bald heads attract as much attention as those with long hair. Those with long hair are harassed for their appearance, while those with bald heads (the "Mr. Cleans") are not. This is the result of being brought up under values of codes hardly consistent with proper means of attaining the goals of education. There can be no openness and freedom of thought when intolerance and prejudice are bred by an unfair code.

In the past, the dress code was perpetuated because of a lack of openness. It was more comfortable for people to view things very narrowly. When prevailing values are automatically accepted, people become defensive in protecting them and intolerance is the resulting outcome. In an honest search for more meaningful human values, prevailing values cannot be automatically taken as relevant. In this way we never stop learning. We never end our education. A free dress code along with the openness of the flexible schedule would be a positive step toward these ends.

We must practice what we preach. A start must be made now. Many students would rather see a short-form, non-specific dress code. Consistent with this rationale for individual expression and human dignity, the following proposal is submitted by the student body of this high school and in turn accepted by the faculty as a standard of dress and behavior within this school program:

Student Body Recommendation for A Dress Code

Philosophy

Our philosophy regarding a "dress code" is that such a code should be designed to protect individuality and individual expression which is consonant with the health, safety, and educational opportunity of all students. Moreover, it is believed that a code which embodies these qualifications not only encourages a tolerance of diversity in dress, appearance and even in thought; but that in so doing it promotes those qualities necessary for the maintenance of an open society.

Provisions

The following provisions are to be observed by all students:
1. In accordance with the California Administrative Code, students shall be neat and clean.
2. Students' dress and/or appearance shall not be disruptive to the educational process.
3. Students shall comply with accepted standards of safety, e.g., this precludes bare feet.

Procedures

The following procedures are to be used in connection with the dress code provisions:
1. Any student may bring a case to the Student Court concerning a dress code infraction for adjudication.
2. The Student Court shall have the power to review and reject cases. All cases will be handled by the Student Court rather than by faculty members or administration.
3. The responsibility for the interpretation of the dress code provisions (and thus the responsibility for the establishment and enforcement of the code) shall rest primarily with the Student Court.
4. The Student Court shall have the power to make recommendations to the administrative staff of the school in regard to the code's enforcement.

Addendum

1. It is recognized that the California Administrative Code states in Title 5:

> *Pupils to Be Neat and Clean on Entering School.* "All pupils who go to school without proper attention having been given to personal cleanliness, or neatness of dress, may be sent home, to be properly prepared for school or shall be required to prepare themselves for the classroom before entering."

2. It is further recognized that by law a student is subject to a faculty member's immediate discretion. In the context of this dress code, this means that a student is subject to a faculty member's immediate discretion: (a) when he disrupts the educational process by his health and/or appearance, and (b) when his safety is concerned. However, it is anticipated by the Student Government and Student Court that the faculty will delegate primary responsibility for the establishment and the maintenance of the dress code to the students and their Court.

3. The stress will be on the "neat and clean" aspect of the code, with the decisions of the Student Court regarding interpretation made known to all students.

4. Finally, this code will remain on an experimental basis. The student body through their elected student body officers will be responsible for reviewing the effectiveness of the code and for making subsequent recommendations prior to the end of the present school year.

THE GUIDANCE–COUNSELING PROGRAM AND THE STUDENT

In attempting to provide a more humanized and individualized environment for students, one other program of the school requires brief consideration. Guidance and counseling services have been created in most secondary schools not only to help guide the student in his academic and intellectual development but also to help him with his emotional and psychological growth. While in theory the function of the typical guidance program looks to be an extremely useful and humanistic process, as well as being an added source for effectively treating individual student needs while at school, in practice this is seldom the case. The main purpose here is to suggest a reorganization of the conventional guidance–counseling functions in order to provide services for students who need help in combating unique problems created by a complex, technological society.

The positions of guidance and counseling, as their titles seem to suggest, should embrace two major functions. These two functions are not identical, despite the fact that they are combined in most secondary schools into one position or role. It is often difficult to find individuals who can adequately function in both roles inasmuch as the two positions do require dissimilar skills and expertise. Briefly, several distinguishing features of the two functions will be given which seem, in part, to characterize these two positions.

Guidance. The guidance function is generally concerned with programming students into proper courses in the spring term and the scheduling and rescheduling of student programs in the fall term. It is based upon a sound knowledge of the curriculum or instructional program of the school and the personality and individuality of teachers and students, as well as the proper "fitting" together of student-teacher-school facilities for the mutual benefit of all concerned. It requires an ability to communicate effectively with students, teachers, parents, and other school personnel concerning the instructional program vis-à-vis the individual needs of the student involved. The guidance person is then a liaison between student, teacher, parent, and school, and often he must show skill as a catalyst in his relationships with those concerned.

The guidance program also encompasses such areas as vocational guidance, academic guidance, college advisement, standardized or individualized testing programs, and so on. It is imperative that any person occupying the guidance role possess basic skills and qualifications in these areas in order to guide students into proper and productive avenues and to aid them in the wise choice of alternatives. Guidance, then, is just that—*guiding* the student into wise educational and vocational channels based upon his individual achievement, interests, and capabilities. This is by no means a simple or menial task. It requires adequate intuitive skill, perceptive insight, and fundamental knowledge of human motivation, particularly knowledge of teenage behavior.

Counseling. Counseling should not be relegated to a secondary role, although this is often the case in many schools. In the conventional school program, if the individual who occupies the guidance–counseling role finds time after having completed the "guidance tasks," he may attempt to work with some students in a "counseling" context. Unfortunately, the counseling activities in many schools are the least understood, most abstract, and least easily conceptualized of the many functions found in larger secondary schools. If ten "counselors" are asked what their role and purpose is in the school program, it is likely that ten different replies would be received. Explanations of the counseling role would range from the guidance tasks already described to just a "friend of students" or "someone for students to talk to."

While it is recognized that it may be difficult to adequately conceptualize what constitutes an "ideal" counseling program or an ideal counselor, it seems that a few prerequisites are fundamental to the program, particularly if an attempt is made to develop a more humanistically oriented program designed to meet the needs and requirements of the individual student. The counselor requires at least three basic skills: (1) the ability to develop a rapid and open relationship with teenagers; (2) a natural sensitivity that displays genuine interest in students, their problems, their interests, their achievements, and their desires; and, perhaps of most importance,

(3) a human sensitivity toward people as people—a person who is genuinely *people-oriented*. In the teenage vernacular, this must be a person who, through his own personality and sincere interest in students, can "turn kids on"; someone they respect, respond to, and will communicate with openly concerning their problems, anxieties, and frustrations.

In the counseling role the individual is less concerned for the moment with the instructional program per se, with school as a required institution, or in fulfilling a predetermined graduation requirement. The counselor is willing and capable of meeting the individual student on his terms and he is skilled in the psychological and behavioral sciences so that he can properly interpret and understand the student's behavior and attitudes. In understanding the behavioral and psychological problems found in many teenagers with intense emotional disturbances, however, he appreciates the limits of his own abilities and he is capable of referring students to the proper auxiliary agencies when necessary. The counselor is sensitive; the student is at ease in his presence and feels free to communicate.

It is necessary for the counselor to be empathetic to a variety of student interests and motivations. He cannot relate only to the typical, well-adjusted, or accepted high school student—those getting the good grades who, in a sense, are "making it" in school. He must develop a rapport and empathy for the so-called social deviate, the non-conformist—those on the fringe of the acceptable social system of the institution. Herein lies the real challenge to anyone aspiring to a counseling role.

When we recognize the complex social problems facing many American high schools today—narcotics, radical dress standards, sex problems, etc.—it is tragic that a more professional, better equipped cadre of individuals who can perform in the counseling role have not been trained. Because of the specialization required in both guidance and counseling functions, it seems that a greater dichotomy is appearing between these two roles than has been recognized to date. It is probably too great a task to expect one individual to be proficient in the skills demanded by the guidance role and at the same time to keep abreast of the psychological, emotional, and behavioral problems confronting teenagers. In order to meet the demands of a rapidly changing society it is necessary to find individuals who are specialized in at least one of these two roles. Therefore, it is suggested that a reorganization of the conventional guidance–counseling program be made, that we separate the guidance role from the counseling or psychological counseling role. Several obvious paradoxes do exist within the combined functions which, in part, have been articulated in supporting such a division.

GUIDANCE AND COUNSELING—PROPOSED REORGANIZATION

This proposal is quite simple. In addition to the present guidance–counseling functions found in most secondary schools, a new psychological-counseling service will be added to the school's program. The number of psychological and emotional problems experienced by teenagers indicates that more specific skills are required in this area than can be expected from the generalized guidance–counselor. If the school is to continue to provide a humanizing and individualizing environment for all of its students, it is necessary to provide greater specialized psychological services for those who require them. Therefore, two departments should be established in larger high schools: (1) a guidance–counseling department with services similar to those found in most schools today and as outlined in the previous section under "guidance," and (2) a psychological–counseling service with the major responsibility of caring for the student's emotional, psychological, and deviant behavioral problems.

The following activities and related responsibilities seem consistent with this proposal:

Guidance–Counselor	*Time*	*Psychological–Counselor*	*Time*
1. Programming, scheduling, related activities	50%	1. Recommendations for programming, scheduling, and courses	10%
2. College advisement, vocational guidance, writing college recommendations	15%	2. Individual testing, problem identification, and test interpretation	20%
3. Group testing and interpretation	5%	3. Individual and group counseling for psychological, emotional, behavioral problems to involve teacher, parent, and student in case conferences	70%
4. Academic counseling, parent conferences	30%		

Inasmuch as the typical guidance–counselor is a familiar position in most schools, it is not necessary to emphasize his responsibilities. However, a little further clarification of the possible responsibilities of the psychological-counselor may be of interest. The psychological-counslor would handle the following activities:

1. Study and assist the individual pupil, using extensive and intensive psychological techniques.
2. Recommend appropriate educational and psychological remediation for exceptional children.
3. Determine eligibility for or recommend pupil placement in special programs and classes.
4. Participation in planning, executing, and assessing programs of education and re-education for pupils.
5. Provide appropriate in-service training and consultive services for school staffs.
6. Plans and execute research projects for the improvement of the educational program.
7. Serve in a liaison relationship between the school, the community, and community agencies in the understanding and treatment of learning and behavior problems.[11]

Above all, the major purpose of this proposal for a reorganization of guidance and counseling functions in conventional schools is to place a greater emphasis upon the counseling role, and to provide greater opportunities for assistance and interaction between students with legitimate psychological problems and qualified school personnel. It is recognized that this proposal may present some fiscal and organizational problems. However, American public education and those elected to monitor and develop the system have always been faced with priorities. Again, consistent with the major theme of this book is this suggestion to provide as many avenues and alternatives as possible for individualizing the school's program as well as for developing an atmosphere conducive to meeting the unique requirement of the individual. The type of guidance-counseling and psychological-counseling program in this proposal would provide one additional alternative route in meeting the individual needs of student and teacher as an important adjunct to the instructional program of the school.

---

[11] These activities for the psychological-counselor are suggested by the California Association of School Psychologists.

ORGANIZATIONAL CLIMATE
AND THE STUDENT

====

11

Public schools have always had their critics. Each generation has produced individuals who vociferously denounced the school's programs and methods. Much of this criticism has come from individuals who, through subjective observation or emotionally charged feelings, have witnessed activities in schools which were personally disturbing. Others, however, with greater insight and objective perceptions and often equipped with the observational techniques of the social scientist, have also been interested in schools and their activities. It is not particularly surprising that some critics with little professional experience or in-depth understanding of schools or their functions have negative impressions of many conventional school phenomena. These impressions often are easily obtained if a person is willing to spend a little time making even the most superficial observations. Perhaps the most disturbing fact is that many of the often justifiable objections raised by some skilled authority have had so little impact upon change in the educational community.

One such observer who has proven to have profound insight into the operation of the typical American high school is Edgar Friedenberg. Anyone interested in the concept of individualization of educational programs, as well as in developing more humanizing school environments, must give some consideration to his observations and subsequent characterizations of two high schools.

> The elements of the composition—the passes, the tight scheduling, the reliance on threats of detention or suspension as modes of social control—are nearly universal. The usurpation of any possible area of student, initiative, physical or mental, is about as universal. Milgrim [ficticious name for one of the high schools in Friedenberg's study] forbids boys to wear trousers that end more

than six inches above the floor, and has personnel fully capable of measuring them. But most high schools have some kind of dress regulations; I know of none that accepts and relies on the tastes of students.

Along with having a less rancorous and choleric atmosphere than Milgrim, Hartsburgh seems to have more teachers who like teaching and like kids. But the fundamental pattern is still one of control, distrust, and punishment. . . . Neither principal respects adolescents at all or his staff very much. Both are preoccupied with good public relations as they understand them. Both are inflexible, highly authoritarian men.[1]

Friedenberg provides very revealing, as well as what may be very typical, characterizations of the social climate of many public schools. Although he has offered interesting impressions through individual observational techniques, the primary purpose of this chapter is to present a similar assessment of the school's environment through more objective procedures and from the standpoint of the students—the indivduals most affected by the social and psychological atmosphere of the school. Moreover, this analysis of organizational climate will be made by assessing empirical data obtained through appropriately designed instrumentation, based on collective student responses, which will measure certain key socio-psychological factors of the school.

The measurement of socio-psychological phenomena within schools has been popularly referred to in the literature as a measurement of organizational climate. In this context, organizational climate may be considered to be analogous with individual personality. A measure of a school's climate may be expressed in terms of a continuum ranging from an environment with high development press, or a school atmosphere that provides opportunities for student self-actualization (open climate), at one extreme to controlled press, or a highly controlled, restrictive atmosphere (closed climate) at the other. Many studies have been conducted in recent years depicting the organzational climate of schools from the viewpoint of teachers and administrators. The extensive use of the Organizational Climate Description Questionnaire (OCDQ) is an indication of the interest in obtaining broad descriptions of

---

[1] Edgar Z. Friedenberg, *The Dignity of Youth and Other Atavisms* (Boston: Beacon Press, 1965).

organizational environments.[2] Unfortunately, very little similar data have been extracted from the students in secondary schools to determine their characterizations of the school's environment as it affects them.

Recently, a student-oriented, socio-psychologically designed questionnaire, The High School Characteristics Index (HSCI), which will assess the environmental press of a secondary school[3] has been developed. Through the use of this questionnaire, schools may be characterized by their students with high development press, or an atmosphere of free-flowing ideas and authentic interaction between school personnel and students. Conversely, those schools with low development press, or controlled press, suggest a rigid, encumbered atmosphere with relative degrees of hostility, resentment, defensiveness, and aggression in the interpersonal relations of school personnel, particularly between students and teachers.

The HSCI has proven to be an extremely useful device for determining what students in any particular school really feel about school life, the general school environment, and related school activities. It is also useful as a predictive tool in determining many of the social and environmental problems experienced in secondary schools today due to hostile and anxious students reacting to a general social milieu of frustration and unrest.

---

[2] The original work with the OCDQ is described in: Andrew W. Halpin and Don B. Croft, *The Organizational Climate of Schools* (Chicago: Midwest Administrative Center, The University of Chicago, 1963).

[3] A complete history of the development of the Syracuse Indices, including the CCI, OCI, AI, and HSCI, are found in: G. G. Stern, *People in Context* (New York: John Wiley and Sons, in press). See also: G. G. Stern, "Student Ecology and the College Environment," *Journal of Medical Education*, 40 (March, 1965); "Student Values and their Relationship to the College Environment," in H. T. Sprague (ed.), *Research on College Students* (Boulder, Colo.: Western Interstate Commission for Higher Education, 1960); "Continuity and Contrast in the Transition from High School to College, in N. C. Brown (ed.), *Orientation to College Learning—A Reappraisal* (Washington: American Council on Education, 1961); "Environments for Learning, in R. N. Sanford (ed.), *The American College: A Psychological and Social Interpretation of the Higher Learning* (New York: John Wiley and Sons, 1962); "The Measurement of Psychological Characteristics of Students and Learning Environments," in S. J. Messick & J. Ross (eds.), *Measurement in Personality and Cognition* (New York: John Wiley and Sons, 1962).

The present analysis reports the use of the HSCI in a middle-class suburban high school after several confrontations had taken place between certain student factions and the professional staff. An advantage of the HSCI as a psychologically derived instrument is its ability to probe and describe environmental situations from a student population with greater significance (at a "gut" level) than is normally undertaken in secondary schools. Generally, the analysis of social or psychological phenomena in secondary schools has been neglected completely or, at best, only treated superficially —as administrative speculation—void of any substantive, objective data base.

THE HSCI QUESTIONNAIRE AND FACTOR STRUCTURE

The HSCI is composed of 300 carefully selected questions descriptive of typical high school activities, student-teacher behavior, and school life. The student responds to these items with a true–false answer depending upon how he feels the description fits his particular situation. Each of the 300 items are assigned to one of 30 different need-press scales which are psychological conceptualizations of personal and organizational behavior (see Table 11.1).[4] In turn, through statistical techniques the 30 scales have been grouped or clustered under seven major factors which describe in more general terms various aspects of school life and the overall school environment or climate. Generally, these seven major factors are used as the basic unit for analysis and interpretation. These seven conceptual categories (factors) are listed below with a brief description or definition of each.[5]

FACTOR 1. INTELLECTUAL CLIMATE

This factor describes a concern with the intellectual activities, social action, and personal effectiveness in academic matters of the school. It indicates the level of concern and interest in intellectual pursuits, such as literary, artistic, and dramatic activities, or interest in political and social issues. It stresses creative and imaginative activities

---

[4] The 30 need-press scales were adapted by Stern for employment in the development of the Syracuse Indices from the original psychological taxonomy developed by H. A. Murray found in: H. A. Murray, *Explorations in Personality* (New York: Oxford University Press, 1938).

[5] The definitions of the seven major factors were extracted in part from G. G. Stern, *People in Context, op. cit.*

as opposed to more pragmatic, day-to-day interests. It suggests an interest in the development of personal values and philosophical thought.

FACTOR 2. EXPRESSIVENESS

This factor primarily suggests a form of aesthetic awareness and emotional participation through a deep concern, interest, and emotional attachment to activities and school life. It suggests an uniqueness about the school which students are aware of and capable of expressing. There is a flexibility and certain excitement in the typical school activities rather than only dull routine. Opportunities are available in the school endeavor for the student to be an unique and creative entity and students are able to express themselves with minimum restraint from adult or peers. This quality of expression is fostered, enhanced, and appreciated by most students and teachers. A lot of energy, effort, and enthusiasm go into the teaching activities.

TABLE II.I

Need–Press Scale Definitions

1. *Abasement–Assurance:* self-depreciation versus self-confidence
2. *Achievement:* striving for success through personal effort
3. *Adaptability–Defensiveness:* acceptance of criticism versus resistance to suggestion
4. *Affiliation–Rejection:* friendliness versus unfriendliness
5. *Aggression–Blame Avoidance:* hostility versus disorganization
6. *Change–Sameness:* flexibility versus routine
7. *Conjunctivity–Disjunctivity:* planfulness versus disorganization
8. *Counteraction–Inferiority Avoidance:* restriving after failure versus withdrawal
9. *Deference–Restiveness:* respect for authority versus rebelliousness
10. *Dominance–Tolerance:* ascendance versus forebearance
11. *Ego Achievement:* striving for power through social action
12. *Emotionality–Placidity:* expressiveness versus restraint
13. *Energy–Passivity:* effort versus inertia
14. *Exhibitionism–Inferiority Avoidance:* attention-seeking versus shyness
15. *Fantasied Achievement:* daydreams of extraordinary public recognition
16. *Harm Avoidance–Risk-taking:* fearfulness versus thrill-seeking
17. *Humanities–Social Sciences:* interests in the Humanities and the Social Sciences
18. *Impulsiveness–Deliberation:* impetuousness versus reflection
19. *Narcissism:* vanity
20. *Nurturance–Rejection:* helping others versus indifference
21. *Objectivity–Projectivity:* detachment versus suspicion
22. *Order–Disorder:* compulsive organization of details versus carelessness
23. *Play–Work:* pleasure-seeking versus purposefulness
24. *Practicalness–Impracticalness:* interest in practical activities versus indifference
25. *Reflectiveness:* introspective contemplation
26. *Science:* interest in the Natural Sciences
27. *Sensuality–Puritanism:* interest in sensory and aesthetic experiences
28. *Sexuality–Prudishness:* heterosexual interests versus their inhibition
29. *Supplication–Autonomy:* dependency versus self-reliance
30. *Understanding:* intellectuality

FACTOR 3. GROUP LIFE

The components of this factor suggest that the typical high school environment is fun-loving, friendly, enjoyable, sociable, and actively outgoing. There is lots of enthusiasm and support of school activities. School is not just academic class routine by many other extracurricular opportunities exist for students to express themselves, to participate and enjoy comradeship and fulfillment. There is opportunity for affiliation and membership in many school-related activities.

FACTOR 4. PERSONAL DIGNITY

This factor suggests that a school environment which encourages individual autonomy should also allow for expressions of dependency and defensiveness. This does not seem inconsistent when we consider that teenagers are in a state of transition, and are needful of opportunities to reassure themselves periodically. This factor is based on high loadings in assurance, development of self-confidence and a genuine school interest in the individual student and his activities. There is objectivity and equal opportunity given to each student; teachers do not play favorites. Students may feel free to express their ideas without indifference and rejection from teachers. School personnel give students the benefit of the doubt. Students are not embarrassed in front of their classmates, and there is no need for defensive behavior.

FACTOR 5. ACHIEVEMENT STANDARDS

The components of this factor reflect a press upon the student for high achievement. Schools high in this dimension stress hard work, perseverance, and a day-to-day commitment to institutional purpose and academic success. This reflects high competition for grades—almost for the sake of good grades—and lots of homework. It suggests that classes and instructional materials, content, and presentations are well planned, well illustrated and well organized. It also stresses student appearance and dress standards as an aspect of achievement in the general school program.

FACTOR 6. ORDERLINESS

This factor is concerned with the control and organizational structure, school procedures as they affect student life, orderliness, and the general level of respect for school authorities in opposition to the general level of rebelliousness and school discipline. The student feels that respect for teachers and other school personnel is important for an orderly, well-balanced environment. Concern may be expressed for general school order vs. disorder, school building and grounds cleanliness, and teachers' attitude toward organizational detail in class activities.

FACTOR 7. PRACTICALNESS

This factor indicates that much of school life and the school environment is reflective of life in all of its pragmatic aspects outside of school. School expectations are community and societal expectations. The school is nothing more than a microcosm of the general community environment of which the school is a part. The practical aspects of school and the need for an education are stressed—financial success, social prestige, community position and status—rather than the more intellectual, aesthetic, or enjoyment aspects of gaining an education. A high degree of ascendance is reflected in the importance of social status, student body positions, belonging to student cliques and groups necessary for prestige.

DATA INTERPRETATION—A CASE STUDY

By utilizing the descriptions or conceptualizations associated with the seven major factors of the HSCI, it is possible to make a meaningful analysis and interpretation of data gathered from the questionnaires administered to a sample of students from any high school. All scores derived from the high school student groups are expressed in standard scores which are computed by comparing the mean scores of the school under study with normative scores which have been extracted from similar high school groups. This normative or reference population is composed of 12 high schools found in various states in the Midwest and East Coast. Thus, in interpreting any individual high school's response in respect to an assessment of its environment, the school would be compared with the responses of approximately 1,000 other students from 12 typical American high schools.

In the high school under study, the student sample consisted of 105 students. The groups were randomly selected from the total roster of students at the high school. The groups selected are shown in Table 11.2. The 105 students represented approximately seven percent of the total student body and was a sufficient sample based on the comprehensiveness of the questionnaire and the sophistication of the statistical techniques employed. It is significant that the

TABLE 11.2

Random Selection of Student Groups

Group description	Number of students
1. 11th grade history, low section	26
2. 12th grade English, low section	18
3. 10th grade biology, med section	20
4. 10th grade history, med section	21
5. 11th grade algebra, high section	20
Total sample	105

number of low, middle, and high sections chosen are directly proportional to the number of low, middle, and high sections found within the total school program.

The mean scores and standard scores received by this high school on the seven major factors appear in Table 11.3. It will be

TABLE 11.3

High School Mean and Standard Scores for the HSCI Data

Factor name	Normative[a] mean score	Sample high school mean score	Sample high school standard score[b]
1. Intellectual climate	43.00	36.29	−3.30
2. Expressiveness	33.01	27.96	−2.70
3. Group life	29.24	23.72	−3.20
4. Personal dignity	35.27	24.74	−5.63
5. Achievement standards	45.81	36.56	−5.24
6. Orderliness	18.74	16.10	−2.63
7. Practicalness	23.87	23.61	−0.18

[a] Norms were made available by the Psychological Research Center, Syracuse University.

[b] $X = 0, \sigma = 2$

noted that in factors one through six this high school received a mean score which ranked well below the mean score of the normative population. The significance of this difference is seen in the negative standard scores in the third column. Only in the area of *Practicalness* do the students in this high school consider their school life and school environment to be average or similar to other high schools.

The two factors of greatest significance or lowest standard scores are factors four, *Personal Dignity* (standard score −5.63), and five, *Achievement Standards* (standard score −5.24). One method of interpreting the significance of these standard scores is in terms of standard deviation.[6] In the case of the *Personal Dignity*

---

[6] The standard deviation is a numerical measure of the degree of dispersion or variability of a score or set of scores from the mean. In any normal distribution the standard deviation may also represent the percentage of cases one would expect to find in this dispersion about the mean score. That is, one standard deviation from the mean represents 68.26% of the population, two standard deviations represent 95.46% and three standard deviations represent 99.73% of any given group. The standard deviation for the HSCI factor data has a numerical value of two. Thus, the formula standard score divided by standard deviation equals the standard deviation range from the mean score on any set of scores.

factor we find that the high school falls almost three standard deviations ($\frac{5.63}{2} = 2.83$ S.D.) below the mean or normative score of all other high schools measured. Statistically, this means we would expect to find a score this low or lower in only one percent of the cases tested. That is, only one percent or less of the high schools measured would be expected to rank this low on the *Personal Dignity* scale. The *Achievement Standards* factor may be interpreted in a similar fashion. A standard score of -5.24 is approximately two-and-one-half standard deviations ($\frac{5.24}{2} = 2.6$ S.D.) below the norm. We would expect a score this low in only two percent of the total population measured.

Now, how may this basic statistical information as expressed in the factor scores be related to the general conceptual descriptions of each factor given previously. In other words, *through these negative scores what are the students in this high school indicating concerning school life and their high school environment?* By way of example, the following generalization of the students' characterization of the school based on the *Personal Dignity* factor is offered.

There is little opportunity for individual autonomy and the school cannot accommodate expressions of student dependency or defensiveness. There is little assurance given students or an opportunity to develop self-confidence within the institutional setting. Little genuine interest is shown by the high school staff in respect to individual student interests. Some might object to this generalization and claim that there is good rapport between student, administration, and staff. However, at the psychological level this rapport between student and staff is viewed or perceived to be superficial or phony. Students are saying that the school gives lip-service to their interests as students, but, underlying this, there is no "real" concern for their desires as individuals. Behavior is not authentic. There is projectivity rather than objectivity in dealing with students, and teachers probably play favorites. Students feel there is little opportunity for free expression of ideas, and they are frequently embarrassed in front of their classmates. In general, the personal dignity of the student as a human being, as a member of a social institution that, above all, should value and respect individuality and human dignity, is considered to be at an extremely low level.

Similar generalizations can also be made from the negative scores received on the factors of *Intellectual Climate* (−3.30), *Group Life* (−3.20), and *Achievement Standards* (−5.24); however, it is felt that this is sufficient interpretation to indicate the general direction of these data and their usefulness to an analysis of the social climate of a school without providing further descriptive generalizations. In summary, the students of this high school are saying that this is not an environment conducive to personal development or self-actualization. This school is characterized by a high degree of hostility, tension, and aggression in the interpersonal relations among students, administrators, and teachers. There are high levels of resentment and defensiveness. The climate is cold, unfriendly, suspicious, and considerable disorder and lack of organization is apparent not only in the school generally but in the instructional program specifically. There is a high work-study oriented atmosphere with a high premium placed on conventional homework activities.

There are two other approaches which may be useful to a school in analyzing the HSCI data. The first is to make a comparison of the individual group standard scores on the seven environmental factors. One might expect that students found in the high achievement groups, for example, the high algebra group, would characterize their school environment quite differently on such factors as *Intellectual Climate, Achievement Standards*, or *Group Life* than students found in the low ability groups. For this analysis, standard scores may be compared in Table 11.4 for the

TABLE 11.4

Comparisons of Individual Group Standard Scores on the Seven Environmental Factors (HSCI)

HSCI Factor	Group 1 11-Hist. low	Group 2 12-Eng. low	Group 3 10-Biol. med	Group 4 10-Hist. med	Group 5 11-Alg. high
1. Intellectual climate	−4.53	−2.79	−2.73	−3.26	−2.78
2. Expressiveness	−3.45	−3.34	−2.42	−2.07	−2.12
3. Group life	−4.05	−2.66	−2.55	−2.63	−3.86
4. Personal dignity	−6.79	−7.28	−3.89	−5.39	−4.77
5. Achievement standards	−6.36	−4.80	−4.54	−4.88	−5.24
6. Orderliness	−2.51	−0.57	−3.14	−3.22	−3.54
7. Practicalness	−0.06	−0.87	−0.02	−0.52	−1.29

five ability groups and the seven HSCI factors. It is particularly interesting to note that, with minor exceptions, little variance or difference exists between the individual group scores. Most of the students, regardless of the ability group with which they are associated, seem to share similar attitudes and perceptions, and in general they are in agreement concerning the school's climate.

A second method of data interpretation is to make an analysis at the item or question level. All questions were analyzed where 75% or more of the students had similar responses. From the 300 items in the HSCI questionnaire, 82 questions (about 27%) fell into this category. This again indicates the strong agreement among the students on certain key issues (see Table 11.5). An item analysis of this nature may serve at least two useful func-

TABLE 11.5

Item Analysis: 75 Percent or More Student Agreement

Student response
T–F	Sample items

T . . . . You need permission to do anything around here.

T . . . . When you get into trouble with one teacher, the other teachers soon know about it.

F . . . . Students don't argue with the teacher, they just admit that they are wrong.

T . . . . Everyone knows who the smart students are because they are in different classes from the others.

F . . . . There is a lot of school spirit.

T . . . . Students seldom get out and support the school teams.

T . . . . The desks are all cut up from doodling with knives and pencils.

T . . . . When students dislike a teacher, they let him know it.

T . . . . Everyone prefers the easy teachers, and tries hard to avoid the tough ones.

F . . . . Most students look up to their teachers and admire them.

F . . . . Students put a lot of energy into everything they do.

F . . . . There are so many things to do here that students are busy all the time.

T . . . . Students who are not neatly dressed are likely to have this called to their attention.

F . . . . Many of the upperclassmen help new students get used to school life.

T . . . . Students are sometimes punished without knowing the reason why.

T . . . . Most students and their families think of education as a preparation for earning a good living.

F . . . . There are frequent displays around the school.

F . . . . Students sometimes get a chance to hear music in the lunchroom or during other free periods.

T . . . . There are no comfortable seats in this school where students can sit and relax.

T . . . . Most teachers prefer that students work out their own problems.

T . . . . Classes are boring.

tions: (1) to focus on those issues or problems which students are most cognizant of and most in agreement with (what's bugging the kids the most), and (2) to use these items as a basis for suggesting improvements to the school program—what minor, and often subtle, changes can be made in the school that would help create better student morale, a more open or anabolic climate, and a more humanizing school environment.

Within the generalizations derived from data such as these there are many serious implications dealing with the social and psychological climate of secondary schools that must be faced by concerned administrators and teachers. While it is recognized that teachers share responsibility with the administration of any school for the establishment of a climate which is open and conducive to healthy student interactions and productive interpersonal relations, the author is equally convinced that the creation of any type of school environment, be it open or closed, must be placed first upon the principal and his immediate administrative staff. If hostility, aggression, suspicion, and defensiveness exist among the students in their relationships with the school and its personnel, then the administrative staff must accept the major responsibility for this perceived climate. Their behavior in relation to teachers, their attitudes, their anxieties and frustrations are readily discernable to students and teachers. Their behavior, although not always overt and conscious, nevertheless strongly influences the subconscious and psychological tone of the school.

In closing this analysis of the socio-psychological climate of high schools and the usefulness of these data to school staffs in interpreting their own school environments, one final quotation from Friedenberg lends itself to the major concern of this section of the book in developing more humanistically oriented environments conducive to student individuality:

> The effects on the students are manifold. The concepts of dignity and privacy, notably deficient in American adult folkways, are not permitted to develop here. The school's assumption of custodial control of students implies that power and authority are indistinguishable. If the school's authority is not limited to matters pertaining to education, it cannot be derived from its educational responsibilities. It is a naked, empirical fact, to be accepted or contraverted according to the possibilities of the moment. In such a world, power counts more than legitimacy; if you don't have power, it is naive to think

you have rights that must be respected. Wise up. High school students experience regulations only as control, not as protection; they know, for example, that the principal will generally uphold the teacher in any conflict with a student, regardless of the merits of the case. Translated into the high-school idiom, *suaviter in modo, fortiter in re* becomes "If you get caught, it's just your ass."

Thus the high school is permitted to infantilize adolescence; in fact, it is encouraged to by the widespread hostility to "teen-agers" and the anxiety about their conduct found throughout our society. It does not allow much maturation to occur during the years when most maturation would naturally occur.[7]

---

7 Friedenberg, *op. cit.*

EMERGENT PROFESSIONAL AND ORGANIZATIONAL PATTERNS

IV

THE TEACHER: DEVELOPING
A CLIMATE FOR INDIVIDUALITY
AND PROFESSIONAL BEHAVIOR

12

In the preceding chapters, several programs oriented essentially toward the student received primary emphasis in discussing the individualization of instruction. The purpose of this chapter, as well as Chapter 13, is to present several concepts for providing the teacher with similar opportunities for individuality, for autonomy in instructional decision-making, and for professional development. Several independent, yet interrelated, themes seem germane to a discussion of elementary and secondary schools and their professional staffs. These ideas include the concept of school system organization, the bureaucratic nature of schools, and the degree to which the school's organizational pattern impedes or enhances professional activities. In public education the clarification of the concept "professional" is pertinent and is in need of definition. Essentially, the question may be posed: "Are public school teachers, technically speaking, professionals?" The latter part of this chapter and the final chapter present several methods for changing traditional, bureaucratic school organizations into more appropriate avenues for providing greater professional development among teaching staffs. This includes concepts such as differentiated staffing, the management of instructional time as a professional prerequisite, and organizational patterns which allow for greater staff involvement in instructional decision-making.

The central theme underlying these two chapters proposes that the teacher, as an emerging professional, should be the manager of the instructional process of the school and should assume a central role in the teaching–learning decision-making process. It is the contention that traditional school structures, which provide the framework for the majority of the instructional programs in this country, rarely allow the teaching staff the degree of flexibility and individuality necessary for professional status. Suggestions are offered here for developing alternatives to the conventional organizational blueprint employed in most school systems. This heuristic approach to developing organizational alternatives seems particularly necessary and consistent with the theme of individualizing educational systems. Few programs for instructional change can function optimally within the constraints imposed by conventional school organizations. Programs for individualizing instruction necessitate complementary organizational support systems which can accommodate greater teacher individuality and program flexibility.

CONTINGENCIES UPON PROFESSIONAL DEVELOPMENT

PUBLIC SCHOOLS AS BUREAUCRACIES

It seems unnecessary at this juncture to present a case for considering public schools, as well as many larger private schools, as bureaucratic organizations. There has been considerable research to date pointing to the fact that bureaucratic components are unquestionably an integral part of the organizational anatomy of most school systems.[1] As schools become larger and more complex in function, and as their operation requires greater numbers of specialized skills, they tend to adopt organizational characteristics identified by the student of organizations as being bureaucratic.

It is not the concern of this chapter to give a lengthy overview of what constitutes a bureaucratic organization. Considerable literature dealing with this subject is available to the interested reader.[2]

---

[1] See, for example: G. H. Moeller, "The Relationship Between Bureaucracy in School System Organization and Teachers' Sense of Power" (unpublished doctor's dissertation, Washington University, 1962); L. K. Bishop, "Bureaucracy and The Adoption of Educational Innovation" (unpublished doctor's dissertation, Claremont Graduate School, 1966); or J. R. George, "Organizational Structure, Teacher Personality Characteristics and their Relationship to Organizational Climate" (unpublished doctor's dissertation, Claremont Graduate School, 1969).

[2] See, for example: Peter M. Blau, *Bureaucracy in Modern Society* (New York: Random House, 1956); Peter M. Blau and Richard Scott, *Formal Organizations* (San Francisco: Chandler Publishing Co., 1962); or Nicos P. Mouzelis, *Organization and Bureaucracy* (Chicago: Aldine Publishing Co., 1967).

The major interest in this discussion focuses on the consequences and impact of conventional school structures as they affect the individuals who participate in the organization. Specifically, the purpose is to look at the relationships between the bureaucratic characteristics of elementary and secondary schools and the opportunity, or lack of opportunity, afforded teachers in achieving professional recognition and status. Central to the study of the organization of educational programs is the consideration of the role of the teacher as a professional. The current model of teacher professionalism originated in the nineteenth century needs considerable reexamination as we consider the problems faced by teachers today.

PROFESSIONAL PARAMETERS

What is a profession? What is professional behavior? Although these questions may appear more rhetorical than definable, some guiding generalizations concerning the dimensionality and parameters of professionalism in the classical definition will be offered. Louis D. Brandeis indicated that the attributes of a profession, in his judgment, were "that the training for its practice be intellectual in character, that it be pursued not for one's own sake but for others, and that the amount of financial reward not be considered the measure of success."[3] Abraham Flexner wrote that a profession should be intellectual, learned, practical, expert in relevant technique, formally organized, and altruistic.[4] He concluded that medicine, law, engineering, literature, painting, and music qualified as professions, but that social work, about which he was writing, did not (one wonders what he would have to say about education).

Other distinguishing characteristics of a profession have centered around the inclusion of systematic theory, authority (accorded by clients), community sanction, ethical codes, and a formally sustained culture.[5] Definitions have also included such essential attributes as a high degree of generalized and systematic

---

[3] This quotation may be found in Kenneth R. Andrews, "Toward Professionalism in Business Management," *Harvard Business Review* (March-April, 1969).

[4] *Ibid.*

[5] *Ibid.*

knowledge, orientation primarily to community rather than individual interest, a high degree of self-control through internalized codes and voluntary organizations, and a system of rewards viewed as symbols of work achievement, not as ends in themselves.[6]

A synthesis of the characteristics and attributes of professional behavior derived from the above definitions is considerably removed from that behavior most often witnessed in many public schools. Generally, in education we have been content with accepting more narrowly defined criteria for establishing professional parameters. These criteria are frequently limited to factors such as sole reliance on formalities of education, admission, ordination, and licensing. More significant and fundamental criteria for professionalism such as systematic theory, expert in relevant technique, a high degree of generalized and systematic knowledge, or a high degree of self-control have had little or no impact upon establishing criteria for professional behavior within teaching.

The process of defining professionalism in the past has confined recognition generally to the three "learned or classical professions"—theology, law, and medicine. It is evident that we must give attention to more refined concepts, as well as to broader-based definitions, in order to evaluate the professional quality of other occupational groups and, particularly, of teaching. An analytic scheme is required which will distinguish more sharply, and in a functional and social context, among professional, semi-professional, and nonprofessional occupational groups.

ANALYTIC SCHEME: THE TEACHER AS A PROFESSIONAL

So far we have offered only general descriptions of professional behavior as a guiding framework, without establishing any analytic differentiation between what constitutes professional or nonprofessional occupations. There has been a general lack of consensus in the literature regarding distinguishing characteristics between these two groups. It is the purpose of this section to employ a scheme for making this distinction; in turn, the criteria proposed will be used to analyze teaching as a profession.

It has been suggested that "previous attempts to differentiate professions from other occupations have met with limited success,

---

6 *Ibid.*

in part because they have offered limited definitions but ignored the social relationship which exists between professionals and their clients."[7] For analytic convenience the entire social framework in which this interaction between professional and client occurs can be divided into three major criteria:

1. The characteristics of the participants in the interaction.
2. The characteristics determining initiation and termination of the interaction.
3. The characteristics of the interaction itself.

Each of the three major criteria for professional analysis contained in this paradigm will be given further amplification.

Characteristics of the Participants. A social relationship always implies at least two participants, each of which occupies a complementary social role. Each of the roles is socially defined so as to indicate the minimal characteristics which persons occupying the role must possess.

> The professional is expected to possess expertise. It is generally a relatively easy matter to demonstrate the possession of the required skills as they are manifested in a variety of symbols: license, diplomas, membership in professional associations, and, in some cases, distinctive wearing apparel.
>
> The clients role is generally without prerequisites, though certain social characteristics do empirically affect access to various client roles.[8]

Characteristics of Initiation and Termination. Social relationships involve not only minimal criteria concerning who may be an incumbent in the various social roles but also norms concerning the initiation and termination of interaction between professional and client.

> The professional-client relationship is governed by norms which require that the interaction be initiated by the client.
>
> The norms governing the relationship also dictate that the termination of interaction be initiated by the professional, though the client is generally free to leave at any time, and thus to terminate the relationship. The norms of the professional suggest the time to break off the relationship as being either when the client's problem

---

[7] Neil H. Cheek, Jr., "The Social Role of the Professional," in Mark Abrahamson, *The Professional In The Organization*, © 1967 by Rand McNally & Company, Chicago.

[8] *Ibid.*

has been solved, or the professional has reached the limits of his capability in aiding the client.[9]

Characteristics of Interaction. Once the role incumbency has been established, relations between client and professional are governed by norms concerning the substantive content of interaction. Within this framework four interaction characteristics can be distinguished:

1. The content of the interaction between professional and client is considered privileged communication. It cannot be divulged by the professional.
2. No transfer of techniques or skills is intended during the interaction. The professional's expertise is based upon a body of knowledge which he alone is capable of interpreting.
3. Decisions made by the professional are limited to the specific interaction period. That is, the professional's decisions are confined both to the "here and now" situation, and to the particular client with whom he is currently interacting.
4. Decisions rendered by the professional are not ordinarily appealable to an "outside" authority. The professional, as a member of a collegial body, acts autonomously in his interaction with his own clients. He is generally subject only to moral and ethical considerations as determined by his professional group.[10]

It can be seen that the characteristics of role incumbency, initiation, content, and termination, as presented in this paradigm, constitute a minimal set of criteria for describing the social role of the professional as well as providing an analytic tool for various occupational analyses. This general theoretical framework may be applied to a broad spectrum of occupational groups in determining their relative position along a professional role continuum. It is suggested that these criteria can be applied to an analysis of teaching as a profession in determining within a context of social interaction to what extent teaching is a professional role.

The following represents an analysis of the teaching occupational role by employing the criteria of this paradigm:

Participants—Initiation and Termination. Is the teacher an expert? The granting of a license by the state can be accepted as evidence of confirmed expertise. . . .

Is the child a client? Children can generally occupy the client's

---

9 *Ibid.*
10 *Ibid.*

role, but they must be "sponsored." The child, sponsored by an adult, does initiate the interaction by going to the teacher. . . . The teacher as professional, routinely interacts with many children who simultaneously occupy the role of client. The teacher does generally terminate the interaction as long as one does not place an arbitrary limitation upon the length of interaction. . . .

Interaction Characteristics. Because the client is not an adult, society does not view the content of teacher-pupil interaction as requiring the sanctity of privileged communication. There are normative restraints among teachers, however, concerning the conditions under which they may enter a colleague's classroom. This indicates an imputed degree of privilege to the activity, but an insufficient degree to meet the paradigm's criterion. . . .

In the teacher-pupil relationship . . . it appears that there is an intended transfer of skills from professional to client. This would be . . . at variance with the paradigm. On closer examination, however, it appears that teachers do not intentionally instruct pupils in how to teach. This is a complex question pivoting around the degree to which teachers are perceived as having an abstract body of knowledge dealing with theories and techniques of teaching. Certainly, in comparison with members of more clearly professional occupations, teachers are relatively lacking an abstract body of knowledge from which they could derive authority.

. . . Interaction between teacher and pupil is appealable to an outside authority which contradicts another criterion. First the teacher lacks the abstract body of knowledge from which professional authority can be derived. Second, the child, as client, cannot make morally binding decisions. Angry parents can mobilize the community to reject a teacher, and principals can over-rule a teacher at many points. . . .[11]

Through the use of this theoretical framework, a set of criteria have been examined which can be applied to the description of the social role of the professional in interaction with a client. In applying this paradigm to teachers as an emerging professional group, we are inclined to characterize them as nonprofessional, or at best as semi-professional, in at least three important aspects of their occupational role. First, they lack a body of abstract knowledge, *qua* teaching. Second, teacher–client interactions are denied the sanctity of privileged communication, and third, the teacher's decisions concerning students are frequently subject to appeal to a higher authority within the hierarchy of the schools from parents or community pressure groups. Thus, it seems clear, at least on

---

[11] *Ibid.*, pp. 15–16.

the basis of this analytic scheme, that teachers as an occupational group are vulnerable in several highly unprofessional situations due to bureaucratic constraints placed upon them by the conventional organizational pattern of the school.

BUREAUCRATIC CONSTRAINTS TO PROFESSIONAL DEVELOPMENT

There is a growing body of literature concerning the emerging education professional which highlights the potential conflict between bureaucratic or organizational demands on the one hand and professional aspirations on the other. It has been suggested that the traditional organization frequently represents a static picture when individuals attempt to achieve professional objectives. Presthus indicated that "the bureaucratic situation . . . is not seen in the same way by all its members. While some individuals perceive the organization as a favorable place in which to assert their career claims, others view its system of authority and status as threatening."[12] School systems which are highly bureaucratic and consequently lean heavily upon "administration by rules" will alienate the professionally oriented teacher who desires autonomy through collegial forms of control. However, the teacher whose professional orientation is weak is more likely to respond favorably to an organization that administers by rules and defines the teacher's role in explicit terms.[13]

General conceptualizations of bureaucracy as an organizational form are not attentive to the character of the human organism within organizational structures. Thus, degrees of ambivalence are fostered by an organizational pattern that is exclusively concerned with precision, reliability, and efficiency rather than the human and self-actualizing potential of the individual. The bureaucratic stereotype has also been accused by some organizational theorists of inducing sterility, indifference, and ineffectiveness; it contains an inherent inability to promote creativity and imagination within organizational structures.

---

[12] Robert Presthus, *The Organizational Society* (New York: Vintage Books, 1965).

[13] Charles E. Bidwell, "The School as A Formal Organization," in James G. March, (ed.), *Handbook of Organizations* (Chicago: Rand McNally & Co., 1965).

Etzioni contends that one of the most serious structural dilemmas is the strain imposed on an organization by the use of knowledge and increased degrees of professionalization, "and it is in this respect that the traditional concept of bureaucracy is least adequate in its accommodation."[14] Within traditional organizations bureaucratic or administrative authority is based on technical knowledge. Subordinates accept the rules of the organization as legitimate because being rational is being right and they regard their superiors as being more rational (more knowledgeable). In professional organizations, or any organization that draws upon a great deal of professional specialization, the hierarchy may not be formed with the most knowledgeable (most rational) people on top. Organizational conflict and role ambiguity can frequently emerge between the bureaucrat and the professional due to the differential in expertise and knowledge base. "Conflict in education, as in many other modern organizations, is between two bases of authority, the profession and the bureaucracy. Within the junior high school the conflict between professionals and bureaucrats is evident at all levels. Bureaucratization and professionalization have been emerging for some time as countervailing forces."[15]

Organizational conflict and role ambiguity may increase because of the diversity of specialization, backgrounds, values, attitudes, and non-oriented organizational interests that the emerging professional brings to the school. As schools create more complex structures, the professional is often relegated to an instructional role in which little latitude is allowed, and routinization of tasks provide less opportunity for creativity and individuality. As the organization becomes larger, relationships between subordinates and superiors increase in complexity and impersonality, and status distinctions are accentuated as additional levels of hierarchy are added. All of these structural conditions influence the social climate under which teachers must work and may ultimately reinforce their tendency to pass on the detached, impersonal

---

14 Amitai Etzioni, *Modern Organizations* (Englewood Cliffs, New Jersey: Prentice-Hall, Inc., 1964). Also, Amitai Etzioni, *A Comparative Analysis of Complex Organizations* (New York: The Free Press of Glencoe, 1961).

15 James G. Anderson, *Bureaucracy in Education* (Baltimore, Maryland: The Johns Hopkins Press, 1968).

attitude of the typical bureaucrat to the clients whom they serve. Willard Waller suggested that the teacher's role by its very nature conflicts with the school's bureaucratic norms. To be effective, the teacher must rely heavily upon personal ties with students. These ties run counter to the rules regarding instruction, which are laid down and enforced by administrators and supervisors and which are intensified as teachers attempt to personalize their relations with the students.[16]

There is also considerable contrast in large organizations between the requirement for bureaucratic control and the need for professional autonomy. One unique characteristic of professionals is their distinctive control structure, which is fundamentally different from the hierachical control exercised in bureaucratic organizations. Professionals typically organize themselves into voluntary associations for the purpose of self-control. In contrast, bureaucratic organizations set norms and need to enforce them; they have rules and regulations and issue orders, which must be obeyed if the organization is to function "effectively." Etzioni states that nowhere is the strain between the organization's needs and the participant's needs—between effectiveness, efficiency, and satisfaction—more evident than in the area of organizational control.[17]

As school systems become more bureaucratic, there is often a tendency toward "over-controlling." As inevitable strain and frustration develop between bureaucratic expectations and professional autonomy, the teacher may abandon his desire for a more autonomous posture and succumb to a bureaucratic orientation. This orientation may be characterized by

> . . . Apathy, a rigid adherence to rules and regulations, an impersonal attitude toward students, and a search for cues from administrators before making decisions. These unprofessional attitudes, though decried by school administrators, school boards, and the public, are the result of bureaucratically structured school systems that foster and reward such behavior.
>
> Whether teachers abandon their professional orientation or not, the administration's refusal to delegate authority to them has its effect on the students, who, in turn, assume little responsibility for

---

16 Willard Waller, *The Sociology of Teaching* (New York: John Wiley and Sons, 1965).

17 Etzioni, *Modern Organizations, op. cit.*

their own education beyond school attendance and a certain minimal compliance with regulations concerning their behavior.[18]

One final point concerning the topic of organizational and professional control requires emphasis. This is related to the primary characterization of professional groups in developing self-regulating techniques for controlling their profession. While teacher professional groups have been very active in demanding a greater voice in educational decision-making and in developing concomitant status, they have neglected, for the most part, an active role in developing appropriate techniques for professional self-control. To a great extent the crux of the problem between considering teachers as "professionals" or as "bureaucratic functionaries" lies with their ability for developing self-regulating mechanisms within their associations in order to provide greater internal quality control. Simply, a system for policing the profession must be established in order for any occupational group to acquire more significant professional status.

It is interesting, and somewhat paradoxical, that in the last decade there has been considerable dichotomy between teacher organizations and administrative professional groups, the inference being that teachers as an emerging profession could not develop the unique characteristics necessary to their "profession" while maintaining a joint alliance with administrators. While generally speaking there is no disagreement with this separatist philosophy, we must question—and to a great extent criticize—teacher "professional" organizations for the limited advances that have been made for instituting internal quality control measures. There is no question that the bureaucratic nature of public education mitigates considerably against the development of significant internal, self-regulating mechanisms within teaching organizations. Interestingly, however, teacher groups have found inroads into the educational bureaucracy in demanding greater latitude, autonomy, and more opportunity for significant roles in decision-making and policymaking in many school systems. It seems consistent to expect that similar inroads could also be made for developing internal control structures within the teaching profession provided that teachers; individually or collectively, were interested in enhancing this important aspect of their professional responsibility.

---

[18] Anderson, *op. cit.*

ORGANIZATIONAL DIMENSIONS OF
PROFESSIONAL DEVELOPMENT[19]

Most concerned administrators recognize the need for and encourage greater professional development among teaching staffs at the secondary school level. Several school programs with which the author is well-acquainted manifest this concern in creating organizational climates which provide for greater staff professional recognition, individual autonomy, and organizational techniques which allow the instructional staff a significant role in the decision-making process of the school.[20] Although considerable progress has been made in a few isolated schools, overall public school teachers continue to be subjugated to roles little different from those held by most subordinate bureaucratic functionaries. To date, educational systems in their organizational designs are extremely limited in supporting models which allow for staff individuality, professional development, or teacher-initiated activities in instructional decision-making.

CONVENTIONAL DIMENSIONS FOR DEVELOPING
TEACHER PROFESSIONALISM

Historically, educators have attempted to ameliorate the problems associated with professional staff development, through one of two methods: (1) by reducing classloads, and/or (2) by attempting to increase teacher salaries. While no one can deprecate the importance of these activities in providing a necessary occupational image for teachers, both avenues are extremely limited in establishing any significant basis for professional agrandizement. There is no argument with increased salaries for teachers, as it is recognized that in some areas of the United States salary schedules are unsatisfactory. However, salary increases per se do not con-

---

[19] Much of the material for this section was rewritten from an earlier article by L. K. Bishop, "The Teacher: Developing A Climate for Professional Behavior," *ISR Journal* (Summer, 1969).

[20] Generally, school systems which have implemented flexible schedules or other similar change programs have found it essential to the success of the program to allow greater staff involvement in the instructional decision-making process. See W. Deane Wiley and Lloyd K. Bishop, *The Flexibly Scheduled High School* (West Nyack, New York: Parker Publishing Co., 1968).

stitute a primary method for providing viable avenues toward professionalism among any occupational group. (In reference to the definitions of the professional considered previously in this chapter, the notion of salary or monetary reward received little or no emphasis.)

In terms of the instructional importance of group size and student classload for each teacher, educators have perpetrated many myths concerning this seemingly "critical facet" of the instructional process. What do teachers do differently in most conventional classrooms with a group of 20 to 25 students that the teacher does or cannot do equally well with a group of 35 or even 40 students? Although schools may vary group size considerably within the conventional, self-contained classroom, this technique alone has had no demonstrable impact upon instructional improvement or teacher professional development. The author seriously disagrees with some professional organizations which, for several years now, have perpetrated the misconception that there is something "magical" about a teaching ratio of 25 students per class with no more than four classes assigned each teacher.[21] In terms of recognizable changes in professional behavior or instructional improvement there is little evidence to date that this formula has had any appreciable effect upon the individuality of instructional method for those school systems that have faithfully employed it. Issues concerning time and its relationship to instruction, individual student learning rates, and interaction processes within groups are not given appropriate consideration with the adoption of such overly simplistic solutions to otherwise complex instructional relationships.

Creative instructional components within educational systems which recognize the interrelationship between the size of a student group and the specific instructional task or activity to be conducted need to be developed. The system must also be flexible in order to accommodate the individuality of the student and the teacher and the day-to-day judgments of the professional staff. To date, some experimentation has been conducted in a few elementary and secondary schools. The deployment of students between large group and small group activities with the implementation of more

---

[21] For example, the National Council of Teachers of English (NCTE).

flexible schedules has provided an initial thrust in this important direction of wedding instructional task to group size and composition. Many teachers are finding that some learning activities can take place in relatively large groups (150 or more students) while other experiences need to be conducted in smaller groups where interaction between student and teacher and, more particularly, between the student and his peer group is more informal. It is the conclusion of the author, developed from several years of personal observation and involvement in innovative school programs, that the conventional, self-contained classroom, regardless of the number of students assigned, is an anachronism; it is, in fact, detrimental to the professional development and needed interaction of teachers.

NEW DIMENSIONS IN DEVELOPING TEACHER PROFESSIONALISM

Traditional elementary and secondary schools require new directions in designing organizational patterns which will provide exploratory techniques for developing greater teacher professional status. The prototypes furnished by the classical professions—theology, law, and medicine—although used on occasion, are not appropriate for providing a theoretical or operational framework for education. Certainly, the unionization movement enhanced through many large metropolitan teaching organizations has not encouraged the development of significant professional status among teaching groups. The union may have been an appropriate model for some industrial occupational groups at the turn of the century, but it seems to offer few professional alternatives for occupational groups approaching organizational problems complicated by the complexities of the twenty-first century. The tactics and methods employed by most teacher unions are little better (in most cases, far worse) than the tactics of the management whom they criticize.

It is ironic that unionization may lead, directly or indirectly, to more stringent controls over teachers. As school administrators perceive opposition and attempts at collective bargaining, they further strengthen and centralize control, and the teacher's behavior is more completely circumscribed than before. If an actual struggle for power between the union and the administration takes place, even less autonomy is permitted individual teachers as both the administration and union leadership exert pressure for the establishment of standard procedures and centralized control. Finally, if the organizational attempt succeeds, the teacher becomes just another member of the union subject to the authority of the school administration and to union officials. Consequently, professional status for teachers may prove to be even more elusive than it is at present.[22]

It is not the intent of this section to offer a complete design for teacher professional development. It is the purpose to present two criteria or elements of a design considered by many educators to be central to any model which attempts to develop professional status among public school teachers in the coming years. These criteria include the management of instructional time and differentiation of teacher responsibility. It is suggested that these criteria also represent primary requisites in attempting to establish open or anabolic climates for teacher interaction and individual expression within any school program.

The Management of Instructional Time. In their enthusiasm to reduce classloads for teachers, most educators have completely neglected to consider other equally significant alternatives. If schools desire to develop a climate for professional activities and to provide teachers with opportunities for greater individual expression, autonomy, and a central role in instructional decision-making, then no other facet of the teacher's school activities seems more crucial than that of time.

We have found few teachers in conventional school situations (teachers who were genuinely attempting to develop exceptional instructional programs) who had sufficient time for these activities. Within the limitations of most traditional school organizations, few teachers have the opportunity to manage or control time in respect to instruction, student groupings, or the specific learning task. One of the critical elements in developing professionalism is the ability of the professional to schedule and manage time in relation to his responsibilities and professional judgments. The best that teachers have been provided in most secondary programs is the inefficacious preparation—counseling period (it is interesting, however, that there are seldom any students available to counsel). Elementary teachers receive little, if any, unscheduled time during the school day.

For any occupational group attempting to develop recognizable professional status, the management of time is a critical dimension.

---

[22] Anderson *op., cit.*

How can teachers display professional behavior in public educational institutions when the organizational structure of these institutions is antithetical to the basic requirements of a professional climate. The teacher, as an emerging professional, requires the opportunity to have more unscheduled time during the school day for their own management and control than is normally provided. Teachers will find it increasingly difficult to assume professional roles within the restrictions of most school programs as they are presently constituted. The teacher during the conventional school day has very little opportunity to restructure activities, to juggle groups, or to be a manager of the instructional process in determining the interrelationship between learning and specific time requirements.

The proposal and emphasis here is simply to furnish teachers with far more unscheduled, informal, out-of-class time during the school day or week than is normally provided. It is proposed, at least as a point of departure, that a 50/50 ratio be established between the teacher's scheduled, formal teaching assignment and his unscheduled, out-of-class time. Fifty percent of the teacher's school week would be scheduled into regularly assigned classroom activities; the other 50% would be unstructured, the use of which would be at the professional discretion and control of the individual teacher.

Because of the restrictions of traditional school scheduling practices, we are well aware of the serious implications inherent in this proposition. However, with the development and implementation of various techniques for scheduling schools flexibly, or team teaching and nongraded programs, this proposed time ratio for teachers is feasible. Several school systems in the implementation stage of a modular or flexible schedule have taken advantage of this aspect of programming by providing a more significant climate for teachers in respect to the control of school time.[23]

Differentiation of Teacher Responsibility.[24]   The present role

---

[23] Wiley and Bishop, *op. cit.*

[24] Part of the information contained in this section was extracted from two sources: (1) Dwight W. Allen, "A Differentiated Teaching Staff," unpublished paper distributed by Educational Coordinates, Palo Alto, California, and (2) from the Policies of the Board of Education, Claremont Unified School District, Claremont, California. It should be noted that John Brinegar,

of the teacher is characterized by no differentiation in responsibilities, assignments, or status positions. "Teachers are generally considered to be interchangeable parts." Paradoxically, education is one of the few social enterprises that rewards excellent performance by moving the individual away from the client he is trained to serve. The tragic situation facing the teacher is that the only way he can gain a promotion and stay in education is to leave teaching and move into administrative positions. No allowance has been made for rewarding the excellent, accomplished instructor. Unfortunately, these promotion methods do not emphasize the professional aspects of teaching or the professional responsibilities that should be attributed to teachers. We need to develop methods of differentiating roles, status, and responsibilities of teachers. Ways are needed to differentiate the responsibility of the outstanding teachers and to use the less competent teachers in supporting roles.

Furthermore, the development of the conventional, monolithic salary schedule found in most school systems has not furnished the financial framework necessary for professional teaching and career development. This type of salary schedule assumes that all teachers at each longevity level are identical and equally competent and that all teaching activities and responsibilities are of comparable magnitude. These salary schedules do not allow for the differences in the intellectual, physical, or psychological attributes that comprise any group of teachers. Some teachers possess greater innate potential, have stronger intellectual powers, and are willing and capable of accepting more responsibility than others. Concomitantly, it is assumed that they should have a more substantial impact upon a greater number of students. Why should the more competent, more effective, more responsible teacher not be rewarded appropriately?

It should be clarified that the present proposal for differentiated staffing is not a form of merit pay. Under most merit pay systems, teachers receive additional pay for being "superior," but retain the same organizational or teaching responsibilities. The more experienced teacher is deployed in exactly the same way as

---

who was superintendent of schools in Claremont, was primarily instrumental in developing a differentiated model in this school system.

the less experienced or less competent teacher. Other than the factor of additional compensation, the merit pay system has had little impact upon developing professional status among teachers. Differentiation of professional responsibilities has not been recognized as a crucial element in this system. In contrast, under the concept of differentiated staffing as a career model, teachers receive additional compensation for the assumption of additional responsibilities which demand advanced levels of experience or teaching competence. Teacher talents can be more effectively utilized by the school system because it has the flexibility to utilize the different levels of skills and abilities in order to meet the varying levels of responsibilities that teachers are willing to assume.

For heuristic purposes, in developing a differentiated professional salary structure five categories or levels of teaching, or five differentiated teaching positions with their complementary levels of responsibility, will be identified (see Figure 12.1).

1. *Intern Teacher.* This is the entering category into teaching as a career. The intern is a beginning, non-certificated student or apprentice teacher. The intern may teach part-time or full-time, depending on the school program and the availability of a master teacher to supervise the intern's activities. Normally one year of service as an intern teacher would be adequate to qualify the individual for the next level of responsibility.

2. *Probationary Teacher.* This would be the entering level into full-time certificated service in the teaching field. The probationary teacher (non-tenure) would typically have at least an A.B. degree, but the category would not be tied specifically to preparation or course units, although it is possible to consider median levels of preparation which are necessary for each differentiated position. General duties assigned to this category would include: (1) general classroom teaching or team teaching assignments, (2) observing the work of other teachers, and (3) attending meetings, study sessions, and in-service or other professionally recognized activities.

3. *Staff Teacher.* The third level of differentiated responsibility might be referred to as staff teacher (tenure). Typical preparation would include a fifth year of college, but may not necessarily include the M.A. degree. Teachers normally would be automatically eligible for this level after having completed their non-tenure

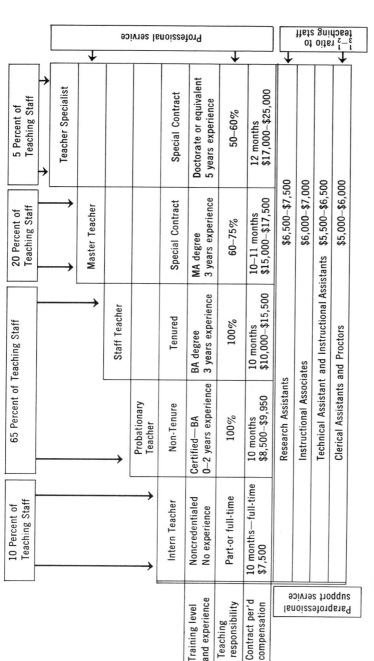

	Intern Teacher	Probationary Teacher	Staff Teacher	Master Teacher	Teacher Specialist
		Non-Tenure	Tenured		
Training level and experience	Noncredentialed No experience	Certified—BA 0–2 years experience	BA degree 3 years experience	MA degree 3 years experience	Doctorate or equivalent 5 years experience
Teaching responsibility	Part-or full-time	100%	100%	60–75%	50–60%
Contract per'd compensation	10 months—full-time $7,500	10 months $8,500–$9,950	10 months $10,000–$15,500	10–11 months $15,000–$17,500	12 months $17,000–$25,000

Research Assistants	$6,500–$7,500
Instructional Associates	$6,000–$7,000
Technical Assistant and Instructional Assistants	$5,500–$6,500
Clerical Assistants and Proctors	$5,000–$6,000

Paraprofessional support service

10 Percent of Teaching Staff

65 Percent of Teaching Staff

20 Percent of Teaching Staff

5 Percent of Teaching Staff

Professional service

1–1 ratio to teaching staff

3–2 ratio to teaching staff

FIGURE 12.1 *Differentiated staffing Model (Career Salary Schedule)*

service. Some duties assigned to this category might include: (1) general classroom teaching or team teaching, (2) specialized teaching duties, (3) serving on curriculum committees, and (4) participating in curriculum research or study projects.

4. *Master Teacher.* The next category could be entitled master teacher or senior teacher; the M.A. degree would be required. The master teacher is a teacher who has demonstrated his qualification to assume responsibility and leadership in teaching. This teacher might be assigned additional duties such as: (1) assuming leadership positions on curriculum committees, (2) assisting in the training of probationary or intern teachers, (3) assisting in research projects, (4) team teaching leaders, and (5) serving in leadership positions in school faculty organizations.

5. *Teacher Specialist.* The highest level in the differentiated model might be designated teacher specialist. Obviously, the title is unimportant; what is important is the philosophy underlying the creation of status positions with appropriate rewards while allowing the teacher to remain in the classroom. The development of this type of salary structure allows the teacher a career line in teaching comparable in status and compensation to administration or other professional activities. This staff level might be associated with the doctorate or comparable post-master's degree work and would enable a person who was interested in classroom teaching to have a full professional career in the classroom.

The teacher specialist is a teacher who, through the quality of his experience, training, and demonstrated ability, is capable of assuming responsibility for teaching and curriculum development on a professional level beyond that expected of the regular classroom teacher. Typical duties might include: (1) demonstration and consultation in areas of his particular competence, (2) research in areas of his specialized knowledge, (3) planning for programs that require system-wide coordination, and (4) performance in experimental teaching situations. The teacher specialist might have some release time from regular teaching duties if his additional responsibilities should warrant this.

Teachers serving in a differentiated staffing structure are afforded opportunities to engage in instructional decision making, a function too often denied them in the past. The vehicle for this service may be in the form of an instructional committee on which the principal, teacher specialists, and master teachers serve, along with representatives of other professional or paraprofessional ranks. In this way the professional expertise of teachers can be brought to bear upon educational problems in a positive manner. This democratic structure serves to assure that decisions will be based on the best possible professional judgment and not upon caprice.

Supporting the professional staff is a four-level paraprofessional ladder composed of four categories. The ladder is designed to provide less highly trained personnel an opportunity to enter instructional work prior to the completion of a four-year college degree. Such an "early-entry" progression can serve to direct many potentially effective instructional personnel who might otherwise drift into other occupations and be permanently lost to public education.

The system also combines service to the schools with on-the-job and in-service training, plus advanced academic studies. Thus, an individual entering the ranks of Clerical Assistants or Proctors receives on-the-job training from the professionals with whom he works, participates in a school district in-service program conducted by district teacher specialists and instructional associates, and attends adult education courses leading to the completion of a high school diploma. Upon the completion of the diploma and in-service programs, plus a minimum period of satisfactory on-the-job performance, he is eligible to apply for advancement to the position of Technical or Instructional Assistant.

Advancement from Technical or Instructional Assistant to Instructional Associate is predicated upon the completion of an additional period of in-service training, a period of satisfactory classroom service, and the completion of two years of college work which would eventually lead to the bachelors degree. Following completion of the B.A. degree and a third period of in-service training and satisfactory service, the associate is eligible to apply for a position as intern teacher or research assistant, depending upon interest and ability. He may, of course, choose to remain at any paraprofessional level but is not encouraged generally to do so. During the intern year the individual completes certification requirements and rounds out his pedagogical and academic training. From this point on, individual progress through the differentiated career ladder depends increasingly upon personal aspirations, talent, and skill development as a professional.

1. Clerical Assistant and Proctor. The clerical aides and proctors provide services which enable the teacher to give more time and energy to the primary task of instruction by undertaking routine supervision, and clerical and materials handling tasks. These responsibilities will include: (1) record keeping, (2) preparation of instructional materials, (3) monitoring of students, (4) scoring of simple objective tests, (5) duplication of materials, and (6) collection of funds under teacher supervision.

2. Technical and Instructional Assistant. This individual carries out many of the same duties performed by the clerical aide and proctor, but because of his greater experience and training he can handle increasing instruction-related responsibilities under teacher supervision. He may, for instance, (1) work with small groups of students in an instructional situation; (2) assist in classroom management, and supervise the library, resource centers, or lunchroom, as well as assist on playgrounds and during bus duty; (3) maintain all teacher-student records; (4) proctor and monitor testing periods, particularly in large group instruction; (5) prepare more sophisticated instructional materials, such as transparencies, overlays, slide presentations, films, and audiovisual equipment; and (6) take charge of the class for brief periods in the teacher's absence.

3. Instructional Associate. An associate is an experienced assistant who acts in a role more directly supportive of the instructional program than those filling the previously described positions. That is, he (1) engages in direct instructional activities on a regular basis with minimal supervision; (2) develops instructional materials and basic lesson plans; (3) counsels students in disciplinary and personal matters; (4) assumes substantial responsibility for class activities; (5) helps supervise other aides and assistants on grounds, bus, and cafeteria duty; (6) participates as an instructor in in-service programs for aides and assistants; and (7) may serve on the instructional committee of the school, thus participating in the decision-making process of the system.

4. Research Assistant. The research assistant is a special category of "teacher aide" which provides special research and materials development tasks for the professional teacher which is not commonly found in most conventional teaching situations. This individual is a specialist in his own right and must possess qualifications and skills necessary for performance as a research specialist. He might perform such activities as (1) historical or philosophical research, (2) empirical and statistical research, (3) evaluation of instructional programs, and (4) research and design studies as directed by the professional staff.

It must be recognized that teachers in most traditional secondary and elementary schools do not enjoy the necessary climate that provides them a basis for developing appropriate professional behavior. It seems particularly incumbent upon the educational community to establish organizational techniques which will allow teachers greater latitude and a broader operational and professional base from which to function. Two dimensions—the management of instructional time and the differentiation of professional responsibility—have been suggested which seem to be fundamental in developing more significant school climates for enhancing professional teacher behavior.

AN ORGANIZATIONAL MODEL FOR INSTRUCTIONAL CHANGE AND PROFESSIONAL DEVELOPMENT

13

This chapter will continue the theme concerning the organizational nature of public schools and the consequences of their bureaucratic design on the individual teacher as an emerging professional. Essentially, the purpose here is to respond to a growing body of literature concerning the dysfunctional aspects of the bureaucratic organizational form and to apply one of these anti-bureaucratic conceptualizations to an analysis and subsequent restructuring of public schools as complex, social institutions.[1]

THE DEMISE OF BUREAUCRACY

Warren Bennis is notable among the proponents of the demise of the bureaucratic model as a functional organizational scheme for the last decades of the twentieth century.[2] In recent publications

---

[1] See, for example, the Selznick, Merton, Gouldner models of unanticipated consequences of bureaucratic organizational structure in: James G. March and Herbert A. Simon, *Organizations* (New York: John Wiley and Sons, 1958); Robert Presthus, *The Organizational Society* (New York: Vintage Books, 1965); Chris Argyris, *Integrating the Individual in the Organization* (New York: John Wiley and Sons, 1964); Robert K. Merton, *Social Theory and Social Structure* (New York: The Free Press of Glencoe, 1957); Amitai Etzioni, *A Comparative Analysis of Complex Organizations* (New York: The Free Press of Glencoe, 1961).

[2] Warren G. Bennis, "The Coming Death of Bureaucracy," *Think* (November-December, 1966); "Organizations of the Future," *Personnel Administration* (September-October, 1967); "Post-Bureaucratic Leadership," *Trans-action* (July-August, 1969); and *Changing Organizations* (New York: McGraw-Hill Book Co., 1966).

he has submitted several intriguing conceptions concerning changes necessary in the blueprint of large, complex social institutions in order for these systems to be brought into focus with the social, political, and humanistic demands required by an increasingly professional and pluralistic society. Inasmuch as most public schools are designed around a typical industrial bureaucratic model, it seems logical that they can be exposed to a critical inspection and analysis in light of several of Bennis's speculations concerning required organizational changes.

Bennis is outspoken in his proposals concerning the "coming death of bureaucracy" as a functional social tool for integrating men and resources toward organizational goals. His forecast is based on the evolutionary principle that "every age develops an organizational form appropriate to its genius and that the prevailing form of pyramidal–hierarchical organization, known by sociologists as 'bureaucracy' and, most businessmen as 'that damn bureaucracy', was out of joint with contemporary realities."[3]

It is not the purpose here to offer a thorough discussion of the underlying rationale proposed by Bennis for the predicted downfall of the bureaucratic form. Briefly, however, Bennis has suggested that the bureaucratic pyramidal–hierarchical structure is vulnerable on at least four counts:

> There are at least four relevant threats to bureaucracy. The first is a human, basically psychological one, . . . while the other three spring from extraordinary changes in our environment: (1) rapid and unexpected change, (2) growth in size where volume of organization's traditional activities is not enough to sustain growth, and (3) complexity of modern technology where integration of activities and persons of very diverse, highly specialized competence is required.[4]

Of perhaps greatest interest to this presentation is the "new concept of organization values" and the basic required changes in organizational philosophy concerning the role of the individual in the organization. Accordingly, the mechanistic organizational man, inherent within the bureaucratic philosophy, is being rapidly replaced by a concept of man "based on increased knowledge of his complex and shifting needs, which replaces an over-simplified, in-

---

[3] Bennis, "The Coming Death of Bureaucracy," *op. cit.*
[4] Bennis, "Organizations of the Future," *op. cit.*

nocent push-botton idea of man." A new concept of organizational power is based on collaboration and reason and replaces "a model of power based on coercion and threat." And finally, a new concept of organizational values is based on "humanistic-democratic ideals" and replaces the depersonalized mechanistic value system of bureaucracy.[5]

> These transformations of Man, Power, and Values have gained wide intellectual acceptance in management quarters. They have caused a terrific amount of rethinking on the part of many organizations. They have been used as a basis for policy formulation by many large-scale organizations. This philosophy is clearly not compatible with bureaucratic practices.[6]

Bennis also states that the real push for these changes in organizations stems from some powerful needs not only to humanize the organization but to use the organization as a crucible for personal growth and development, for self-actualization.

THE ORGANIC-ADAPTIVE STRUCTURE

Bennis's conceptualizations are not the only criticisms which have been leveled at the bureaucratic form of organization in recent years; however, he is one of the few critics who has attempted to present alternative approaches to the bureaucratic phenomenon.[7] Even though his proposal only provides a rough framework for considering organizational changes in the future, his concepts are sufficient for provocative speculation in suggesting alternatives in structure, roles, and interpersonal relationships among professional staffs in school systems. (Bennis's ideas on organizational change might be compared to an impressionistic painting in which much of the detail of structure and form must be completed by the imagination of the viewer.) The purpose now is to adapt this basic framework to a possible organizational model for secondary schools that will be more appropriate for the future. This type of organizational development seems particularly pertinent and consistent with the general theme in considering the concepts of professional staff development and individualization of instructional programs.

---

[5] *Ibid.*

[6] *Ibid.*

[7] See, for example: Victor A. Thompson, "Bureaucracy and Innovation," *Administrative Science Quarterly* (Summer, 1965).

Briefly, some of the fundamental components of the Bennis proposal for future organizational change are as follows:

The social structure of organizations of the future will have some unique characteristics. The key word will be 'temporary'; there will be adaptive, rapidly changing temporary systems. These will be 'task forces' organized around problems-to-be-solved by groups of relative strangers who represent a diverse set of professional skills. The groups will be arranged on an organic rather than mechanical model; they will evolve in response to a problem rather than to programmed role expectations. The 'executive' thus becomes a coordinator or 'linking pin' between various task forces. . . . People will be evaluated not vertically according to rank and status, but flexibly and functionally according to skill and professional training. . . .

Adaptive, problem-solving, temporary systems of diverse specialists, linked together by coordinating and task evaluating specialists in an organic flux—this is the organizational form that will gradually replace bureaucracy as we know it. As no catchy phrase comes to mind, I call this an organic-adaptive structure.[8]

Furthermore, Bennis suggests that the tasks and goals of organizations in the future will be more technical, complicated, and unprogrammed. Essentially, they will call for the collaboration of specialists in a project of a team-form of organization. Because of the increased level of education and mobility of individuals, the values we hold about work will change. People will be more intellectually committed to their professional careers and will require more involvement, participation, and autonomy.

RATIONALE FOR ORGANIZATIONAL CHANGE

In employing the Bennis framework in an operational context for secondary school organization, the basic underlying theme of an organic–adaptive structure based upon overlapping, flexible, interdisciplinary *task–force teams* appears to be highly germane in organizational functions within secondary schools as well as some larger elementary schools. To what extent these teams will be "temporary" systems with the same degree of fluidity as suggested by Bennis will be assigned for the present to the realm of conjecture and not treated in depth in this discussion.

In light of our considerations in Chapter 12 for providing more open or anabolic organizational climates in order to accom-

---

[8] Bennis, "Organizations of the Future," *op. cit.*

modate greater professional staff involvement, the organic–adaptive system with its concepts of "collaboration of specialists" and "humanistic–democratic ideals" seems extremely pertinent. The concept of power equalization—the distribution of organizational power among organizational members, and particularly among the emerging professional group—has long been a critical issue in designing more functional, humanistic organizational forms. There is little doubt that more creative organizational schemes are necessary within educational systems for providing more humanistic environments. The concept of an organic–adaptive organizational structure appears to be consistent with the overall theme of individualizing instructional programs. Exploratory techniques for organizing educational resources must be developed in order to provide greater individuality to professional staffs and students, especially in terms of instructional decision-making, flexibility in modes of teaching and learning, and interactions between student and school programs.

BASIC UNDERLYING ASSUMPTIONS FOR CHANGE

Several basic assumptions must be clarified in adapting the organic–adaptive structure to secondary school organizations. These assumptions are concerned with the primary purpose for the existence of public schools as complex, social institutions. The assumption basic to this rationale for organizational change supports the conviction that schools exist primarily for the purpose of instruction. That is, the instructional process—curriculum development and individualized methods of teaching and learning—are the primary and essential components, the *raison d'être*, for the existence of any school program. All other activities and programs of the school must be considered peripheral or secondary to the central instructional function of the school.

The second assumption, a natural outgrowth of the first, is concerned with the level within the traditional organizational hierarchy where the primary responsibility for the development of curriculum and the instructional program should be placed. This proposal supports a "grass roots" approach to this basic responsibility. The contention is that this responsibility, and subsequent decision-making concerning the instructional process, must rest with the instructional staff within each school—in other words, with the teachers. Correspondingly, the third assumption is concerned with the instructional leadership of a school. Again, the contention is that this leadership function must be at the building level and that latitude and autonomy must be granted to each functional unit of the overall school system. Reason seems to dictate, however, that this leadership function must be a shared responsibility. There has been considerable debate in administrative circles in recent years concerning the principal's role as an "instructional leader" of his school. We would strongly contend that this function must be more of a collaborative effort—a task–force team endeavor—than the total responsibility of any one individual or organizational role.

Finally, there are basic assumptions inherent within this proposal for organizational change which suggest the rapid and early demise of the conventional, self-contained classroom. If teachers are to enjoy a central, dominant role in the development of instructional programs, then a great deal more teacher interaction, collaborative associations, and interchange opportunities must be designed into the basic organization of schools. These assumptions also imply that teachers will accept a greater professional role in this interchange process. It is assumed that they will find greater creative potential in collaboration than in isolation, and that they will be willing and eager to assume a greater professional role in the instructional decision-making process, particularly as they work collectively toward discovering more unique methods for individualizing that process.

THE NONRATIONALITY OF CONVENTIONAL ORGANIZATIONAL PATTERNS

These assumptions for organizational change raise several concerns which deal with the rationality of the conventional pyramidal–hierarchical structure of most secondary school systems. Reflection upon the typical organizational positions from teacher, through principal, to superintendent and board of education highlights several inconsistencies between the degree of expertise held by each role incumbent and the forgoing assumptions concerning the level of responsibility for developing individualized instructional programs within any school.

An analysis of the traditional pyramidal–hierarchical structure (Figure 13.1) makes it apparent that the teacher in this organizational design cannot occupy the primary decision-making

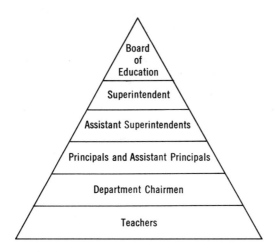

FIGURE 13.1
Conventional Pyramidal–Hierarchical Secondary School Structure

role in influencing the development of instructional programs. Essentially, the teacher's occupational role is little different from that of any other bureaucratic functionary found in most bureaucratically organized systems. Following the logical and rational order of the bureaucratic model in respect to the decision-making process forces one to conclude that control must flow from the top of the hierarchy to the lower levels of the organization. As indicated in Chapter 12, bureaucratic or administrative authority is based on technical knowledge. Subordinates in the hierarchy accept rules and decisions of the organization as legitimate because being rational is being right and they regard their superiors as being more rational (more knowledgeable). Thus, in the pyramidal–hierarchical organizational model, decision-making and leadership functions are commanded from the top hierarchical levels. This structure, if "rational," demands that the greatest expertise and knowledge concerning organizational goal accomplishment be located at the top of the hierarchy. The higher up the hierarchy one ascends, the more rational—and thus the more knowledgeable—the role incumbent must be concerning the operational aspects of the organization.

Today most educators would agree that few superintendents, not to mention boards of education, possess the required knowledge base or expertise to function in the role of instructional specialists. In terms of curriculum development and instructional leadership, however, conventional bureaucratic structures demand that this "rationality" and knowledge base reside with its top administrative positions as suggested by the pyramid design.

A basic dilemma exists between the assumptions concerning the teacher's role in the instructional decision-making process and the bureaucratic organizational design of most schools. One method of resolving this dilemma, which would appear to be more logical with the pyramidal design, would be simply to invert the pyramid, thereby placing the teacher at the top of the hierarchy. An inverted pyramid, although more "rational" in a bureaurcratic context for allowing the teacher the central role in instructional decision-making, would not find wide educational acceptance. Therefore, an alternative approach is necessary for designing an organizational system which will properly integrate the teacher into the instructional decision-making process of the school. Bennis's concepts of the organic–adaptive model with its formulation of collaborative task-force teams seems at least to offer one solution for the inclusion of teachers as professionals in the instructional process in a collegial form of organizational development.

APPLICATION OF THE ORGANIC–ADAPTIVE MODEL TO SECONDARY SCHOOL ORGANIZATION

Again, the basic notion underlying the use of the organic–adpative model in secondary schools assumes that the primary purpose and emphasis of the school is on the development of instructional programs. Inherent within this assumption is the necessity for shared, collaborative instructional leadership and, further, that the teacher as an instructional specialist and emerging professional of the teaching–learning process must play a dominant role in the instructional decision-making process of the school.

THE PROFESSIONAL TEACHER CORE

The professional teacher core constitutes the essential and primary functional component of the school's program and, sub-

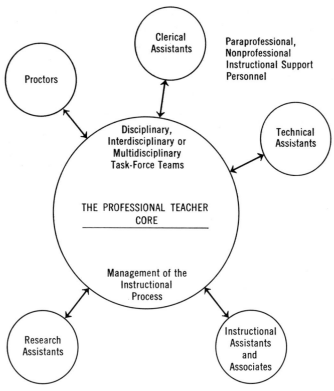

FIGURE 13.2
The Professional Teacher Core—Basic Instructional Component of the Organic–Adaptive System

sequently, the basic component of this organizational model. In attempting to visualize the interrelationship of the constituent parts of this component of the model, Figure 13.2 provides a simplified schematic. The professional teacher core consists of a differentiated professional teaching staff with supporting nonprofessional personnel (see also Figure 12.1, p. 243).

Included within the body of the teacher core are various combinations of disciplinary and interdisciplinary task–force teams of teachers with corresponding levels of responsibility. In some cases, these task force units would be similar to present concepts of team teaching; however, if the organic–adaptive model is applied to its fullest potential, one would expect to find more flexibility and over-lapping of team members. This would allow greater degrees of interdisciplinary activities than is normally found in most conventional team teaching programs. Also, some teams would be "temporary" task–forces formed for specific problem-solving situations involving the instructional program or curriculum development. After the completion of a specific instructional task, these task–forces might be disbanded or reorganized for other problem-solving situations.

It must be noted that the organic–adaptive process of creating functional, temporary problem-solving teams cannot be equated with the conventional "teacher committee" which is often found in public schools. Generally, the administration is responsible for the formation and appointment of these committees. In the task-force team concept, it is conceived that these temporary problem-solving teams would be formed by the teacher core as curricular problems are identified and require solution. Thus, the teaching staff could exercise their professional prerogatives and autonomy for the solution of instructional problems as needed.

> Individuals in organizations, and teachers apparently are no exception, want and need a certain amount of autonomy if they are to contribute meaningfully to the organizational endeavor and at the same time avoid the anxiety and conflict endemic in modern organizations. Such a demand cannot be satisfied through rotating positions of titular authority, such as that of department chairman, or through nominal participation in decision making, such as appointing teachers to the innumerable committees that advise administrators. Teachers want to make decisions that they consider within their professional domain, and they are not satisfied with participation in decision making at the discretion of administrators.[9]

Ideally, the professional teacher core would constitute a flexible, collegial group of men and women dedicated to the sophistication and furtherance of the instructional enterprise. Their activities would consist of an open, continuing interchange of ideas. Professional opinions and decisions would be reached through rational, collaborative responses to common curricular and instructional problems.

---

[9] James G. Anderson, *Bureaucracy in Education* (Baltimore, Md.: The Johns Hopkins Press, 1968).

There appears to be a good deal of compatibility between the concepts of differentiated staffing, presented in Chapter 12, and the organic–adaptive, task–force team-oriented system. Each task–force found within the body of the teaching core would be composed of teachers with various degrees of specialization, experience, and willingness to accept instructional and leadership responsibilities. Compensation on the basis of this willingness to accept additional responsibility seems consistent with the development of this organizational scheme. Auxiliary or paraprofessional personnel as support staff to the professional teacher would also find appropriate semi-instructional roles within the task–force team design.

Paraprofessionals and Instructional Assistants.[10]   Present concepts of teacher assistance, supervision, and acceptance of responsibility dates back to a nineteenth-century normal school concept, where the teacher typically had completed a ninth grade education and one year of normal school. There was a valid assumption that the teacher was probably not able to cope with the educational problems confronting him. Thus, close supervision for the teacher was included in the conventional organizational models for schools. This consisted of a hierarchy of "professionals" who were available to teachers as consultants in order to supplement their inadequacies.

The training of teachers today is not even remotely similar to that of a century ago. Teachers now have four or five years of college education and are better equipped to deal with both their teaching subjects and their students. Yet assistance for the teacher remains the same: supervisors, consultants, curriculum coordinators, and administrators.

Consistent with the design for an organic–adaptive task–force team organizational system within public schools are the new concepts of help and assistance for the teacher. These positions will consist of nonprofessionals and paraprofessionals (teacher aides) which may take the form of clerks, proctors, technical assistants, instructional assistants, research assistants, and so on. The emphasis should now be on the teacher as an instructional professional—

---

10 Part of the material for this section was extracted from an unpublished paper written by Dwight W. Allen, "A Differentiated Teaching Staff," Standford University, Stanford, California.

a manager of the instructional process—with various kinds of instructional and technical assistants to help the teacher perform his specialized responsibilities. In the conventional school system we fail to differentiate between instructional competence which requires five years of college experience and the competence needed to run a ditto machine or motion picture projector. The teacher today is cranking his own ditto machine, typing his own stencils, proctoring, and acting in the capacity of technical assistant as well as instructional expert. (We might also add that in many school systems teachers are the highest-paid babysitters in town.) Thus, an undifferentiated staff exists that is reminiscent of the medical profession at the turn of the century, when the family doctor was responsible for the full range of medical services without the aid of nurses, laboratory technicians, or other assistants.

> While it is proper to translate public concern for the importance of public education into truly professional salaries for teachers, it is also obvious that the continuing escalation of wage packages for huge armies of city employees can only lead to an impossible budgetary problem unless high salaries are followed by improved productivity. In the case of teachers, this can be accomplished if in the years ahead the ranks of the highly paid professional instructors and administrators are augmented by paraprofessional support. An imaginative redeployment of staff and resources and an effective redefinition of teaching functions can do much to help solve urban educational and fiscal problems.[11]

Instructional Space. In developing an organizational design for schools based on the organic–adaptive model we immediately realize that present concepts concerning the design of instructional space are obsolete. For example, we still consider it desirable to identify a teacher with a specific classroom in the school. With the proposed scheme for developing task–force groups, it is mandatory that we define the role of the teacher independent of a permanent room assignment. Teachers and their respective teaching activities can only be identified with classrooms for specific instructional purposes. The teacher's base of operation should be an office, work area, or planning area, not a classroom standing empty during a preparation period. Proper facility design becomes even more crucial as the proportion of the teacher's formal, in-class time

---

[11] Editorial "Teachers' Settlement," *The New York Times*, June 26, 1969.

diminishes. As proposed in Chapter 12, a 50/50 ratio is recommended between the teacher's structured and unstructured instructional time. Thus, the concept of the thirty-student capacity classroom with a single teacher is undoubtedly an anachronism.

Furthermore, the school plant must be conceived in terms of a new openness and flexibility which will encourage both casual and formal observation of instructional situations. The professional teacher operating in the task–force unit cannot feel threatened by outside observation; indeed, the organizational design suggested here demands professional collaboration, frequent interaction, and cooperation among teachers and other instructional assistants. If we expect teachers to develop as professionals, to engage in collaboration and significant interactions, to encourage individualization of instruction, and to confer with individual students and their colleagues, then appropriate space and specific instructional facilities must be provided.

> One concept is the systematic inclusion of experimental space in each building. Space that is designed for maximum changeability. Here teachers can come to develop innovations in space configuration for pilot programs or special layouts for existing programs. If the school has some portion of its facilities set up with modular units, making it easy to change its size, shape of space, electronic circuitry, and equipment, it can have a laboratory for continuous space innovation, thus encouraging the staff to frequently examine their instructional requirements. This should increase both efficiency and effectiveness of the use of space. Design can encourage change by creating alternatives within a single building to provide a perspective on use of space. Teachers in general have narrow notions of the use of school space. To them, instructional areas are stereotyped and they are not looking for alternative possibilities. We need to encourage a period of empirical development in education wherein teachers are exposed to alternatives. After this, or at best, concomitantly, more systematic examination and hopefully specific recommendations can emerge for future construction.[12]

The school of the future needs to be free from the sterile institutional form of today in order to make it an exciting and more dynamic place for student and teacher. It needs to be a place that is aesthetically designed to create pride and pleasure and that provides a base for humanizing and individualizing the activities of

---

[12] Dwight W. Allen, "The Continuous Progress School Building," unpublished paper distributed by Educational Coordinates, Palo Alto, California.

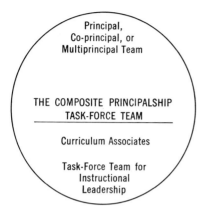

Principal,
Co-principal, or
Multiprincipal Team

THE COMPOSITE PRINCIPALSHIP
TASK-FORCE TEAM

Curriculum Associates

Task-Force Team for
Instructional
Leadership

FIGURE 13.3
The Composite Principalship Task-Force Team

student and professional staff. It must be compatible with, and adaptable to, the organizational scheme by which men and resources are brought together to accomplish the goals of the institution.

THE COMPOSITE PRINCIPALSHIP TASK-FORCE TEAM

As public secondary schools become larger and as school-related functions become more complex and diversified, the leadership and coordinating functions in turn become more critical. While the professional teacher core constitutes the primary functional component for the instructional program of the school, the composite principalship task–force offers comparable specialization to the functional dimension of the leadership-coordination-administrative component of the organic–adaptive system (see Figure 13.3). Obviously, the necessity within any complex organization structure for the coordination of activities, general goal delineation, and leadership functions must be taken into account. For lack of a more imaginative concept we will refer to this component of the system as the composite principalship task–force. It is recognized that this is a rather awkward title; however, there are several important inferences in this concept concerning the basic elements of its design. Simply, we will refer to this unit of the model as the principalship or leadership task–force. The composite principalship task–force is composed of two essential components

which will be discussed in this section. These are the principal–
co-principal team and the curriculum associates.

The basic assumption underlying the formation of the principalship is an outgrowth of the complexity and diversification of the
educational services demanded in most large public schools. The
concept of the single "principal," an outgrowth of the "principal
teacher" concept at the turn of the century, is no longer appropriate
for the degree of specialization required today. A more flexible
leadership unit must be devised for combining professional skills
in coordinating the complex, specialized tasks of school programs.
The leadership function of any complex organization with diversified demands placed upon it by a pluralistically oriented society
must pool its leadership resources into a shared, collaborative management unit. The formation of the composite principalship component of this model as a leadership task–force unit will supply
this aspect of specialization to the functional operation of the
overall system.

The principalship team is responsible for the long-range decision-making and policymaking of the institution. It provides
general administrative directions as well as specific instructional
leadership to the school program. It must be emphasized that this
office is no longer held by one individual designated the "principal"
but rather by a group of highly skilled professionals who will share
in a collaborative fashion the day-to-day exigencies of the school
program, as well as the important aspects of long-range planning
and decision-making.

The chairman or coordinator of the leadership task–force
could continue with the title of principal or co-principal, depending upon the circumstances and the size of the school. The title is
not nearly as crucial as the specific role expectations engendered
within the concept of principal as employed in this model. The
emphasis of this role, as well as the total principalship team, is to
provide leadership and coordination to the instructional program
of the school and to develop a climate within the school for the
professional agrandizement of the instructional staff. Other aspects
of the school program, for example, public relations, student affairs,
or athletic programs—are relegated to a lower priority level.

In addition to the principal or co-principal team, within the
principalship task–force are a group of instructional or curriculum

experts called curriculum associates. These are teachers who have reached professional excellence, who possess the requisite expertise to be leaders in their respective instructional areas, and who can provide direction and supervision in curriculum development. The curriculum associate, although highly involved in the leadership-management-administrative aspects of the school, remains committed to the teaching role and devotes part of the school day to basic teaching activities and interaction with students.

It is envisioned that the principal or co-principal component of the principalship task–force unit would provide relative stability to this team organization (Bennis's stable coordination and linking pin element). On the other hand, the curriculum associates could provide a more flexible or fluid element as suggested by the temporary system concept. Positions and roles in this aspect of the principalship could easily change as new requirements and demands are determined within the process of developing instructional programs and specific curricular content. For example, a school which initially was organized along more conventional lines with a curriculum associate for English and another for history may decide that an interdisciplinary approach is more appropriate. Thus, one curriculum associate with an interdisciplinary orientation could be appointed, constituting a needed and justifiable change to the composition of the principalship team.

The Curriculum Associate. The concept of the principalship generally and the curriculum associate specifically is dedicated to the conviction that greater teacher involvement must exist in the management of the instructional program and the supervision of the teaching-learning process. The curriculum associate is an instructional expert in a specifically defined area of the curriculum. He performs the specialist's role in offering leadership and direction, as well as representation and coordination, to a specific area of the instructional program. This leadership may follow conventional disciplinary lines, but preferably it would be organized along an interdisciplinary approach to instruction. The curriculum associates are instructional specialists within the composite principalship team, while in contrast the principal, co-principal unit are instructional generalists who provide specialization in administrative functions, organizational skills, and interpersonal relations among organizational members.

At this point, it is important to show the interrelationship between the differentiated staffing model proposed earlier and the role of curriculum associate. Conceivably, the curriculum associate could be placed at either the "master teacher" or "teacher specialist" level of the salary proposal (see Figure 12.1, p. 243), depending on the degree of responsibility assumed by him and the size of the instructional area to be coordinated. More importantly, with this degree of salary flexibility it would be feasible to attract highly competent professionals to these important positions. It is not inconceivable that individuals holding advanced degrees—Ph.D. or Ed.D.—would be attracted to these school programs.

Generally, the curriculum associate would be appointed for a one-year period. Under ideal circumstances he would be assigned this position after collaboration and mutual agreement had been reached by his peers from the instructional area that he must represent on the leadership task–force team. If the curriculum associate is appointed from outside the school, then a representative team of teachers from the specific instructional area should be involved in the interview process. Each curriculum associate is directly responsible to the composite principalship team and the specific instructional area he represents and from which he would obtain the necessary authority to function and perform his duties.

For example, a partial listing of these responsibilities might include:

1. Instructional Program
   a. Development, supervision, and evaluation of the instructional program
   b. Evaluation of teachers
   c. Orientation and assistance to teachers
   d. Staff development and in-service training
   e. Participation in the interviewing, selection, and assignment of teachers within the instructional area.
2. Coordination
   a. Work with the principalship team and other curriculum associates to insure coordination of all instructional activities
   b. Provide internal coordination within instructional area for staff and facilities
   c. Maintain liaison between the principalship task–force and the instructional staff
   d. Coordinate the development of all instructional materials.
3. Planning

     a. Participate in research and planning for curriculum development, textbook selection, and class scheduling
     b. Provide leadership for instructional meetings and develop participation in disciplinary and interdisciplinary interchange among staff
     c. Provide liaison to counselors concerning the welfare of students
     d. Conduct instructional area meetings for coordinating and planning of curriculum development.
4. Reporting and Communication
     a. Keep the principalship task–force informed of instructional area operation
     b. Keep area teachers informed of policies and decisions adopted by the leadership task–force unit

The Principal, Co-principal Team. In larger conventional high school organizations the administrative unit of the school is usually composed of a principal and one or more assistant or vice principals. We have purposely neglected to consider the typical assistant or vice principal position in our model simply because this position does not exist. Essentially, we are suggesting the elimination of these positions in favor of a team approach to the central administrative unit. We have chosen to call this subsystem, or component, of the composite principalship task–force team the principal, co-principal team. In smaller secondary or elementary schools this position would be filled by one individual; therefore, the *team* connotation would be ιappropriate. However, in larger secondary schools, where a principal and one or more assistants are normally employed, we are proposing the development of a co-principal or multi-principal team organization. The co-principal team would share the authority and related responsibilities usually assigned to the single conventional principal.

One member of the co-principal or multi-principal team might serve as chairman of the team and, concurrently, chairman and coordinator of the composite principalship task-force unit. In a more sophisticated unit composition, this chairmanship would be rotated among the members of the multi-principal team, thus allowing each member the experience and responsibility of this office. Ideally and in an evolutionary context as individuals become more secure in this type of administrative leadership, it would not be necessary to designate a chairman of the co-principal team. Rather, through their professional expertness and sense of logical administrative procedures, the team would function as a collectivity.

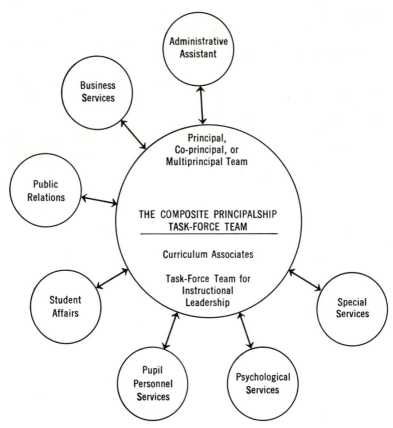

FIGURE 13.4
The Composite Principalship Task-Force with Supporting Subsystems

performing the administrative tasks as a "team" unit or through management by collaboration.[13]

Supporting Units. Inasmuch as the principalship team is primarily responsible for leadership in the instructional program of the school, we envision all other school-related functions as peripheral or supporting subsystems to this central decision-making body

ris, *Mastery of Management* (Homewood, Ill.: Dow Jones,
).

(see Figure 13.4). The model suggests that such functions as student affairs, pupil personnel services, or business services are only conceived as support services to the instructional program of the school. The individuals occupying these roles do not participate in the central decision-making process of the school. As supporting personnel they may be called on at any time to offer direction and expertise concerning their area of specialization. Frequently, they may be influential within the principalship team in providing guidance and direction in specific program development. Their impact upon the instructional program of the school is derived only in relationship to decisions and program development as constituted in the principalship task-force unit.

The number of supporting subsystems generally will be determined in relation to the size of the school and the number of auxiliary services the school can support financially. In most larger secondary schools we would expect to find, as minimal supporting services, a pupil personnel program, student affairs, and some type of business-office management service. Inherent within this model is the conception that individuals occupying roles such as administrative assistant to the co-principal team or business-office managerial services are not required to have previous educational experience or typical certification. It is expected that in many cases it would be preferable to employ individuals with specialized training in the specific position rather than to transfer teachers from the classroom in order to fill these positions.

THE ORGANIC–ADAPTIVE MODEL—LINKAGE AND FEEDBACK

The key linkage and feedback roles for facilitating communication and coordination to all aspects of the system lie primarily in the curriculum associate position. This position supplies a vital and pivotal link to all other components within the organizational model. The curriculum associate obviously commands greater responsibility and status than his conventional counterpart—the anachronistic department chairman. In respect to the effective functioning of the instructional program of the school, no other position is more crucial than that of the curriculum associate. He provides the essential liaison, coordination, communication, decision-making linkage, and feedback between the principalship task–force and the professional teacher core. The overall effecti-

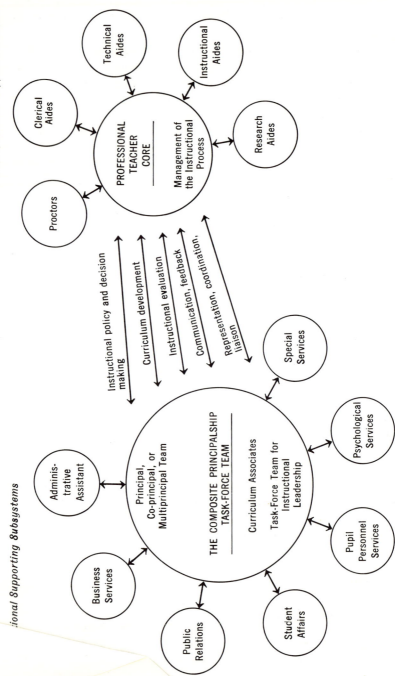

FIGURE 13.5 *The Expanded Model—The Organic—Adaptive System*

Paraprofessional Support Personnel

Technical Aides

Clerical Aides

Instructional Aides

Proctors

Research Aides

PROFESSIONAL TEACHER CORE

Management of the Instructional Process

Instructional policy and decision making

Curriculum development

Instructional evaluation

Communication, feedback

Representation, coordination, liaison

ional Supporting Subsystems

Adminis-trative Assistant

Business Services

Public Relations

Student Affairs

THE COMPOSITE PRINCIPALSHIP TASK-FORCE TEAM

Principal, Co-principal, or Multiprincipal Team

Curriculum Associates

Task-Force Team for Instructional Leadership

Special Services

Psychological Services

Pupil Personnel Services

ness of the total instructional system of the school—curriculum development and evaluation, appropriate staff involvement, and staff representation—is dependent upon the leadership ability of each curriculum associate functioning either individually within his respective curricular area or collectively as a task–force team member.

SUMMARY—AN ORGANIZATIONAL MODEL

In order to accommodate more individualized instructional programs in the near future, alternatives to the current bureaucratic structure found in most elementary and secondary schools must be developed (see Figure 13.5). Any new organizational scheme much recognize that the instructional program is the central function of the school and that those individuals responsible for its development must be placed in key decision-making positions. This assumes, of course, that the professional teaching staff will occupy a dominant role in this organizational design.

For heuristic purposes, in designing an organizational system for secondary schools we have chosen an organic–adaptive model composed of interrelating task–force teams of specialists. The central leadership-decision-making level of the school is composed of a task–force team of professionals working in collaboration in what might be referred to as a composite principalship. This aspect of the organizational system consists of two main components—the principal, co-principal team and several curriculum associates. The curriculum associates provide representation, coordination, liaison, and feedback from the professional teacher core. They are instructional specialists and offer leadership in the development of specific components of the instructional program. They are experts in their respective fields and, preferably, have an interdisciplinary orientation. Their positions in terms of status and compensation would be comparable to the master teacher or teacher specialist positions found in the differentiated staffing model.

The principal, co-principal team, as a component of the composite principalship, is an instructional generalist and an administrative–management specialist. These individuals are responsible for the overall administrative, logistical, coordinative functions of the school program. This position in the model performs the *e*⁻

tive "linking pin" role described by Bennis. Changes in staff organization and personnel will be made as the team members within the principalship identify the need for change; thus, "temporary" systems of diverse specialists are created to collaborate in solving specific, complex instructional problems.

Several subsystems evolve about the principalship task-force, either as temporary or permanent units, in order to supply specialized support to the instructional process. These non-instructional positions might consist of an administrative assistant (executive secretary) to the principal, co-principal team, business administrator, psychological services, pupil personnel services, student affairs, public relations, and so on. The key to this organizational design, however, is that the instructional program and instructional specialists occupy the central decision-making positions in the structure. All other school-related activities are peripheral or supporting services to the instructional program. The curriculum associates, as specialists representing the teacher core, and the co-principal team, as administrative specialists, share equally as a collaborating task—force team in the decision-making, policymaking process of the school program.

INDEX